RICK HANSEN
MAN IN MOTION

Rick Hansen and Jim Taylor

Douglas & McIntyre
Vancouver/Toronto

Second revised edition

Douglas & McIntyre Ltd.
2323 Quebec Street, Suite 201
Vancouver, British Columbia   V5T 4S7

Canadian Cataloguing in Publication Data

Hansen, Rick, 1957–
  Rick Hansen

  ISBN 1-55054-759-3

  1. Hansen, Rick, 1957– 2. Paraplegics—Canada—Biography. 3. Spinal cord—Wounds and injuries—Biography. 4. Wheelchair sports—Biography. I. Taylor, Jim, 1937–   II. Title.
RD796.H35A3   1999   362.4'3'092   C99-910919-7

Editing by Saeko Usukawa
Design by Barbara Hodgson
Cover photograph by Roger Gould, used courtesy of NIKE International Ltd.
Design by Barbara Hodgson
Typeset by The Typeworks
Printed and bound in Canada by Friesens
Printed on acid-free paper

All care has been taken to trace the ownership of photographs reprinted in this book. If any omissions have occurred, they will be corrected in subsequent editions, provided notification is sent to the publisher.

Canada
The publisher gratefully acknowledges the support of the Canada Council for the Arts and of the British Columbia Ministry of Tourism, Small Business and Culture. The publisher also acknowledges the financial support of the Government of Canada through the Book Publishing Industry Development Program.

A Special Thank You

The Rick Hansen Institute is pleased to share with you a story of long-standing and far-reaching support. It began when Royal Bank became one of the first corporate sponsors of the Man in Motion World Tour and mobilized its employees to donate their time and money in support of Rick's dream: to raise funds to support spinal cord injury research, rehabilitation and wheelchair sport, and to raise awareness of the potential of people with disabilities.

Employees accepted donations and counted the thousands of coins that poured in to branches across the country; they organized and attended dozens of events, and they became a key group of cross-Canada volunteers as the tour proceeded westward. Royal Bank's generous donation of a van and its secondment of an employee (Dan Northam) to the Tour were important factors in collecting donations from Canadians.

After the tour ended, Rick Hansen, with the support of the federal government, established National Access Awareness Week, and Royal Bank became a corporate partner. Royal Bank has also provided funds for wheelchair athletes competing in the 1994 Commonwealth Games and is the sponsor of the BC Life Skills Program and Role Model Resource, produced by the Rick Hansen Institute and now in all BC schools. These programs provide life skills education for all students, helping them to make good life decisions, manage change and overcome obstacles. In addition, Royal Bank has supported the NeuroScience Network (now NeuroPartners Canada), which has helped to build the neuroscience industry in Canada and will ultimately have a major impact on discovering cures for spinal cord and brain injuries.

In 1997, Royal Bank Financial Group helped Rick Hansen celebrate a decade of achievements and chart a vision for the future, by presenting the Man in Motion Tenth Anniversary Tour. The tour saw Rick Hansen revisit 17 Canadian cities, to thank Canadians for their original contributions and to let them know what their donations had accomplished. It resulted in the creation of two new legacies: the Rick Hansen Neurotrauma Initiative and the Rick Hansen Insititute. Perhaps most important, the Tenth Anniversary once again demonstrated the importance of helping people with disabilities reach their full potential.

In 1998 and 1999 Royal Bank Financial Group was a partner of the Rick Hansen Fishing Challenge, a networking, fishing and fundraising event whose proceeds support the work of the Rick Hansen Institute. Royal Bank's most recent contribution is this special print run of the updated version of *Rick Hansen: Man in Motion*.

The Royal Bank partnership has been a key to our success, and we'd like to take this opportunity to say a special thank you to Royal Bank Financial Group for its incredible support of our journey, and for its belief in the power of a dream.

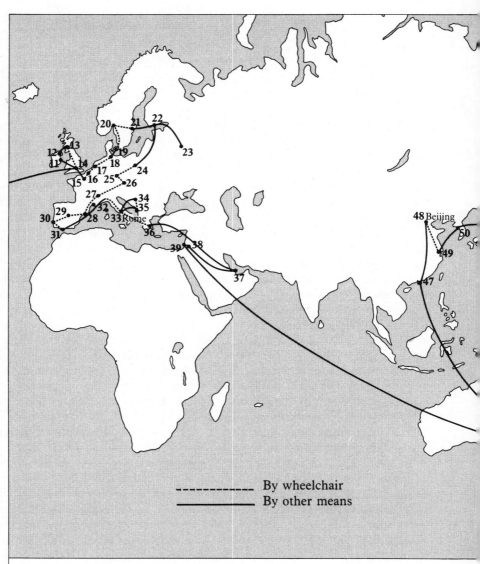

_____ By wheelchair
_____ By other means

1985	
1	Vancouver/March
2	Seattle/March
3	Portland/March
4	San Francisco/April
5	Los Angeles/April
6	San Diego/April
7	Phoenix/May
8	Dallas/May
9	New Orleans/June
10	Miami/June
11	Dublin/July
12	Belfast/July
13	Glasgow/July
14	London/July
15	Paris/July
16	Brussels/July
17	Amsterdam/July
18	Hamburg/August
19	Copenhagen/August
20	Oslo/August
21	Stockholm/August
22	Helsinki/August
23	Moscow/September
24	Warsaw/September
25	Prague/September
26	Vienna/September
27	Geneva/October
28	Barcelona/October
29	Madrid/October
30	Lisbon/November
31	Gibraltar/November
32	Marseilles/November
33	Rome/November
34	Belgrade/November
35	Dubrovnik/November
36	Athens/December
37	Bahrain/December
38	Amman/December

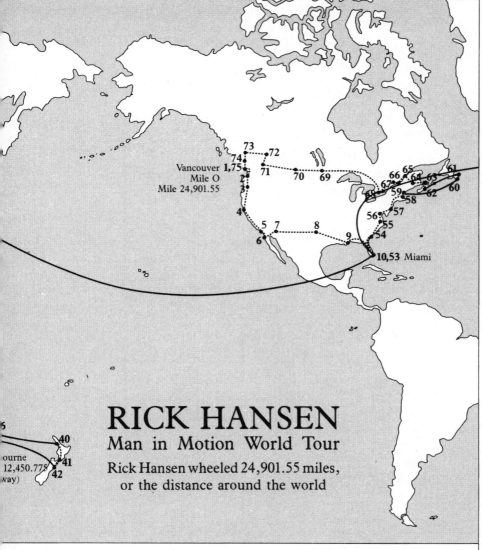

73
74 •72
Vancouver **1,75**
Mile O
Mile 24,901.55
71
70   69
66 65
67 64 63 61
59 58 62 60
56 57
55
54
5 7   8   9
6
10,53 Miami

40
41
ourne
12,450.775
vay)
42

RICK HANSEN
Man in Motion World Tour

Rick Hansen wheeled 24,901.55 miles,
or the distance around the world

39 Tel Aviv/December	**51** Sapporo/May	**64** Fredericton/October
1986	**52** Tokyo/June	**65** Quebec City/October
40 Auckland/January	**53** Miami/June	**66** Montreal/October
41 Wellington/January	**54** Savannah/July	**67** Ottawa/October
42 Christchurch/January	**55** Richmond/July	**68** Toronto/November
43 Adelaide/February	**56** Washington, D.C./July	**1987**
44 Melbourne/March	**57** New York/August	**69** Winnipeg/January
45 Sydney/March	**58** Boston/August	**70** Regina/February
46 Brisbane/March	**59** Bar Harbour/August	**71** Calgary/March
47 Hong Kong/April	**60** Cape Speare/August	**72** Edmonton/March
48 Beijing/April	**61** St. John's/August	**73** Prince George/March
49 Shanghai/May	**62** Halifax/September	**74** Williams Lake/April
50 Seoul/May	**63** Charlottetown/September	**75** Vancouver/May

For the team—
those at home and on the road,
and the thousands in thirty-four countries
who helped transform the dream into reality

1

"You'll be all right, son. You'll be fine."

He was sitting on the stage in the auditorium of the Oakridge shopping mall in Vancouver, a smile frozen on his face, praying that the fear didn't show.

In a matter of minutes he'd be wheeling down the ramp and out onto the road, his escort vehicle tucked in behind him, to begin a journey most in the room considered impossible: 24,901.55 miles through thirty-four countries in nineteen months — in a wheelchair powered by nothing but the strength in his upper body and the conviction in his heart. Rick Hansen, paraplegic. Age: twenty-seven. Weight: 140 pounds. Condition: numb.

One by one his supporters were trooping to the microphone to make presentations, offer good wishes and tell him what a great thing he was doing — the premier, the mayor, civic dignitaries, corporate sponsors, friends. He tried to listen, but their voices faded in and out as his mind flew in other directions. The wheelchair wasn't ready. He was injured, had been for four months, and nothing was getting any better — not the shoulders, the elbow or the wrist. There wasn't enough money to get him past Los Angeles, let alone around the world. What was he doing here?

His mind snapped back. Betty and Rollie Fox were there, Terry's parents, adding their good wishes. Terry, his buddy, taken at twenty-two by cancer in 1981 in the midst of his one-legged run across Canada. Not beaten. Never that. He just wasn't granted enough time. Terry would understand what he was feeling. Maybe he'd felt it himself, back there on the coast of Newfoundland as he was about to take the first step west.

He looked out over the faces, and some of the numbness melted away. All these people, all the others who'd taken part in the radio telethon outside, people he knew and people he didn't, all there to support this kid who said he was going to wheelchair around the world. He knew that a lot of them probably didn't think he could do it. They were there not be-

cause he was likely to succeed, but because he had the guts to try. Somehow, that made the feeling even warmer.

God, he was tired. So many things to do, so little time to do them. Four hours sleep, tops, in the past thirty-six. The apartment a madhouse of partially packed gear, the wheelchair in pieces on the floor at midnight, TV cameras, people coming in and out to say good-bye or give haircuts or do interviews or shove something under his nose he'd forgotten to sign. The crew going over check lists, Amanda scrubbing the bathroom to get the place ready for the guy who'd be subletting it . . .

Amanda. "How dumb does a guy have to be," he wondered, "falling in love just before he's about to go wheeling off around the world?"

Emotionally he was wrung dry. This thing was such a roller coaster. Yesterday he'd been honoured at a reception in the Faculty Club at the University of British Columbia. Because the place had no wheelchair access, he'd wound up being stuffed into a dumbwaiter. They'd hoisted him up to the wrong floor, so no one was waiting there to let him out. Finally he'd managed to pry the door loose, scaring the daylights out of a cook who had her back to the opening. At that moment his crew had arrived, put him back into the dumbwaiter and hoisted him one floor higher to the reception. "Not exactly a sweeping entrance," he thought wryly, and wondered how many people realized how often stairs and doors become insurmountable barriers when you look at them from a wheelchair.

The speeches were winding down. It was almost time. He said his final thanks, waved, and spun the chair toward the ramp, exhausted, frustrated, and suddenly overcome by the enormity of what he was about to attempt. There was no way they were ready. They were poorly prepared, underorganized, underequipped, underfunded. If they'd started two weeks ago as scheduled, the winds from the north would have blown him halfway to San Diego. Today the wind was from the south, in his face, and somehow he knew that's the way it was going to be.

Logically, he was too hurt to start, but if he didn't start now it might never happen. But how tough would it be on the road ahead? How tough, really?

The chair jolted to a halt, the wheels tight against the metal strip set into the floor as a doorstop. Absent-mindedly he rolled a half-turn back, put his arms into it, and surged over the first bump and out to challenge the world.

"What the heck," he thought. "The road that got me this far hasn't been any picnic . . ."

I could give you a dozen reasons why it should never have happened, point to a dozen places where choices—simple choices—logically could have been made another way and I'd be walking today instead of wheeling. I've had a lot of hospital time on a lot of sleepless nights to count them.

What if I hadn't gone fishing? I had a good reason not to. What if the gas tank on the truck hadn't developed a hole? What if we hadn't stopped to help the hippie change his tire? What if the *first* accident had delayed us another five minutes, or even another two or three? What if it had been my turn to hold the fish? What if . . . ?

What if can drive you crazy, if you let it.

You could call it God's will if you like. Personally, I don't know whether I really want to believe in God. It implies someone up there controlling my life and I like to believe that control is mine. But I do believe there's something up there, and a reason why we're down here. So call it bad luck, or fate, or anything else you like. In the end it doesn't matter a rat's rectum. All that matters is that on June 27, 1973, on a hot summer evening about 8 P.M., I was bouncing along a gravel road in the back of a pickup truck with my buddy, Don Alder. Two kids—me fifteen, him sixteen—hitchhiking home from the kind of week city kids can only dream about.

And everything fell apart.

When you grow up in small towns in British Columbia, Canada, in the heart of the mountains and forest and some of the finest fishing and hunting grounds in the world, fishing becomes second nature. I'd lived in Port Alberni (pop. 11,500), Fort St. John (pop. 3,600), Abbotsford (pop. 7,500) and now there I was in Williams Lake (pop. 4,500), a kid with three obsessions: fishing, hunting—and sports. Always sports. If you could throw it, hit it, bounce it, chase it or run with it, I wanted to play it. And usually I could do it pretty well.

That didn't make me unusual. In smaller communities—particularly the out-of-the-way places in what city kids would probably call wilderness—there isn't the specialization in the early years you find in the big city schools, where the guys who play basketball might not play football and the track guys concentrate strictly on running. I had a sort of a plan in the back of my mind that in grade eleven and twelve I'd concentrate on one sport, but that was down the road.

That weekend there was a volleyball clinic at 100 Mile House, about 60 miles south of Williams Lake, the first of a series for people who wanted to try out for the Pacific Rim and Canada Games team. Volleyball was my favourite sport, and if getting there had been essential I'd have been there no matter what. But there was going to be another tryout camp later, and I knew I could get a shot at it then. So the trip to 100 Mile wasn't vital. And I had what seemed like a better option.

Between Williams Lake and Bella Coola 290 miles to the west, the country is loaded with rivers and lakes, many of which you can reach only by four-wheel drive or on foot. Don and I and another friend named Randy Brink had planned to take off in Randy's dad's truck to spend a week exploring and fishing our way to Bella Coola, stopping wherever and whenever we felt like it. I have to admit it was my idea, although they sure didn't need any coaxing. So: go to a volleyball clinic I could afford to miss, or spend a week with my buddies bopping around catching fish and having a great time?

No contest. I went fishing. I didn't know it, but I'd just blown the first choice.

We loaded the truck and took off. The week was everything we'd figured: plenty of fish, plenty of laughs. Oh, there was one thing that we could have taken as an omen if we'd believed in such things. On our way to One-Eye Lake we rounded a corner and found a bunch of guys sprawled all over the place, some of them cut up pretty badly. They'd rolled their jeep—a Land Rover type with a hardtop. Nobody really seriously hurt, but everyone fairly shaken. They were on a fishing trip, too—heading for Bella Coola. If it was another alarm going off, I still wasn't listening. We drove them to the nearest lodge where they could get treatment, and kept right on going.

Remember the really great summers when you were growing up, the ones that just stretched on and on, when every day was sunshine and school was so far down the road it wasn't worth even thinking about? This was one of those and that week was the best of it. We just kept on fishing and camping and hiking and laughing. When getting the hole in the gas tank fixed put us off schedule a couple of days, we shrugged it off. No big deal. We were fishing. More important, we were *catching*. Which is probably why we were in such a good mood when we came across this hippie-type guy about twenty-five and his girlfriend looking down at a flat tire on his old '54 pickup, stalled in the middle of nowhere.

Hey, no problem! We helped him change it, he gave us a beer, and we headed off down the road. As it turned out, another bad choice.

And then it was time to head home. We'd had our week or the best part of it. Don and I wanted to stay on in Bella Coola and fish some more, but Randy had had enough. And you know how it is when you're kids. You get an idea, you want to do it *now*. He not only wanted to leave, he wanted to leave *then*, which happened to be around midnight. We tried to talk him out of it, but he got pigheaded (he's a lot like me) and it was his truck, or at least his dad's. So here we went in the pitch black, climbing out of Bella Coola canyon, 200- or 300-foot cliffs on either side, narrow road full of switchbacks and a sheer drop to nowhere if you got careless.

We got careless.

We were all dead tired. Randy started to nod off at the wheel once and almost killed us right there. The truck nosed out toward the drop, and he jerked awake just in time to wrench it back. Suddenly, I wasn't sleepy anymore. I figured it would be a great idea to stay awake and keep *him* awake. But Don fell asleep, then I fell asleep, and I guess Randy must have looked over at us because *he* fell asleep. And we went over the side of the mountain—at the only spot on the canyon with a ledge just below the road.

I've thought about that a lot. We don't land on that ledge, we're history right there. And it wasn't all that wide a ledge. A few feet to either side and they scrape whatever's left of us off the bottom of the valley. Do you think somebody was trying to tell us something? Like, for instance, "Get some sleep, you idiots. This is your last warning!" ?

But we were alive. Sleepy, ticked off, but alive, and it was all part of the adventure—even being stuck on the ledge with no way to get the truck back up onto the road. Cars went by all the time and some of them stopped, but never one big enough to haul a truck off a ledge. We dug and shovelled and cursed and got nowhere. And then fate or whatever offered me another choice. A friend of mine named Duncan Boyd drove up in a camper with his dad. They'd been fishing in Bella Coola themselves and offered to give us a ride. But there wasn't enough room for all three of us. I could have gone with them. Lord knows it was tempting at that time of the morning. But what kind of a guy would leave his friends at a time like that? No, I decided to stay with Randy and Don. Wrong again.

Finally a dump truck came along, the guy hauled us out, and we drove on to Kleena Kleene, which was a combination post office, general store, gas station and farm, all run by Randy's dad. And there Don and I got really stupid.

Randy suggested we stay there a day or two because his dad would be going into Williams Lake then and we could go the whole 150 miles home with him. It made sense, but he'd been kind of grumpy and we'd been scrapping a little—not physically, just snapping and nattering the way friends do, especially when you've been together without a break for a long time. Forget it. We'd hitchhike the rest of the way.

"Well, at least come up to the house and get some sleep first," he said. But not us. We'd stay right there on the porch of the general store where we could see the cars coming.

It made no sense. It was still early, but hot and dusty. We'd been up all night. We were absolutely bushed, so tired we could barely stand, and we could have been stretched out in bed. But where were we? Sitting on a porch waiting for cars and falling asleep anyway.

I don't know how many cars went by that we didn't even notice. One man stopped and offered us a lift as far as Riske Creek, but that would have left us still 35 or 40 miles out of Williams Lake, so we said no. We probably slept through a bunch of others, because to this day I remember snapping awake, looking down the road, and feeling a strange, eerie sensation sweep over me when I saw that cloud of dust coming toward us about a mile away. All right, it sounds weird, but it looked, well, ominous.

But that was silly. We'd missed enough rides already. I shook Don awake. "Aw, let it go," he protested. "I'm tired." I shook him again, we stumbled out to the road—and a truck roared right by us.

Well, to heck with it. I still felt kind of creepy about it, anyway. There'd be other rides. We could wait.

We'd just turned around to head back to the porch when we heard the brakes squeal. The driver had caught sight of us in the rearview mirror. It was the hippie and his girl, the ones we'd helped to change their tire. That's the only reason he stopped, he said. He didn't normally pick up hitchhikers. But he'd recognized us, and after all, we'd helped him change that tire.

So we had our ride. Damn it, we had our ride.

The guy cracked a couple of beer. He wasn't drunk or anything. It was hot and he'd been pushing it, so he had a couple. And then darned if we didn't get another flat. We fixed that and took off again, the guy and his girl in the cab, Don and I in the back of the pickup, perched on top of a pile of stuff so high we were closer to the top of the truck sides than we were to the floor. I think the guy was moving or something. We were both dozing, but taking turns holding the fish we'd caught. On that gravel road it was so bumpy it was hold them or lose them. The one with the fish would sit on the floor of the truck, or as close as he could get to it, while the other one stretched out on this big steel tool box and tried to sleep.

It was my turn on the tool box. I gave the fish to Don and wriggled around on my back, looking for the most comfortable position. And finally, I dozed off.

A scream woke me. The girl, I guess. Up in the cab she'd have been able to see it all happening.

We were skidding down the road out of control, swerving from one side to another while the guy fought the wheel trying to straighten us out. Apparently we'd been coming out of a long, gradual corner onto a straight stretch when we hit some washboard road and went into a skid. We were only doing 35 or 40 miles an hour, but being a city driver not used to that sort of thing he may have oversteered trying to get back in control.

Whatever he did, it didn't work. Two more skids and we were flipping end-over-end, side-over-side, bouncing on an angle toward the right-side ditch. I just had time to look over at Don and think, "This is it, I'm gone," and I was flying out of the truck bed.

But not far enough. Not quite.

There was a crunch. I distinctly remember hearing a crunch. I guess the tool box went first and I was slammed down on the edge of it. I heard the crunch, and blacked out.

It was only for a couple of seconds. I woke up and thought, "Hey, I'm alive!" Then I thought, "Whoa! Something's wrong here. Something's definitely wrong." Because I tried to move, and I couldn't.

There were boxes and junk all over me. I was propped up against this tool box, and I couldn't move. It didn't hurt. Not then. I guess I was in shock. All I remember clearly is the dust settling around me. But suddenly there was this searing pain—pain like I'd never felt before. And I'd never in my life been so afraid.

As Don and I pieced it together later, it was the type of crash just made for one of those TV movies where they go slow motion so you can watch the pieces flying in all directions.

The two of us, the tool box and every other piece of stuff the hippie had piled into that truck all went flying at the same time. The box landed first, then me, then all that junk on top of me. Don had flown farther because he'd been sitting on the higher side of the truck and got a better trajectory, but he had troubles of his own. He'd hit the road rolling and bouncing—and here came the truck, rolling and bouncing along after him and gaining every second. Fortunately he rolled into the ditch and scrambled out of it on the other side. The truck hit the ditch, stopped, and gave one final roll before it came crashing down about two feet from his head.

Don pulled himself up and wobbled back up the road looking for me. Actually, I was his second choice. As he admitted later, his first worry was whether his guitar had survived. He could hear me yelling his name, but he couldn't see me. I was buried under all that junk. Finally, I worked a hand up through the pile and waved. He rushed over and threw the stuff around until I was clear, anxious as a puppy dog, not knowing what to say.

"I can't move my legs," I told him. Then, as the realization hit me, I screamed it again: "I can't move my *legs!*"

At fifteen I weighed 165 pounds without an ounce of fat on me and my legs had been like iron. Now I poked them, and they were like jelly.

Still, it hadn't really sunk in. A little bell in the back of my head was sounding, but I wasn't going to listen to it. Not yet. It was temporary. It had to be. The hippie guy is there, patting me on the head and saying, "You'll be all right, son. You'll be fine." Don's telling me not to worry, because he'd broken his pelvis in four places a year earlier in a car accident and it felt the same way, and I'm yelling, "Get our stuff! Get the fishing rods! Don't let anybody get the fish!" And the pain is just washing over me in waves.

The rest of it is a blur.

Cars were stopping, people gathering. The fire truck came, the police car came, and about an hour later the ambulance came. One guy who'd had first aid checked my back and said it was broken. Somebody offered me a shot of gin. I asked for water, and a little kid ran all the way to and from a farmhouse about half a mile away to get some, and when he tried to give it to me, I screamed, "I don't want any water! Get it out of here!"

I started to swear a lot, telling the hippie that he'd screwed me up and what a jerk he was. I'd pass out for a while—which I think made everyone just as happy because there were a lot of little kids around—then I'd wake up and start in on him again. Everyone wanted to be helpful, but no one knew what to do. What do you say to a kid with a broken back? Not "Hey, watch your mouth. There are children here!"

The ambulance crew tried three or four times to transfer me without doing much but making the pain even worse. Finally, they got a board under me. Then it was into the ambulance and down the mountain at 90 miles an hour to the Cariboo Memorial Hospital at Williams Lake, which I guarantee was not a fun trip. Well, we'd wanted to get home in a hurry . . .

It didn't get any better at the hospital. They couldn't give me anything for the pain until they knew for sure what was wrong. So they X-rayed me, then put me on this table, and suddenly we're not talking ordinary broken back. This is severe. The doctor gave it to me straight:

"It's really serious," he said. "I doubt you'll ever walk again."

I told him he was full of shit.

Okay, so I had this tube going up my nose and into my stomach and I kept gagging on the thing, and I was peeing into a catheter and my mom and dad were by my bed crying and they were going to have to operate. Fine. I could handle that. But not walk again? Don't be ridiculous.

Walk or no walk, there'd have to be an operation. I had some strong opinions on that.

"If you've got to operate, you get me out of here," I yelled. I'd heard stories of people dying of hepatitis in Williams Lake. I didn't know if they were true, but I'd heard them. So after a couple of hours trying to arrange a mercy flight (there were no planes available), it was back into the ambulance for seven hours to Royal Columbian Hospital in New Westminster, just outside of Vancouver.

If it hadn't hurt so much I might have laughed. Here I am, this little fifteen-year-old kid from the boonies, all messed up and on morphine, and they couldn't operate on me right away because it was the July 1 long weekend and people were mashing each other all over the place. It was a question of priorities. I was hurting, but I was stable. They couldn't help it, that's just the way it was. You want an operation? Take a number.

But they did put me under. They made the pain go away and fixed it so I didn't have to think for a while. And when I came out of it, the first thing I saw was this beautiful girl.

She was my private nurse. I fell instantly, totally in love. Lying there on a table, woozy and full of drugs, I saw The Girl For Me.

Then they took me away and operated, and I never saw her again. When you're hot, you're hot.

All I remember is always being in pain. They'd give me morphine, it would wear off after ninety minutes, and then it would be ninety minutes in pain until they could give me some more morphine.

Apparently what they'd done in the operation was called a "decompression laminectomy and spinal fusion," in which they roughen up the appropriate areas of the spine, insert little chips of bone against the roughened spots so they and the spine hopefully will fuse together on their own, put metal plates on each side of the spine and bolt them together. It's about all they can do with that type of injury: immobilize it and hope things fuse together to provide support. They weren't too precise about the extent of the injury. The guy at Williams Lake had been blunt; the people at Royal Columbian were kind of head-patting vague: "We have to try hard, hope for the best, anything can happen." That sort of thing. Not that it mattered. I wouldn't have believed them anyway. Besides, I had a few other problems at the moment.

I had this tube up my nose and they were draining this awful gunk away and all I could drink was water. I kept harping at them to take out that stupid tube until they finally did it, probably just to make me shut up. And, of course, I'd convinced them too soon and I got sick again.

I was in a bed they called a Stryker, something invented to allow patients to be turned over without actually turning the body. It had two mattresses—the one under me, and the one they would clamp

15

over me when it was turning time. If I was on my back they'd clamp it on my chest, turn the bed over until I was facing the floor, then remove the mattress that was now pressing down on my back. To get me face up again they reversed the process and took the mattress off my chest. For eight weeks I felt like the filling in a sandwich.

They were supposed to flip the Stryker every three hours, but sometimes on night shift they'd forget. When that happened I could spend all night on my stomach. I have bony hips and the pain would be just brutal.

And sometimes I'd get scared. Not all the time, but sometimes. At night, mostly. I remember waking up once at 2 A.M., face down and filled with fear. I threw up all over the floor. I kept flicking the light off and on and yelling for someone to come turn me over. But no one did, and for the rest of the night I stared down at this stuff on the floor that I'd heaved.

You can't be brave all the time. Sometimes, you just have to cry.

But no one saw that Rick Hansen. He was nighttime. The daytime Rick was upbeat, uptempo, utterly convinced this thing was only temporary. I was a fighter. You break a bone, it heals. I twisted my ankle once. It healed, didn't it? I wrote letters back to Don and other friends at school telling them I was having dreams about walking again and that it would be pretty soon.

I really believed that. I was so sure of it that when people came in to cheer me up I'd wind up doing it for them. I'd be home soon. I'd be back in school. Hey, the service here is great! Old friends from Abbotsford, cousins, my coaches from Columneetza Senior Secondary School in Williams Lake, they all looked so *sad* that I found myself doing things to loosen them up.

The first time Bob Redford, my volleyball coach, stuck his head in the door, I pointed my finger at him and yelled, "This is your fault! You should have made me go to that clinic!" But he knew me better than that. He gave me some smart-aleck crack right back, relaxed, and I gave him my sales pitch: "Hey, coach, no problem! I'll be back next semester! Sorry I can't make the team this semester, but I'll be back!"

I was a tough kid. I wasn't going to let this affect me. Give me a bullet to bite on. My friends, the doctors, the nurses, the other patients were all really impressed. He's so bright! So pleasant! Hey, is this kid brave or what?

And then my parents would come in, and I'd dump all over them.

I didn't know why at the time. They were there, trying the best they could. My dad, Marvin, got a temporary transfer from B.C. Telephone so he could work in Vancouver for as long as I was in hospital. They'd come in to see me every day, and it was just hell for them. All my frustrations, all my anger at this *thing* that had happened to me, this un-fair, unnecessary, scary *thing*, would be thrown at them. The rest of the world got the daytime Rick, boy hero. My parents got the angry, inwardly terrified nighttime Rick, the one looking for some way to strike back, something or someone to hit.

They took it. At what price, I don't know. I was too caught up in myself to notice.

Every single day, two or three hours a day, I would try to make it happen. I'd stare down at my toes and *will* them to wiggle. Move! Just once! Then I'll know it can happen, that all it will take is work. But *move!*

It never happened. Not a twitch. I might have gone nuts eventually with nothing else to distract me. But there were fringe benefits at Royal Columbian, a lot of lovely looking, sweet-smelling fringe bene-fits. Royal Columbian had student nurses.

It was kind of a two-edged sword, having them there. Here I was, a fifteen-year-old kid just beginning to get into the boy-girl thing at home when the accident happened. I liked girls. I'd even asked one out. She turned me down because she said I was too shy. Heck, I didn't have time to be anything but. I mean, girls are cute, guys, but let's get to the gym and shoot baskets. Now I'm sitting in hospital sur-rounded by these gorgeous eighteen-year-old girls who are spoiling me rotten. They thought of themselves as big sisters. I thought of them . . . well, I thought of them.

I remember one day some friends brought in some "Go, Rick" stickers to cheer me up. When a beautiful young nurse named Wendy leaned over to adjust my blankets, I gave her a little pat on the bum.

"Rick!" she said. "Don't get fresh!" I apologized—but she didn't know she had a Rick sticker on her bum until someone asked her who this guy Rick was. She looked in the mirror and there it was: a fifteen-year-old kid had put his brand on her backside.

From the first day in hospital I'd set myself goals. I'd promised my-self I'd be out of that Stryker bed for my birthday, August 26, and I was. I had my sixteenth birthday in a normal bed, sitting up. That may not sound like much, but it was a big deal for me. I remember them putting me on this incliner bed and slowly bringing me up. They'd say, "Well, you'll pass out here, everybody does." And they got me up to sixty degrees, then seventy, and I wasn't passing out. For the first time since I was up against that tool box in the back of the truck, I was sitting up straight.

"Piece of cake," I told them. "Beat the odds again."

Later that night my cousin smuggled in a beer (just one, that's all his pocket would hold), and I drank it with a straw to make it last. Hey, kid, you're sixteen! It's your birthday. Don't think. Just knock it back.

And then I was in a wheelchair. It was like giving me a parole.

By that time I'd met a couple of other kids around my age who were in for a while through accidents of their own. One of them was Mike Ozan, who'd broken his leg when his Volkswagen lost an argument with a trailer. We'd get out of the hospital once in a while for parties, have a few beer, that sort of thing. Or I'd arrange to get out to watch a volleyball or basketball game.

The student nurses knew what it meant to us to be able to laugh and joke with people close to our age in places outside the hospital environment. For me particularly, it meant a chance to forget and be normal. We weren't in hospital anymore. Heck, Mike forgot so well one day that when we were horsing around he reached out, grabbed the front wheel of my chair and just flipped me over backwards, tail over teakettle.

Once in a while the girls even smuggled us into the student nurses' quarters. It was great. They weren't more than a couple of years older than we were. We'd talk, play records, make plans. For a while, the wheelchair was just a chair and there were no battles to fight. And getting there was half the fun.

The route led through a tunnel linking the residence and hospital basements, and that tunnel ran right past the morgue. I guess the whole thing was set up to discourage unauthorized visitors, because the elevator from the residence basement stopped automatically at the main floor and the doors opened to give the duty nurse a clear view of the occupants.

They got around it. The door would open and there would be three students all in a row, waving and smiling at the supervisor—and blocking her view of the two guys crouched behind them.

So figure it out. Here's this sixteen-year-old who's never had much time for girls, surrounded by eighteen-year-old girls who are making a fuss over him. Suddenly I became very interested in women, and very frustrated. I was disabled. My legs didn't work—I mean, what kind of girl is going to want to go out with me, especially a little guy with a Williams Lake attitude? And what if I *didn't* get better? What if . . . ?

It couldn't happen that way. I wouldn't let it.

The wheelchair changed everything. I had a form of transportation. I had some independence. I put miles on it, up and down the hallways and outside when I could. I learned to do a wheelie, building up speed, leaning back and hoisting the front wheels as though I was on a motorbike. Even then, I was fooling around with a basketball. The urge to compete was there, but there was no outlet. So I just kept working.

I'd spent about two months in the orthopaedic ward. Now there was a decision to be made. It was time to move on to a more extensive rehabilitation program. There was no room for me at the moment at the G. F. Strong Rehabilitation Centre, but they were building a new unit. I could go home and wait, or I could stay at Royal Columbian in M1, a sort of acute rehab ward full of elderly people. Dr. Hunt recommended that I stay. He said he'd give the same advice to his own son. So I stayed.

When I arrived at M1 I was put in a room with four or five other guys. Right beside me there was an old guy named Joe who'd broken his hip in a fall. He kept calling out: "Jessie! Jessie! I love you, Jessie!" There was also a paraplegic named Bob, a nice guy in his forties who was getting drunk all the time, looking for his own way out. It wasn't the most encouraging, upbeat environment, but eventually I got my own room. It was great—so great that if I'd stayed there much longer it might have become a trap.

There I was with my own room in what was becoming a very secure environment. My meals were served. I had cute nurses around me. I could sneak out of the hospital to the pizza parlour, take some correspondence courses. My friends would take me to basketball games, or my parents would take me home for visits. I was starting to build up a very secure world. I didn't have to go into the real one if I didn't feel like it. And believe me, I didn't feel like it.

Look, I was optimistic, but I wasn't stupid. All my life I'd felt that if you worked hard enough you could get what you wanted. I wanted to walk again, I was working my butt off—and there was no improvement. Worse than that, nobody would tell me anything, not even my friends the student nurses.

So I broke into the files to find out.

I picked a time at night when no one was in the nurses' station, wheeled in, hauled out the drawer with the H files in it and read mine. It said, "Acute paralysis, secondary to thoracic spine 10 and 12 fracture"—10 and 12, as I discovered later, meaning the two points of fracture on the spinal cord.

I put the file back, closed the drawer and wheeled out. Then I went looking for a nurse and asked her what "acute" meant. "Serious," she said. So now I knew: the kid who believed he could do anything was a serious paraplegic.

I went back to my room to think about it. But first I stole a couple of old Bob's beer.

2

"I didn't come here to make cookies."

When Avril Corbet pictures Rick Hansen, he is always standing up and always walking. The braces are on his legs, the crutches are pushing up into his armpits, and he is thumping his way down endless halls, looking for nothing more than an excuse to thump his way even farther.

Avril Corbet is a physiotherapist, and physios see them all: the temporarily incapacitated taking the exercises to strengthen a broken limb before they go home and get on with their lives; the resigned ones who've pulled the blanket of institutional living around them and sit waiting out the days; and the stubborn ones like Hansen to whom quit is the vilest of four-letter words.

Physios hear every patient's story, from the endless chain of traffic accident victims to some whose sentence is worsened by the knowledge of the incredible odds against it ever happening. The drunk who fell asleep with both legs sprawled across the railroad tracks and was now a double amputee struggling to master artificial limbs. The pot-smoker who climbed a tree, stretched out on a high branch to stare at the stars, fell asleep, and at some point in the night rolled over. The teen-ager who forgot to set the parking brake, felt the car move while he and his girl were necking in the back seat, and couldn't scramble to the brake in time as the car gained momentum and rolled off a cliff.

After a while nothing surprises them. But sometimes . . .

"I was at G. F. Strong when Rick arrived," Avril Corbet recalls. "And he came in fighting. He worked so hard you'd get irritated. Once he finally got braces he just never sat down — and very few people stay up on them all the time, except those with enormous drive. Everywhere I'd go, all day, it seemed he was behind me, walking God knows where. I remember whirling on him once and saying, 'Don't do that! Go and sit down!' But it was no use. He just wasn't geared to the system, or maybe *it wasn't geared to him. He had this way of looking at what you were trying to do to help him, knowing you were on his side. Then he'd say, 'Yes, I understand that, and I'm with you. But there's this part of me that says I have to do this!' And then he'd stand up again."*

Avril Corbet calls herself extremely fortunate.

"Physios aren't the most popular people, because you're working with patients, making them exercise, trying to get them better equipped for the rest of the battle. Sometimes that process can be painful to them, but you have to make them keep going. I remember once a bunch of us were working on the mat, and one patient said, 'Boy, I really hate Avril.' Someone else said, 'Yeah, let's have a party and bring back everyone who doesn't like Avril.' And the first one said, 'No, the rental on the coliseum would be too high.' "

In a period of a few months she had two patients who overlapped— Hansen and Knut Nordlie, a Vancouver ski flyer who'd been injured in a meet in Ironwood, Michigan. Ski flying is ski jumping with one major difference. The highest jump in the Olympics is 90 metres. In ski flying it's 160. There are only five ski flying hills in the world, and you have to be invited to compete.

"Knut told me that as he was coming down he knew he was going to fall, because the wind was lifting his ski tips," she says. "So he had to decide which way to fall that would do the least damage. The one he chose left him a paraplegic. The fall was so terrible that the CBS 'Sports Spectacular' used it as part of the introduction to the show. Sometimes in the hospital if the show was on, he'd sit in front of the TV and watch himself fall.

"The point is, I don't think he had a chair very long, either. (He didn't. 'I gave it away,' he says. 'It was important to me to be able to stand.') He was there before Rick and was an outpatient, but from the first day Rick came in, I saw the similarities. They knew what they had to do, and nothing was going to be allowed to get in the way . . .''

I left Royal Columbian in tears. It was the old comfortable environment thing: I'd had my sixteenth birthday in that hospital. My new friends were there, and the nurses I'd come to know—and to love, in a way. I was *safe.* Moving to G. F. Strong meant leaving a comfortable, secure environment and going out into a world I was unsure of. But off I went, and wheeled into what looked like everything I didn't want, wrapped up in one big package.

The new building wasn't finished yet, so we were all housed in the old part—a dark, dingy looking place, sort of like those army barracks you see in the old war movies. And that's where I was from the start: at war.

They were teaching things that were humiliating even to discuss, like bowel and bladder control. Later on I'd learn one of rehab's facts of life: that you check your pride in the locker room and pick it up when you leave. But there I was, a sixteen-year-old kid being taught how to go to the bathroom. I was angry, I was embarrassed, and it just strengthened my conviction that leaving Royal Columbian had been a terrible mistake. This wasn't a rehabilitation centre. This was a place to kill time. Or so I thought.

From the minute I'd wheeled through the doors I'd made myself another promise: I'd be out as fast as I could. That was the only reason I was there, to get functional enough so I could go home. Otherwise, why bother? Apparently a lot of people didn't feel that way. Not that I was the only one with my attitude. There were people working as hard as I was, but there were also guys all around me just going through the motions. They had a place. They felt secure—as I'd felt secure at Royal Columbian. They had insurance settlements coming and life didn't exactly look like it was going to be a bed of roses, so what the heck? Relax. Just sit back and let it happen.

I couldn't live that way. There had to be a goal, and from my point of view the people running the place weren't letting me work toward it. At least, not as hard as I wanted to.

For me, rehab broke down into three major areas: occupational therapy, physiotherapy and remedial gymnastics. I loved the last two. They were what I was there for, to get stronger and better equipped physically. But the administrators wanted me to get into occupational therapy as well. They were after me to do woodworking and bake cookies and things like that. I took it with my usual calm.

"I never wanted to do woodwork and make cookies when I was *healthy!* This is a waste of time. I'm an athlete! This is crazy! I'm not going to take this!"

The fight was on. They insisted I should be taking OT and I insisted I wouldn't. "Forget it," I said. "I'm here to get *out!* I'm here to do the best I can physically. I'm not going to waste my time building little boxes and baking cookies, and that's *it!*"

Years later while we were on the Canadian portion of the Man in Motion tour, that cookie crack would come back to haunt me. I was quoted in a newspaper article—I don't recall making the statement, but I guess I did—and the letters started coming in from OTs. They were angry, and they had a right to be. But I was an adult recalling my perceptions as they were when I was sixteen. You grow up, and part of growing up is learning that the adults weren't nearly as dumb as you thought they were. I know now how important all phases of rehab can be in an integrated program. All I knew then was that the fastest route home lay in getting fit, and these people were getting in my way.

And I won. They conceded, probably for the same reason they'd taken the tube out of my nose at Royal Columbian. We'll do it, Rick, only please, *shut up!* I focussed everything on physiotherapy and gymnastics. But for a while it was still a case of batting my head against a wall. With the best intentions in the world the staff just didn't believe it was the proper approach to take and, naturally, since they held that belief they weren't exactly encouraging. The funny thing is, about three months later I did make cookies. Chocolate chip. I went into that kitchen and I made them. The difference was, I was doing it then because I wanted to. It was a difference they never understood.

Take the fight about the leg braces.

Now, leg braces do not allow you to walk. They're kind of like very stiff plastic boots fused to two metal splints, one running up each side of the leg. There's a hinge at the knee that locks when you stand, and two leather straps that secure them around the upper thigh. What they do is give the leg support enough to allow a person to stand, as long as he's on crutches. People with high spinal cord injuries can't use them. The person wearing them must be prepared to put in the work to lift and swing that essentially useless lower body forward. It's not the strength, although you need that. It's the work. They're inconvenient in that you always have to have the crutches with you, and as a method of transportation they're nowhere near as fast or as efficient as a wheelchair.

But if I could learn to use them, I could stand up. I could tackle stairs. I could look out at the world instead of up at it. From the minute I heard about them, I *needed* them.

Some people at G. F. Strong tried to discourage me, but once I got into that gym the staff really turned it on for me. I had a physiotherapist named Avril Corbet who was just brilliant and a gym teacher named Tadeusz Kasprzak who knew when I was down and never let me stay that way for long. Tad had arrived from Poland a couple of years earlier, and although I didn't know it at the time I was his first patient in his new job. They figured that since he had been a volleyball player, it might give us some common ground. They were right. We hit it off right away, and Tad and was a tremendous help in improving my technique with the braces once everybody learned I was serious.

That took a while. I got the feeling it was an administrative thing: braces aren't the best way to go, so don't encourage patients to use braces. Avril describes it perfectly. "At G. F. Strong," she says, "you have to do it the GFS way: You're in the chair from three to six months and then you get the candy—the try at the braces." Me, I wanted the candy right now.

Forget it, they said. Braces are impractical. They're too tough. You'd never be able to use them.

I thought that was pretty funny, since I'd been using them for months.

It had started back in Royal Columbian when I first got into a wheelchair. Mobility meant more opportunity to work toward getting better, and I worked all the time—on pulleys in the gym to build up my strength, in the halls putting miles on the chair, or just in my room staring down at those toes that still wouldn't move. The staff knew that I wasn't fooling and wouldn't quit. Then someone mentioned that when I got to G. F. Strong I'd probably be moved along a step and tried on braces.

"Braces? You mean like on my legs braces? You mean I could stand up?"

"On crutches, yes. But they're really not all that . . ."

I was barely listening. If I was going to start using braces, why wait? It might be months before I got transferred. Why waste all that time? Why not get started?

They didn't have any braces. Okay, we'd make our own. I coaxed and wheedled and people got interested. Before long both my legs were in plaster casts, then the casts were cut in half lengthwise to make two shells that would fit around my legs. We put straps and bandages on them so they'd stay on. Suddenly, I had custom-made braces.

The first problem was what to do with my toes. I had no control down there. I could lift my foot off the ground by using my arm strength on the crutches, but the toes would just flop down and drag and I'd be forever stubbing them. So, we tied me up like a field goal kicker. When I was barefoot we'd tie a string to my big toe, haul the string up until it lifted the toes clear, then tie it just below my knee. If I wore runners, I tied up the toe of the shoe the same way.

Maybe those improvised braces didn't look like much. But one day I got between the parallel bars and lifted. My arms were shaking and I don't know how long I could have stayed there—but I was standing on my own two feet with no one holding me. To me it was the victory stand at the Olympics, and I'd just won the gold.

Rehabilitation is peaks and valleys. I could beat the system and get leg braces, but I couldn't beat the loneliness.

24

People tried to help. We moved into the new building in December, which made a huge difference as far as atmosphere and facilities were concerned, and for all that I didn't like the system and fought every step of the way to get what I wanted, the hospital and the staff were good and good to me. (Later on, when the Man in Motion tour looked like it was dead before it started, I had another opportunity to find out just how good.) It just seemed as though nobody wanted out as badly as I did.

Rehabilitation went from 8:30 A.M. to 4 or 4:30 P.M. After that, everything shut down. It was like everyone was asleep. Sometimes the only sound you'd hear in the halls after 4:30 was the whip . . . whip . . . whip as that crazy Hansen kid hauled his way up and down four flights of stairs, trying to improve his brace walking, telling himself that every step up or down was a step closer to going home.

It would have been so much easier if there'd been someone with me, someone I could talk to or joke with to make the time go faster. I'd had that at Royal Columbian in a boy named Dan Wesley. He was about twelve when he tried to hitchhike on a train and got caught under the wheels. The double amputation of the legs was about as high up as you can go. Danny had just received his artificial legs and was beginning to learn how to get around on them. We'd jack around in the halls having races on our walkers. Because he was using a four-point walker he was a little bit slower. I remember once I got through a door just before he did, reached behind me, and closed it. You make your humour where you can.

At G. F. Strong I was surrounded by people, but essentially alone. Sometimes having people try to help only made it worse.

A kid named Les Timar and I had reached the doubles quarter-finals in the provincial badminton tournament in Victoria just a few months before the accident. He and his dad came to the hospital, and we batted the bird around for a while in the gym, me in my wheelchair. It was a nice gesture on their part and it was really good to see him, but I wanted to cry. From the provincials to this. They never came back to the rehab centre, and I didn't see them again until Christmas 1984. I guess it was hard for them, too.

Or take the time our school volleyball team was in Maple Ridge playing in the provincials. I managed to get over there to watch them play Mission. That was a peak, but the tumble into the valley was quick and painful. There were my friends, guys I'd been playing with the year before, battling it out in the quarters or semis. It was all I could do not to break down, knowing that I could have made the difference, and knowing I could never play again.

Peaks and valleys . . .

Given enough time you build a social life in hospital. It's your world. You can't just sit there. I met other patients, liked some, didn't like others, pulled the occasional joke. (One night I sneaked into the nurse's station and changed the time on a wake-up call for a guy named Bill. They woke him at 5 A.M. I gather he didn't take it well.) There were opportunities to break the routine. Sometimes I'd get out to spend a weekend with Aunt Betty and Uncle John Jones and my cousins, Wendy, Mike, Hartley and Bill. I even took driving lessons through a special program set up by the rehab centre at a driving school where they had driving simulators with hand controls for paraplegics or those with other physical difficulties.

I was trying to cope, but I kept banging into the system. For instance, I'd go out at night sometimes, on my own or with friends, and get in a little late. I'd be sitting there after a good evening, trying to phone my parents—and the nurses would be trying to get me into bed. I did not go quietly.

"Hey, I'm sixteen years old! Just what is this? I work all day on my braces, go out at night for a little relaxation, and when I've finally got a chance to phone my parents you're shoving me in bed? Get out of my life!"

And then there was the night one of the nurses and her husband took me out for dinner and a movie. *Jonathan Livingston Seagull,* it was called, and I gather there was supposed to be something significant about it. Not for me, there wasn't. But I found something significant in the dinner. Oh, yes.

We went to a restaurant called the Keg on Granville Island, a steak-and-salad bar, no-reservation place that was very popular. It was also very dark and had a slope in one part of the floor, probably a wheelchair ramp. But I wasn't in my wheelchair. I was using my new braces and crutches, and still not as steady or as confident as I'd be later. My feet hit that slope, and suddenly I was skidding on my nose.

The waiter, the lady and her husband got me up, and we enjoyed our dinner. As we prepared to leave, the waiter suggested I use the back door in order to avoid the slope. All I'd have to do is walk between two tables.

Perfect. I was a little self-conscious with the braces anyway, and here I'd already fallen flat on my face. The back door was fine. So they opened the door onto the lane, one of my crutches caught on a table leg, and I pitched out the door and fell face down into an overflowing garbage can.

Welcome to the real world, Rick. This is how it's going to be.

I worked my tail off at G. F. Strong. In three months I was ready to leave—I'd have been out in two months if I hadn't had to wait for my braces, which naturally had to be custom-made for a proper fit. They didn't want me to go. Normally it took five or six months to go through the rehab process, and I'd cut it in half. It took a lot of squabbling with the administration to get sprung, but it happened soon enough for me to fulfil half of the commitment I'd made to myself and to Bob Redford back at Royal Columbian: I got back home in January in time for the second semester of grade eleven, though I wasn't playing on the team as I'd said I'd be.

But the hospital days weren't quite over. Months later there was a postscript. On my seventeenth birthday I went back to Royal Columbian. The metal plates they'd bolted to my spine were giving me a lot of problems and pain as I grew more active. I guess the muscles were grating over the plates. The doctors X-rayed but couldn't see through the plates to see if the bone was really stable. So they made me an offer: if I wanted to go through it, they'd go in and look. If the bone had really healed, they'd take the plates out. If it hadn't, it was a wasted operation.

"Go for it," I said. "This is driving me crazy."

So they put me under, I woke up, and there was the doctor, throwing the plates onto the bed next to me and saying, "There you go, Ricky. Solid as a rock."

I started to cry. Maybe it was postanaesthetic depression. But I'd had a year of dealing with it. I had a girlfriend now and tons of things were piling up on me. I guess I'd forced most of it into the back of my mind, and lying there on the bed it all came rushing out and hit me at once. Steady as a rock, and just as mobile . . .

Anyway, they brought in a counsellor, a guy in a wheelchair himself who worked for the Canadian Paraplegic Association. He talked to me for a while, asking me what was wrong. When I told him, he said yeah, he knew what I meant.

I just looked at him.

"No you don't," I thought.

But that was later. Right now, seven months after the accident, I was going home. In a way it was the end of one battle and the beginning of another. I was strong for a young kid. I'd built myself back up pretty fast. I could walk on braces and crutches and I could scoot around in the wheelchair. But for all its frustrations, hospital life had carried with it that built-in security. Now I had to go and get the answers to a couple of questions: could I accept life as a paraplegic at home and, more important, would life at home accept me?

It was time to go and find out. I was happy, nervous, excited and scared all at once, which is why the trip home took a lot longer than I'd figured. Because the first thing we did was get into another accident.

To understand how it happened you have to understand a little bit about my dad.

This is a man who's worked all his life for B.C. Tel, starting with the line gang in Port Alberni when he was sixteen. The line gangs were the elite, the big boys. They'd dig all the holes and plant the poles—no mechanical lifters, just muscle. There was no place in there for whiners. You were tough and fit, or you were gone.

Dad knows about accidents and pain. He was climbing a pole up in Fort St. John in the winter of 1964 when he heard a cracking noise and felt the thing start to go on him. When he tried to swing around so he'd at least be on top of the thing where he could ride it down, his climbing spikes locked. He shattered his hip in three places. Actually he was lucky to come out of it at all, because it happened in a desolate area in brutal cold. Fortunately, a car happened along and he was rushed to hospital.

So here is this no-nonsense, get-on-with-it guy, come to take me home to Williams Lake in my brand new 4x4 Ford Bronco, which I think I'd had for about six hours. Things were so rushed with me trying to get home for second semester that I'd bought it without even seeing it. I just saw some pictures, figured that was the one I wanted, and shopped by phone.

We kind of finished in a dead heat. I got the licence (I was one shaky farm boy, learning to drive in city traffic and over bridges—the instructor said I needed more work but he'd let me have it because I'd be driving up around Williams Lake where there wouldn't be much traffic). We arranged for the truck, G. F. Strong got the hand controls installed, and now here it sat out front, waiting to take us home.

I flipped the keys to my dad. He flipped them back. "If you're gonna drive this thing," he said, "then drive it."

I drove.

The hand controls consisted of one straight lever down the steering column, with connecting levers that pushed one rod down onto the gas and another onto the brake. When one pushed down the other lifted off, so you couldn't wind up hitting the gas and brake pedals at the same time. The main lever jutted out at the top on the left side of the column. I steered with my right hand and operated the controls with my left—push forward to brake, haul backward and down to accelerate.

I learned to love that Bronco. It took me everywhere. When the pressures got too tough at home, it took me to the woods or the lake where I could fish or just sit and think. But on that first day what I had was a new truck with new hand controls that had just been installed and thus were a little sticky. And off we went to Williams Lake.

We drove through the evening and into the early morning, and the farther we got the tougher the driving became. There'd been a thaw and then a freeze-up in the area between Clinton and Williams Lake, turning the road slick with black ice. We hit it about 3 A.M.

I wasn't doing much more than 30 to 40 miles an hour, but the accelerator was sticking at 35, so I had to push down hard with the hand control to get any acceleration. That was fine, except that every once in a while it would quit sticking, the rod would plunge down on the gas pedal, and I'd have a sudden burst of speed I wasn't expecting. That's okay on normal roads, but on black ice it just sends you into a spin.

Well, I had a few memories about spinning on roads around Williams Lake. I really didn't need to find myself driving a truck that was spinning like a top down Highway One at three in the morning. I looked at my dad, literally threw both hands in the air and yelled: "*All right!* What do we do now?"

He reached over, got the thing under control, and we pulled to a stop.

"You drive," I said. "I've had it."

He looked at me for a second.

"Don't be such a wimp," he said. "You'll do fine."

So I started her up and kept driving—but only at 25 or 30 miles an hour this time. My dad fidgeted until he couldn't stand it any longer.

"Look," he said, "you keep this up and it'll take us forever. Go faster."

"But it'll *stick* again!"

"The road's fine," he assured me. "Go ahead."

I hit the gas, and we were spinning again. This time it was my turn to get it under control. When I'd finished, we were up to the door handles in a snowbank.

Well, no big deal. That's why I had a four-wheel drive. I'd just power us out. When I finished trying that, all I could get out of the wheels was a spin. So we sat there in the cold for a couple of hours, just me and Dad, alone in the middle of the night somewhere between 100 Mile House and Williams Lake, until a couple of trucks with sanding crews came along and hauled us out.

We went on to Williams Lake. I was still driving. As we pulled in, my dad had his final word on the subject.

"See?" he said. "I told you you'd do fine."

3

"The only wheelchair in town."

*H*e'd wheel out to the middle of the floor at the school dances," Patti Lueke recalls, "and for the first couple of dances he'd cool it, letting people get over the shock. Then, bit by bit, he'd start working the chair to the beat, doing wheelies, that sort of thing. Gradually, people would move back to give him a lot of space, and then he'd really flash out — wheelies, 360s, 180s. When he fell — and he would fall — and someone tried to help him, we'd say, 'Oh, leave him alone. He'll be fine.' And he'd pull himself to the chair, climb back in, and start all over."

No one had a better view of Rick Hansen's struggle to rebuild his life in Williams Lake than soft-spoken, dark-haired Patti Lueke. She was his schoolmate and his first serious girl, part of the gang of kids who swept him up and took him along, doing their best to keep things as they'd been before. She saw it all and remembers it fondly.

"He had to be scared, coming home like that," she says. "But if he was, he never let anyone see it.

"The dancing in the chair, that was a breakthrough. For the longest time after he came back he'd come to the dances, all right, but he'd come in his braces because he was so terribly self-conscious about being seen in that chair. He'd use it for sports, then hop out and get right back into the braces. So he'd come to the dances and just stand there by the wall sort of swaying on his crutches, bopping along to the music. It wasn't much, but it was all he had.

"I think what changed things for him was the sports. As he got back into them he had to learn to use the chair as something more than transportation. He became so physically adept at moving it around, so agile in it, that I guess he just figured if he could play games in it, why couldn't he dance in it? From then on, for everything, it was just throw the chair in the Bronco and go."

Ah, yes, the Bronco. Brad Hansen remembers it as the hub of his brother's social life.

"He drove that thing like a tiger. One of the first things he did when he came back was try cross-country rallying, him driving and me navigating. I think we even won the first or second time out. The Bronco was an outlet. We'd jump in after school and go hunting. Weekends we'd get a gang together and go out in it and party. There'd always be someone around the liquor store who'd bring out some beer for us, and away we'd go.

"Rick wasn't usually much of a drinker. One or two beer would do, but when he had more, oh boy. I can remember once in a while we'd pull up to a stop sign, and Rick would use the winch on the front of the Bronco to pull it out by the roots and leave it lying on the roadside. It didn't happen often, but when it did it was like all the anger and frustration had built up and was pushing its way out."

Mostly, the anger stayed inside. Marv and Joan Hansen look back on the time after his return as being pretty much the same as it had been before he left. Their marriage was in the process of dissolving—nothing to do with the accident, insists Marv, who remarried in 1981, just two people going in different directions. Oh, they'd jump at the first sound of a thump, feel their hearts lurch when they'd find him crumpled at the bottom of the stairs he'd almost climbed, worrying over and treating the sores he got on his legs from the rubbing of the braces. But basically, life went on as before. "If anything," Marv says now, "it might have been toughest on the kids."

Brad was fourteen when Rick came home, too young, really, to understand. Neither he nor his brother had ever been very good at expressing their feelings for one another—perhaps, Joan says dryly, "because Rick kept breaking him. Once they were fooling around with a rope over a tree branch where one was supposed to go up as the other came down, and Rick landed on him and broke every toe on his right foot. Another time when they were wrestling on the carpet, Rick lifted him by the legs and dropped him. Brad landed nose first, and broke it."

But there was an unspoken closeness.

"I kept waiting for the doctors to come and operate and he'd be better," Brad recalls. "All these years, that's always been in my mind. When I biked beside the chair in Australia and he mentioned, quite casually, that whatever research this triggered would be too late for him, that he would never walk again, my mouth just fell open. I guess, down deep, I'd never quit believing . . ."

Cindy, eleven at the time, can remember sneaking up on her brother to squeeze his emaciated legs or tickle his feet or pinch his toes "because, just once, I wanted him to say ouch. But he never did."

Bob Redford, Hansen's high school gym teacher and a major influence on his life, offers a slightly different viewpoint of Hansen's road back. To him the chair and the sports made a difference, but perhaps not as big a difference as the kids who were there when he needed them.

"That group of kids—Patti, Don Alder, the kids who'd been on the team and had been his friends before he got hurt—were a special bunch. They always wanted to help but they were never condescending about it, and they always seemed to know when to back off.

"When Rick came back, he came back stubborn. I guess inwardly he was having a lot of problems, but he very seldom showed it, always tried to give the impression that he had everything under control even when it was obvious that he didn't. It made a lot of people uncomfortable, not knowing what to do. They'd try to help him up a flight of stairs, that kind of thing, and he wasn't having any of it. But these kids just rode right through all of that. He'd been part of the gang and gone places with them before, and now he was back, so naturally he'd be going places with them again. They didn't ignore the accident, they just didn't let it get in the way. If anyone was self-conscious about the situation, it was Rick.

"I've often thought about that. Another group a year or so younger, or just a different collection of kids, might not have handled it that well. And who knows how differently things might have turned out . . . ?"

Back at G. F. Strong, getting ready to come home to Williams Lake, I'd made three decisions:

I'd give up athletics, because what else could I do?

I'd give up on women, because what girl in her right mind would want to go out with me?

I'd concentrate on school. I was a semester behind, so I'd take a lot of courses and catch up.

Social life? Don't be silly. I'd been a star athlete. Everything I'd done had pivoted around sports. I was part of the team. How many kids were going to hang around with a guy in a wheelchair? They had things to do. I knew—I used to do them with them.

It was a matter of facing facts, and from the instant the Bronco pulled up in front of the house, there were a lot of facts to face.

Fact one: the house was totally inaccessible for a wheelchair.

Fact two: I wasn't sure I wanted to live there anyway.

The house looked fine from the outside—flat driveway and only one step up to the front door. But once through that door, on a landing barely big enough to take a chair, let alone provide room to swing one, you ran smack into steep, seven-step stairs up to the living area and seven steps down the inside stairs from the living area to the basement. Sundeck off the kitchen to ground level in the back yard: twelve steps. Back yard to the outside entrance to the basement living quarters my dad had put in for me: six steps down into a concrete stairwell. Wheelchair accessible? Forget it.

Not that it worried me. I hated the chair. Just being in it told the world I was disabled. Worse, it told me. I'd use the braces and the sticks. As long as I was standing, I wasn't quite that disabled. So I attacked the house the way I'd attacked the halls and stairs at G. F. Strong.

The house fought back.

I could get up and down all right if I wanted to bum-hitch, going up sitting down backwards and lifting my butt stair to stair. But that was too slow, and after all, the inside stairs did have handrails on top of the banisters. Why couldn't I go up on the braces and crutches, pulling myself along on the handrails?

Because the house didn't want me to. Those handrails were held to the banisters with screws. I'd put so much pressure and twist on the railings pulling myself up that they'd rip right out of the banister and send me head first and backwards down to the landing. I'm not talking occasionally, I'm talking often. Up the stairs at the front, down the inside stairs to the basement—they ripped out on me. The house got me anyway. The outside stairs to the basement had no railings, only a banister. One day the banister broke off in my hand and I went head-first into the concrete stairwell. I could have broken my neck.

The battle never stopped. To this day, there's a dent in the plaster shaped just like my forehead, next to the bed in one of the upstairs bedrooms.

I was trying to develop a new, faster system for getting up on my braces by lifting myself on the crutches from a sitting position to allow my legs to swing free. That way I could swing them back until the knee braces locked. It was tricky, it was even a bit dangerous. That's why I chose a practice room where the bed was close to the wall: fall backward and I'd land on the bed. Fall forward and I could brace myself on the wall. At least, that was the theory. In practice, I slipped so often I literally dented the plaster with my head. Eventually I mastered it, and use it to this day. As for my battles with the house, I guess you could call that one a tie.

It wasn't just the house, it was everything.

Outside was a joke. We'd come home in snow season. When there's ice under the snow and a crutch hits it, I don't care how good you are, you fall. And when it came to the braces, I wasn't too good. I'd try to walk, my crutches would stick, my feet would keep on sliding, and I'd wind up hopping along on the crutches hoping they wouldn't slide and watching my legs go every which way. It was maddening, so frustrating I could barely stand it. And underneath, whenever I let my

33

guard down, there was this little inner voice giving me the word: forever. It's going to be this way forever . . .

A newly disabled person suddenly in a wheelchair can put on a big, brave front, as I'd been doing with everyone but my parents, spend every minute looking on the bright side and telling people this isn't going to slow you down, and generally being so optimistic about it that they'll swear you should be up for sainthood. A newly disabled person might even believe it. But the hard fact is that you are tied to that chair or to those crutches, and facing it for the first time can make you the loneliest person in the world.

Inside the house there was another hurdle that had nothing to do with stairs or railings or accessibility: I wasn't coming back to a happy home, I was coming back to a house in which two people were tearing each other apart.

My mother and father's relationship had been steadily deteriorating for five years before the accident. I resented it a lot, and being the kind of person I was, I just wouldn't put up with it. I was thirteen or fourteen. I'd lie awake and listen to two people I loved yell and scream and tear at each other all night, and it would just eat me up. So I'd jump out of bed, pound on their door and barge right in. Mom would be crying, Dad would be angry, and I'd stand there in the doorway and yell at them:

"Look, you two, either fix this up or get a divorce!"

I knew it was difficult, otherwise they probably would have split already—but I couldn't just lie there night after night listening to it and not do anything at all.

I couldn't stand what they were doing to each other and to the family. In my opinion, it was over. I knew there just couldn't be any love left there. Why keep hurting one another?

You could say they should have booted my tail down the stairs or set my my butt on fire and thrown me back into bed for interfering. But really, what could they do? They'd have been justified if the fight was a one-time thing, an isolated instance—but what could they say when they were aware of the situation but trapped in it, and here was their son telling them they'd better get it straightened out? They couldn't brand me; I was right. It was a last, desperate way of saying this wasn't just their fight anymore, it was ours.

But I was young enough to remember how it used to be, and old enough to ask myself what went wrong . . .

From the time I was a little kid I'd been so darned independent. I was the first of four. Each new one became a priority. I was nineteen months old when Brad was born. Three years later there was Cindy, and fifteen months after that there was Chris. And for the first six years of my life I was literally surrounded by relatives.

My father's roots were Norwegian, my mother's English. My grand-parents had settled in the Port Alberni area. My maternal grand-father, Joe Gibson, was a drill sergeant in the army (a blasting cap accident cost him his trigger finger and one other, and kept him out of the war) who worked for the city and in the pulp mill until he de-cided at age fifty that he wanted to be a farmer, sold everything he owned and bought a 640-acre farm in Fort St. John. Grandpa Magnus Hansen had been a miner, a longshoreman, then a fisherman. Talk about your huddled masses: within the space of ten acres there was our family, Grannie and Grandpa Gibson, and Uncle John and Aunt Betty Jones. Uncle Leonard and Aunt Fern Gibson and a raft of other Gibsons and Hansens were scattered around Port Alberni, and count-ing all the families there were twenty-six kids. (If I've miscounted, folks, forgive me.)

We were all very close, always visiting each other, but under those conditions you learn early to go your own way. My dad took me fish-ing a lot, and he and Grandpa Gibson taught me about hunting and respecting the land, and the ethics of discipline and hard work. I got love and I got support, but probably not as much attention as I needed, given the kind of kid I was. (Mom says I needed so much that I should have been an only child or she should have waited longer to have the rest.)

Moving as much as we did was no help. We bounced from Port Al-berni to Fort St. John in 1962 just after I started grade one; then in 1964 after Dad's accident to Abbotsford (where we changed houses and schools three times) and then to Williams Lake in 1971. There never seemed time to make really close friends in the early growing-up years. I wasn't a loner. I just chose my friends carefully and de-cided how close I was going to let them get to me, because what the heck, we'd probably be moving again anyway. In self-defence, or maybe as a substitute, I focussed all my attention outward, and deeply resented any parental insistence that it be any other way.

Take school. Kindergarten was fine, although Mom says it took two adults to get me there the first day. But the last thing I wanted to do was go to elementary school. She had to drag me into grade one, too. Or take church. My parents made me go every Sunday. Then, about grade six, I decided that was it. My Sundays had become too valu-able. I wanted to hike and hunt and fish and play sports, and church was getting in the way. One day I put my foot down and that was that. There was some flak, but I guess they realized that forcing me to go wasn't the answer, so they gave in.

Sometimes I'd even get into trouble trying to be good. Like the time I was five years old and decided it was time I started fishing and bringing home the catch to help save on the food budget the way Grandpa and Dad were always doing.

My friend Mikey Boyden and I went down to the creek at the foot of Grandpa's property, me with my little rod, determined to land a big one. There were big fish in that creek, all right. What we didn't know was that it was spawning time, and fish just don't bite then. Still, we got one—a big dead one that had spawned and flopped out onto the bank Lord knows when. Well, I was ecstatic. The thing must have weighed thirty pounds. To two five-year-olds it was a monster. We each grabbed an end and lugged it, all slippery and slithery and wet, up the bank toward my house.

We got as far as Uncle John's and collapsed. There was just no way we could go any farther. There was only one thing to do: I went to Uncle John and asked him if I could borrow his bread knife. I probably didn't mention why I needed it. Then I went back and started hacking that fish into steaks, until someone came along and told me a fish like that couldn't be eaten.

So I left it there. Hey, I had things to do.

Uncle John was not impressed. I'd loused up his bread knife, his lawn was covered with rotting fish, and I was nowhere to be found. But then, I seldom was.

It was like a burning in me to do things, to accept challenges, to stretch out and go looking. In Port Alberni I was always getting grounded for coming home filthy dirty or soaking wet because I had to prove to the other kids I could run over the log booms faster than they could. If I couldn't, well, okay. But I had to try. In Abbotsford I'd bike 20 miles on my little three-speed to find a new place to fish. I'd get the gang together, catch dew worms at night and fish the next day. We'd hike the valleys in what amounted to wilderness, find a creek no one knew about and follow it until there was no creek left. We'd explore caves or just pick a power line and follow it, never knowing where it was going or when it would end. And once I saved enough money from part-time jobs to buy a little Honda 70 motorbike, forget it. I was gone.

I had to have the bike, had to get away, because by that time we'd moved to Williams Lake, and I hated it. We were miles from anywhere, with unpaved roads that made it almost impossible to bike. I fought that move tooth and nail, but when you're thirteen you don't get a vote.

But you adjust. We moved closer to town and school. I made friends, got involved in basketball and volleyball again. I played some baseball, pitched softball for the men's "C" division team, fished and hunted when I could, and still found time to raise my share of teen-age hell.

For instance, you know how some kids have a clubhouse or a fort? We had a house.

The yellow house across the street from ours had been vacant for a year. We never damaged or took anything (except the key, from where the agent always hid it), we just used it as a place to hang out. And we felt pretty secure, because it had been vacant for so long we figured no one was ever going to buy it. One night a bunch of us were waiting for one of the guys to finish arguing with his girlfriend in her house, which was next door to ours. I guess the argument didn't go too well, because when he came out he picked up a rock from a gravel driveway and hurled it at the front of the deserted yellow house. Boom! It hit the aluminum siding. Great sound! Suddenly we're all hucking rocks at the house.

Boom! Boom! It was so dark outside we couldn't tell whether we were hitting siding or glass. I found out the next morning. The windows were gone. All of them. The siding had more craters than the surface of the moon.

Then I noticed something else. The For Sale sign was gone, there was a car in the driveway and a man was staring at the wreckage as though he didn't know what had hit him. His name was Frank Moore. As it turned out, he was a prince of a guy. When the police came and took us to the station (naturally, the neighbours had seen what was going on and who was doing it), he never laid charges. The house insurance covered the damages, and we felt as stupid as we'd been.

Fortunately, there wasn't much time for trouble, not with all the sports and the job and the outdoors calling me. The only ongoing trouble was caused by my determination to go my own way. My dad didn't have the time to take me fishing as often as I wanted to go? Okay, I'd hop on the bike and go myself—fishing, or anywhere else I felt like going.

My attitude didn't always sit well at home. There came a day not more than a year before the accident when my dad sat me down to discuss freedom and independence. Translation: he wanted me to spend more time at home. Well, I didn't need that. I ran away. Hitchhiked to my cousin's cottage. I'd show them, boy.

A couple of hours later, in comes my mom. She'd figured where I'd go, and she came and hauled me back. My dad was waiting.

"If that ever happens again," he warned, "you're gone for good."

"Don't worry about it," I shot back. "If it ever happens again, I *will* be gone for good."

So that was the Rick Hansen who came home to Williams Lake in a wheelchair: a sixteen-year-old who'd never developed a really strong family bond, never really gotten to know his parents, never learned to communicate with them or with his brother and sisters, never learned to show the love he had for them; a kid who'd gone his own way, a doer and a leader who'd lived for his independence and freedom to roam.

And now I was helpless and needed everyone.

I'd had a taste of it at Christmas. I'd been flown in from G. F. Strong, bundled up in what amounted to a cart and carried on and off the plane because I wasn't good enough yet on the braces. The humiliation of it just burned at me.

Now I was back to stay, or so everyone thought. Me, I wasn't sure. In my mind I'd phased myself out of the house and was on my own before the accident. The house was there and was handy, a place to eat and sleep, but I'd always been out as much as possible. Some of that still applied once I was home, but it was a two-edged sword. The house was still handy, there were still good reasons for staying, but I could never be independent because it was so inaccessible. I couldn't pop in and out and go my own way. In a sense I was a prisoner.

My family rallied around. Dad had the basement renovated to give me my own room and bath. Mom and Dad had their own problems, but there was no doubt who was the first priority. I was still being tough on them, but they never pushed me, never tried to overprotect me.

A lot of people have asked me whether the family stress over my accident was a factor in my parents' separation. Actually, it worked the other way around. For a while I think it kept them together through their concern for me. But the stress might have been the final blow, particularly for my mother, who'd had more than most of us ever encounter.

First there was Dad's accident. Then Brad severely burned one leg when firecrackers exploded in his pocket and tobogganed head-on into an oncoming car, breaking the bones around both eyes; he required surgery and was lucky to escape with his eyesight. And a year before my accident, Grandpa Gibson died in a horrible farm accident. He was wearing a wool work shirt buttoned at the neck. The sleeve caught in the combine, and as it twisted into the machinery his shirt literally strangled him. Grandma Elsie found him when she brought his afternoon tea. His hat was on the ground, the combine still running. She climbed aboard and found him lying in the bin.

People can take only so much pressure, particularly when the family life is deteriorating and the support systems aren't there. It was especially tough for Mom because she'd tried to stop me from taking the fishing trip. Grandpa Gibson had travelled that road shortly before he died and had told her, "Don't let the boys drive to Bella Coola." And of course we did, and she was riddled with guilt because she thought he'd had some sort of premonition and she hadn't some-how kept me at home, as if she could have.

My parents hung in there for a couple more years. I was settled into university when they separated and ultimately divorced. For me there was no sorrow, only the hope that they'd both find happiness, and a sense of relief that something that should have ended a long time ago was finally over.

Of all the things I remember about my parents, through good times and bad, I remember this most: when I needed them, they were al-ways there. I loved them then, I love them now, and I always will.

Meanwhile, there was the outside world to be faced. The outside world—and school.

I almost didn't go. Downtown was bad enough. Williams Lake was a small, work-oriented town whose people had never had to deal with something like this. Mine was the only wheelchair in town, and the town wasn't geared for it. Wheelchair access was unheard of, and the smallest trip had to end with my being pushed or lifted.

People thought my life was over. Worse yet, so did I.

Well, maybe I could handle all that. But school? Go back to the place where I'd been an athlete and a leader, like this? Go back into the gym? All that big talk at Royal Columbian about coming back, about playing again. I'd played the scene over and over again in my mind. This was reality time. This wasn't the star athlete com-ing home. This was the cripple. How would my friends act? How would I act?

The first day was a horror. There was snow all over the ground and I wasn't sure how I was going to get through it and into the place, let alone get around inside. Once I managed that, there was another little surprise for me—a portable school annex set down beside the main building, the two joined only by a footpath. Oh, school was go-ing to be wonderful.

The kids were nervous, the teachers were nervous, I was self-conscious and scared stiff. They were staring at me—trying not to, but I could feel it. I could read their minds: "What's he thinking? How's he going to handle this? Poor Rick . . ."

It took me weeks to get over that sense of the eyes drilling into me. Once, thumping up the stairs between classes, I met a boy with polio heading down. I remembered seeing him before my accident and thinking how sad it was, and how terrible it would feel to be that way. And it struck me, not without a touch of bitterness, that he was probably looking at me now and thinking the same thing.

But if that was tough, going back into the gym was devastating. I avoided it as long as I could. Then one day I screwed up my courage and peeked through the door. There they were: Bob Redford and the volleyball team. Same coach, same guys, only now I was on crutches and out of it. It was going to be awful.

I underestimated them. I thumped across the floor and started talking to Redford. The guys said hi, Randy made a face at me, and for a few moments it was like I'd never been away. The practice continued, Redford still talking to me, asking me to assess the talent and the skills of the individual players. (Even then, I think he was trying to ease me back into athletics in some other form.)

Suddenly, I just lost it. I was shaking on the crutches. If I stayed one more minute I was going to cry. So I just turned and thumped out. I climbed into the Bronco, powered out to the country and did my crying there.

When I think about it, I guess I underestimated all of them.

The first day back at school, heading from the main building to the annex, I ignored the path and tried a shortcut across the snow. Naturally, I fell. While I was sitting there spitting snow and wondering if I'd be found before spring thaw, around the corner came a couple of kids named Ken Rich and Rob Graham. They got me back up onto my feet as though it was the most natural thing in the world, and off we went to class. Just like that, I had two new friends.

Once the initial shyness was overcome, my old friends were there as they'd been before. Randy and Don had the toughest time, Don in particular because he'd been in the truck with me and had escaped without a scratch, and there I was in the chair. But they made the effort. They'd come over. We'd take a pellet gun to the basement and shoot ping-pong balls off bottles. I got my dad to hang a trapeze from the ceiling so I could hang by one hand while standing on my braces and play ping-pong.

My friends were going to be fine. It was just a matter of educating them. But first I had to educate me.

Thank God for the Bronco. It was my recreation, my escape, my four-wheel-drive thread to what I'd been before. I drove it every chance I got, and I drove it hard. Maybe I couldn't push myself in other ways, but when I was behind the wheel I was on even terms with everyone in it—and I was in control. Every weekend and a lot of weeknights three or four of us would throw a case of beer in the back —stupid thing to be doing, drinking and driving—go booming off through the back country at breakneck speed, fish or party it up, and come flying back. If we got stuck, that was part of the thrill.

Once, doing 60 miles an hour down a roller-coaster back road, we hit a cattle guard so hard we were airborne. My head banged into the roof *and* I rebounded and landed under the dash. There I was, flying blind, steering by reaching up for the wheel while I fumbled around trying to find the brake. We missed a head-on collision with a telephone pole by about a quarter-inch. On another night when we didn't have enough gas or money to go fishing the next day, one of the guys suggested we siphon some from the cars on a used-car lot. They'd do it, I'd be the lookout. As it turned out, I had the good job. I just got moved along by a security guard who wondered why I was parked by myself at midnight with the lights out. Brad and the other guy were chased by police, complete with tracking dogs and flashlights, and had to hide under the railway trestle for four hours until it was safe to sneak home.

Juvenile delinquent? No, just bored and scared. I was on the edge of getting myself into real trouble, feeling out my options and finding none of them too bright. It was craziness — but maybe it was necessary, because for all the hell-raising I was at least socializing, taking an equal part, learning that even if athletics was a lost cause there were still things I could do on equal terms with my friends, even if they did require accepting help. Just being there, the guys had come through for me in a way they probably never understood. Without them, I might have just pulled the hole in after me and quit.

When the hope dies, a terrible thing can happen to a disabled person. You get it into your head that you can't do things, and you never let yourself forget that you're handicapped. It's not just the things you can't do, it's the things you can do given enough time, things other people could get done for you much faster. If you're not careful, you start trading off the independence for the service. Either that, or you get stubborn and do things yourself when you should be asking for help. Every so often you have to stop and give yourself a kick in the butt, or become a pain in the butt.

I remember once on that first Christmas after I came back to stay, a bunch of the kids decided to go to Blue Lake for the weekend. It was all snowed in, and I was put off because I couldn't make it. But they got a toboggan, grabbed the ropes and hauled me in. We could have had the greatest time — but I was sitting there sulking because I had to be tobogganed in. I wrecked the entire evening. We stayed overnight and came back the next day. It was okay, but I'd acted like a little wimp.

I know part of the reason. It was the old boy-girl thing and I was self-conscious. Because by that time, I had a girl. Yet, I was still in the chair, or on the braces and crutches. Why was she going out with me? How long before she dropped me for someone else? What did the other kids think about it?

Yeah, I know: I'd written off women before they could write off me. It was funny the way I changed my mind. Brad had a crush on a girl named Kim Belcher who played on one of the school volleyball teams, but was too shy to ask her out. I razzed him about it and kept telling him I was going to phone her and set up a date for him. He thought I was kidding until I did it.

Well, she said yes, and the thing was a lock until I told Brad. He wimped out, phoned her, and explained that the whole thing had been my idea and he didn't want a date. So where did that leave me? Obviously, I owed her an apology.

I got as far as the phone when it hit me: this is a cute girl! Why am I asking her out for him? I want to ask her out for myself. So I did, we went for a drive, and that's how I had my first kiss at the ripe old age of sixteen.

That was a bit of a confidence builder, but I still didn't think any girl would go steady with me or anything like that. Then one day in grade eleven science I noticed this girl named Isobel at the back of the room who kept looking up front at me and smiling. At first I didn't smile back. She couldn't be smiling at me. Then I noticed there was no one in front of me but the teacher, and she couldn't be smiling at him. "Hey," I thought. "She *is* smiling at me." Then I gave it up. Probably just felt sorry for me.

But she'd come up and talk to me, and one day she drove up in her friend's old car to where I was lying on the grass. She asked me out to a show, and we wound up dating for about three months. Wait a minute! Maybe they didn't just feel sorry for me. Maybe girls weren't out of the question.

I started asking girls out instead of waiting to be asked. Son of a gun! It worked. By grade twelve I was going steady with a girl named Patti Lueke who played on the grade eleven volleyball team I was helping to coach. We went out rather seriously for about the next three years. In fact, it was Patti I was with on the Blue Lake expedition.

So why was I being such a jerk? Because through it all I was still pretty insecure. I was jealous of the other guys. I'd look at Patti and think, "What can she possibly see in me? Why is she with me when she can be with one of them?" At parties I'd just sit back and watch. I was embarrassed over my legs, which had wasted away to next to nothing after being so big and solid and well defined. We'd go to the lake, and the gang would be saying, "C'mon down! We'll carry you to the bank." Not me. I'd sit in the truck on the road waiting while they were down in the water swimming. We'd go on a picnic, and I'd barely make an effort to do anything. I was just sitting there feeling sorry for myself and trying to make as many people as possible feel sorry for me.

There was no future in it. Deep down I think I knew that. But my education was just getting started.

There's nothing wrong with being carried down a bank by your friends so you can go swimming. What's wrong with taking your clothes off and going in shorts and letting people see that you've got skinny legs? It's no big deal. I had to realize that there weren't too many things I used to do that I couldn't do again, but that some of it wouldn't be the same. All I really had to do was adapt, to try my hardest and accept the bumps and frustrations as part of the payment for what I could do.

Take hunting and fishing. They'd been a huge part of my life. I'd been running away from a lot of things because I was disabled. My old fast-track life had slowed to a crawl, and it was only going to get worse unless I did something about it. Hunting and fishing gave me the opportunity to get back in touch with myself and my old friends and lifestyle, to focus on targets, to get back a sense of responsibility.

I can't remember life before fishing. I started spincasting when I was three, and Mom says by the time I was six I was doing it as well as a man. It was something I had to get back to. When we decided it was time, Dad and Brad took me to a place we used to go to on the Thompson River. To get there we had to get across an old swinging bridge—and I was on my braces.

Well, what the heck? I wanted to be independent, didn't I? I hopped out onto the bridge. It's swaying, I'm swaying on the crutches, my feet are sliding around, and I can see the river below quite clearly thanks to the knotholes in the rotting timbers I'm trusting will hold my crutches. All I can think of is, "What am I doing?"

But I made it. I handled that part, and the mile or so down the railroad track, then let them help me with the part I couldn't handle: carrying me down the bank, putting me in a life jacket and tying me to a tree so I could fish without falling in. We caught some fish and really enjoyed ourselves. Adaptation.

Kayaking, which I'd never done before the accident, presented the same story, and the same solution. I had to attack it a little differently. Put kayak on car. Put chair in car. Drive to boat ramp. Take chair out of car, pull kayak off car. Throw gear out of car. Put chair back in car. Drive car to parking lot. Take chair out of car, wheel to kayak, climb in and go.

Oh, yes—be sure chair is left above high tide line. One day I left at low tide with my keys sitting on the chair. When I came back, the tide was up, my chair was sunk and my car keys were gone. But assuming you come back and haven't been that dumb, getting home is simple. Wheel to car. Put chair in car. Drive to kayak. Take chair out of car. Hoist kayak on top of car. Put chair back in car. Drive home. Take chair out of car. Take kayak off car. Wheel inside. Relax.

Later on I eliminated a lot of the hassle by renting space at a marina and leaving it moored where I could just drive down, hop in and be gone. The point is that when I wanted to go kayaking I went, and my method wasn't any different from that of other people except that I had to add a few steps. For instance, I learned to use gravity to my advantage in loading and unloading. Moving the kayak to the marina was just another logical step up, learning to go about it in the easiest way for me. Adaptation.

Hunting is more difficult, but not impossible. I love to hunt. I'm not bloodthirsty. It's not the thrill of killing something. My family has always hunted for meat, and for the challenge, and for the pure joy of getting out into the wilderness. I've hunted from the time I was old enough to be taught how to handle a rifle properly and safely. And the time came after my accident when I wanted to go hunting again. The question was, how?

When you're in Fort St. John in Alaska gumbo mud, you can't go anywhere in a wheelchair, let alone try to walk on crutches and braces. So when we go hunting I don't use a chair, I use an all-terrain vehicle, a six-wheel drive that can go over water, snow, swamp or hill. Now, I can hardly sneak up on a moose in an ATV with a sixteen-horsepower Tecumseh spouting exhaust fumes. There aren't that many blind moose with head colds out there. So, rather than chase the moose, I let the moose come to me.

You can cover a lot of ground in an ATV. We scour it until we find tracks, then follow them to find the crossing and feeding areas and watch where they're browsing, and get down wind or high up. We set up camp nearby, return to the area we've selected—and wait. Sometimes I'll sit out there six, eight, ten days waiting for a shot. It gives a guy time to do a lot of thinking. There are even certain advantages.

It's tough to get around in camp. I can't skin out a quarter as easily as I used to because holding the carcass with one hand and cutting with another while balancing on crutches isn't easy, and I can't get the cutting angles I need. So, I do what I can, and then I get to play foreman. You think I don't get shots from Brad and the old man about that?

Adaptation. We're out there in the wilderness breathing in the clean air and working and camping and going to bed with that special tired feeling that comes with it. It's freedom in some ways, and in some ways it's frustrating because it throws back in my face the things I can't do.

Like the time Rob Graham and I threw a couple of dozen beer in the ATV and headed out from camp. We weren't hunting. We didn't even take our guns with us. We just wanted to see some country. After about three hours we'd seen so much of it that we'd cut through a couple of swamps, the road had petered out, the beer was two-thirds gone, and the ATV was perched on top of a beaver dam with the nose sticking out about three feet over the water.

"You wanna turn around?" Rob asked.

I thought about it for a few seconds.

"Good idea," I said.

So we turned around, got to within a couple of miles of camp—and the ATV broke down. No problem! We'd walk in! What the heck, I had my braces and crutches. Why not? Except that the road was gumbo mud, and every so often one of my crutches would sink clear up to my armpit, the tip would come off, and I'd be face down in the mud. I lost track of how many times that happened in two miles. It's the simple things that get you down, like a nice little hike that turns into a stumble through the mud that grabs at your crutches like quicksand and takes you with them.

No, it's not easy. But I'm hunting! I'm having a great time. And I usually get my moose.

These things didn't all come to me in a flash. There was no blinding revelation. The educational process was painfully slow, and it came in stages. My thinking was being shaped by my experiences, and I was making progress. I was learning to do some things on my own. But I was still going about it the wrong way. I still didn't appreciate the things I could do. Instead, I was focussing on the things I couldn't do. And though I didn't realize it, that kind of thinking was getting me nowhere fast.

Then I burned my foot. Thank goodness, I burned my foot.

It was June of 1975, my grad year. By that time I was beginning to discover that competitive sports, like girls, weren't really out of the question. A man named Stan Stronge had lured me into wheelchair sports (we'll get into that later) and there I was in Montreal, a third-string basketballer in the Canadian Wheelchair Games.

It was really an eye-opener. I was tremendously impressed by the sheer athletic ability of these people. I'd had a wonderful time, and now I was in the shower still half asleep from a late night, racing to make the plane home. So I turned on the hot water tap, expecting it to take a while for it to heat as it did at home, and dozed off. It came out hot from the start. My left foot was under the spout, and because I had no feeling in my legs I couldn't feel the flesh scalding.

There was no permanent damage, but in the month it took for the foot to heal, I was hit with a whole new set of frustrations—and a new appreciation of the things I'd been able to do before it happened. I'd made gains, gains that I'd taken for granted. I could drive, so I had transportation. I had crutches and braces, so I wasn't bound to the chair. Now those edges were gone.

I could drive, but with the wound on the foot I couldn't get the braces on, which meant using the chair all the time if I wanted to get anywhere, and in the house the wheelchair was worse than useless. I wasn't just back to square one. It was worse than that, because I'd had a taste of what I could accomplish myself. Now my family had to help me everywhere. And again, I came to expect it.

One day I drove up to the house and honked the horn for Brad to come and help me into the house. Without the braces I couldn't do it myself. He'd already helped me from the house to the truck when I left. Now I was back, and ready to go in.

"There in a minute!" he yelled. "I'm busy."

Busy? What did he mean, busy? Furious, I honked the horn again, but louder. He didn't come. Now I was spitting nails. I threw open the Bronco's door, lowered myself to the ground, and started bum-hitching toward the house. Where was everybody? I'd honked. Why weren't they there?

But there was a small difference. I was ticked off. I was furious. But I was getting to the door. And suddenly it hit me. "Hey! You don't need these guys. You can do it yourself." And I realized I wasn't mad at them at all, I was mad because I needed someone again. I was dependent again because I didn't have the braces. When I had them, I could do things. And if I could do some things, maybe I could do others . . .

You see how it worked out? Because I burned my foot I lost the braces, lost the independence I'd gained—and learned to appreciate it. It changed my focus. Now I could concentrate on the things I could do while learning to accept help with the things I couldn't.

The next plateau—learning to do special things totally on my own—was reached in another series of steps over a couple of years. It was one of those steps that left me face down in the Fraser River with my wheelchair on top of me, miles from anywhere and wondering just how I was going to get out.

By that time I was living in Vancouver and attending the University of British Columbia. Life was working out pretty well. I had wheel-chair sports. I was working toward a degree in physical education. I had friends and a social life. But every once in a while that old feeling of dependency would pop up and nag at me.

On that particular day I had an itch to get back up-country and fish, but everyone I asked was wimping out. And I caught myself thinking, "Jeez, if they won't go, I can't go!"

Then I realized how stupid that was. I was in a totally different frame of mind in those days than I'd been in Williams Lake. I'd been going places on my own for quite a while. Maybe not into the wilderness, but that was no big deal. I'd grown up there. Fishing hadn't changed. Why should I?

I loaded up the little Honda and drove clear up to the Fraser River to a spot I used to go to when I was a kid in Abbotsford. (In 1979 I'd traded the beloved Bronco for a Chevy 4x4, which I later sold to Brad dirt cheap on the condition he retain the hand controls in case I wanted to use it, and bought a Honda Civic. It made more sense: my life was in the city now.) I got to the dike—and the gate was locked. Okay, city boy, what do you do now?

Hey! I'd come to fish! I parked the car, strapped on the braces and threw the chair and the fishing rod over the gate, which was about five feet high. Now I had to go fishing.

I pulled myself up by the arms, manoeuvred my body over the top of the gate and lowered myself to the ground on the other side. Then I wheeled along the dike to a meadow plateau, overlooking a spot where a slough entered the Fraser. I powered the chair through a ditch, went through the gate climbing routine again, only this time over a barbed-wire fence, and rolled down to the edge of the river. Didn't catch much—a few bullheads, things like that—so I went down the slope very slowly to another plateau, worked my way back up and more or less wandered from place to place. Finally, I decided to go back down to the first plateau. Only this time I got cocky.

I threw the rod down, kicked the chair into a wheelie and coasted down the hill. Naturally, I was moving far too fast. When I tried to turn the chair from the path onto the plateau, the momentum caused me to roll the chair, and we both flew off the bank and four feet down into the water—first me, then the chair on top of me.

My first thought was, "Save yourself," which was brilliant. There wasn't a soul for miles. If I didn't save myself, who would?

The water wasn't particularly deep, and I wasn't being swept away, so I threw the chair off and scrambled to the edge. My next thought—"Save the chair"—came just in time. It was slowly sinking out of sight where I'd flipped it off. I leaned out, grabbed it and hauled it in.

Well, I wasn't going to drown. Starve, maybe, but not drown. Don't forget, I was still below that four-foot bank, and we are talking mud-bank, slick and slippery. Okay, Hansen, get yourself out of this.

I started to crawl, clutching at tufts of grass. "I'm never gonna make it," I told myself. I got embarrassed. Then I got mad. "Off by yourself and can't handle it. Wimp!" I grabbed another chunk of turf, powered to the top, reached down and hauled up the chair. Then I set it up, rolled back down to that same ledge—more cautiously this time—and stayed until I'd caught a couple of fish.

The return roll was easy. I followed the rod and the chair over the fence and the gate, wheeled to the car and headed back. As fishing trips went, I've had better. But I smiled all the way home.

4

"Hey! These guys are *good!*"

"*T*he truth is, Rick wasn't that great an athlete in high school," admits Bob Redford, Hansen's coach and friend. "He was a good athlete—good co-ordination, good skills, highly coachable—but not great in the sense that he was going to be a pro or a superstar. He was a kid who could play a lot of sports at a better-than-average level, played them all and worked his tail off to get better."

There is no doubt in Rick Hansen's mind that the discovery of wheelchair sport turned his life, that with no outlet for his burning desire to compete, the Man in Motion tour might never have been attempted. He was used to being the leader, the one the others looked to. He didn't just accept that responsibility, he needed it. Once the outlet was provided, he threw himself into it—and from the beginning it was a no-nonsense proposition.

"Competitive?" says Stan Stronge, the man who first got him involved in wheelchair sport. "Oh, yes, he was competitive. In everything else, he was painfully shy. He'd win something, and I'd have to drag him to the banquet to accept it. But get him in a game, give him a challenge, and look out. Second place was something he didn't understand and wouldn't accept.

"He had a puppy-dog look about him then—you know, the eyes looking up at you from under the brows—and feet so big we'd just stare at them. But he was smart, and full of questions, and wouldn't let anything get in the way. Once he asked me to meet him for lunch and showed up with this lovely girl. He wolfed down the lunch, said 'I've got to go now. Got to work on my racing chair,' and just left us there. I drove her home, and as we passed his apartment, there he was on the balcony, working on that chair.

"He wasn't being rude. Not by his lights at the time. She was beautiful —but he had a chair to get ready."

Peter Brookes had plenty of opportunity to see that competitiveness in operation. Brookes is a close friend, a Delta, B.C., native now living in Los Angeles with his wife, Candace Cable-Brookes. They are both paraplegic, both track and marathon racers, Candace among the best in the world.

"Rick was the king on the circuit," he says. "If Hansen crossed his legs for a race to cut wind resistance, all the Canadians did it. And he knew he was good. Hell, he wasn't stupid. It bordered on arrogance. What saved it was that he was always working with the other guys, helping them, offering advice. He'd party with the best of us, but before the race he'd shut it down. Racing was all business, and you don't party in business hours."

And even when Rick partied or relaxed, Marv Hansen recalls, business was never neglected.

"He was always working on his upper body, weightlifting, getting stronger. I used to give him hell. He was pressing far too much. He got so he could press two hundred pounds seven or eight times. I'd scream at him: 'You trying for a rupture, for god's sake?' He'd just grunt and keep lifting.

"Even when we went hunting, way up in the bush, he insisted we hoist that three-hundred-pound training rig of his into the van at home and out again in the middle of nowhere so he wouldn't have to screw up his workout schedule. Every fall I'd say, 'Rick, there's no room!' And every year he'd say, 'We'll make some.'

"Brad and I wanted it to be a hunting, fishing, beer and BS trip. But no—two and one-half hours every day on that machine, in the middle of a moose hunt!"

Tim Frick, an able-bodied friend who was "dragged" by Hansen into coaching a wheelchair volleyball team and soon found himself playing with him, the two of them against full teams, Hansen in his chair, says Hansen was always fussing over his chair, always late or nearly late for a competition.

"Once, in an 800-metre race, I was actually pumping a tire with a slow leak at the starting line when the gun went off. I yanked the pin, and he took off and won, going the last 100 or so with the tire flat.

"But the sport was developing so quickly we learned early that to win you needed the best preparation, the best equipment and the best mental attitude. Rick was always into chair design, and because he was such a perfectionist and such a worrier, he was never sure he had it just right. He was never really happy, because in his mind he knew that there had to be a way to make that chair a little bit better or to change his technique to make it fractionally more efficient. Even when he was the world champion he was always looking, and I know he'll never stop. That's just the way he is."

49

Postscript: Going over the manuscript of this chapter, Hansen said: "There's too many plays in here—playing tennis, playing basketball, playing volleyball. Find another word. I don't play. I compete."

I came back to competitive athletics through the back door, urged and coaxed and encouraged by a coach who cared and an old man in a red convertible who had a dream of his own.

From the day I first forced myself to go back into that gym, Bob Redford was steering me into the other side of sport, the coaching and management side. He'd say, "Why don't you come out and help me coach these guys?" When I said I couldn't, he'd look at me and say, "Why not?" It was that way with everything from coaching to convincing me I could still go to college. He and Jack Burgar, my old basketball coach, kept at me, and every time I hesitated or tried to back off, one of them would come at me with "Why not?" Eventually, I'd run out of excuses and wind up doing it.

One of the projects was the training of Glen Burrell, a kid I'd played volleyball and basketball with before the accident. It was ironic in a way. Remember the volleyball camp I'd skipped so I could go fishing with Randy and Don? Glen was picked to go in my place. It really turned him on to the game, and he'd worked and pushed himself to a spot on the provincial team. Now there I was, helping him get ready for tryouts to be a setter on the Canada Games team and then the national team.

We spent hours in the gym. I'd encourage him as he lifted weights, grab a ball and play catch with him, or toss balls in the air for him to hit or set. When we weren't in the gym, I'd be chasing him up the side of a mountain in the Bronco, working on his wind and endurance.

We became very close. We coached a grade seven girls' team; he even boarded at our place. So did a lot of the guys—Don, Randy, Rob Graham. With my mom and dad, the door was always open. And gradually, what with all that coaching and training and playing some table tennis, I began to wonder if I'd been wrong about sports being out of the question for me, just as I'd been wrong about girls.

I hadn't just been sitting around while Glen worked on the weights. I'd worked on some myself and done a lot of sprint work in the chair, zooming it up and down the back corridors of the school. To coach the volleyball teams, speed wasn't enough. I needed mobility. I had to be able to stop, start and turn quickly on the court. The ball didn't care who was trying to run it down. It had no special easy bounces for paraplegics. I moved, or I missed it. Out of necessity, I became more and more adept at handling the chair, and less and less self-conscious about using it.

Maybe I could compete.

Oh, I didn't figure it would be much. I knew there was a wheelchair basketball team in Vancouver, and a wheelchair sports organization, but I didn't have much respect for it, because I still had the same attitude that most people do: gee, look at the people in wheelchairs playing. Isn't it nice that they can have a little recreation and rehabilitation?

Serious? Competitive? Don't be silly. But any level of competition was better than none.

And then, in the spring of 1975, I was crutching my way to class when this red convertible pulled up and an old man leaned out.

"C'mere, kid," he called.

I thought he must be some kind of pervert until I spotted the wheelchair in the back seat and the Canadian Paraplegic Association decal on the windshield. Then he said the magic words: "I hear you were a good athlete. I also hear you play table tennis and like other sports. Why don't you come down to Vancouver and compete . . . ?"

And that's how I met Stan Stronge, one of the true pioneers in the field of wheelchair sport, and a man who would become a life-long friend.

Stan broke his back on a stormy, wind-swept and rainy day in November 1940. A tree fell on his car as he slowed to pass through a school zone. He came out of the accident a paraplegic, paralyzed from the chest down. He was newly married, a month shy of his thirtieth birthday.

There was no B.C. Paraplegic Association in those days, no sulpha, no wonder drugs, limited medical knowledge in the area of spinal cord injury, and virtually nothing in the way of a support system. Stan didn't just survive, he contributed. He'd been a good athlete before the accident; now he devoted his life to helping the disabled, working as a counsellor and developing and building the wheelchair sports program. He did everything for me, and for more people like me than I could ever hope to name. In 1981 he received the Order of Canada, and I can't think of anyone who deserved it more.

Stan was manoeuvring me into position that first day. Technically he was there as my counsellor on behalf of the BCPA, checking on how I was adjusting to being at home. And he did want me for table tennis, all right, but that was just for openers. He had a wheelchair basketball team in Vancouver called the Cablecars, and he was always on the lookout for recruits. He let me nibble on the table tennis and the chance to compete, then hooked me into coming down for the basketball on the promise that there might soon be a wheelchair volleyball team. That set the hook and changed my life, because there I was in late May, in the table tennis singles final at the Pacific Northwest Games for the Disabled in Seattle.

51

I won the gold medal, but only because our entire basketball team surrounded the table in the final, cheering me and hissing at my opponent and completely psyching him out. Hmmm. Maybe this whole business was more competitive than I thought . . .

Actually, that was my second competitive event since the accident. Three months earlier, four of us had jammed into the Bronco and taken off for Fort St. John and the Northern B.C. Winter Games. We were not what you'd call highly organized—we ran out of gas somewhere in the boonies and wound up waking a farmer at 3 A.M. to get enough to go the rest of the way—and I didn't make it past the first round in table tennis, but I think I taught my opponent a little something. He was able-bodied, and when he saw the wheelchair he started out taking it easy on me until I laid a few killer serves on him. Then he buckled down and beat me, treating me as an opponent instead of a guy in a chair. Which, of course, was what I wanted in the first place.

The win in Seattle qualified me for the 1975 national Wheelchair Games a month later in Montreal. Two table tennis tournaments, and I was in a national competition. Hey! This thing had possibilities. The dates would conflict with my high school graduation—but who needed grad? I was competing again!

Montreal was an eye-opener. I was there more or less as a rookie, playing table tennis and on the Cablecars as they represented B.C. and won the gold medal in basketball. I was a terrible basketball player. I'd been the school Most Valuable Player in 1973, but this was a different game—the shooting from under the hoop, the balance in the chair, everything—and who could I work out with in Williams Lake? At practice I'd fall out of the chair twenty times. When the coach tried to get me into the final with two minutes left and the game already won, I looked down at my scalded toe, considered my skill level and said "Naah!"

But I knew I'd be back. Because now I'd seen athletes like Pete Colistro and Kevin Earl and Eugene Reimer, Canada's male athlete of the year in 1972, competing not just in basketball but in the track events, wheeling in ninety-degree heat. They were in tremendous shape, as physically and mentally tough and competitive as any athletes I'd seen in any able-bodied sport. "Hey," I thought, "these guys are *good!*"

Two years almost to the day since my accident, eighteen months after I left G. F. Strong convinced that my athletic life was over, I had a whole new sports world to conquer, and I couldn't wait to get at it.

I didn't get off to the greatest start. My summer in Vancouver lasted two or three days, until I found out there really were no definite plans

to form a volleyball team and no competition planned at the international level even if we had one. I went home in disgust. In September
I was back at Columneetza, taking a couple of subjects and upgrading
a couple more to have a better shot at university. I also did a little
substitute teaching the rest of the school year, thanks to Redford.
The man just wouldn't let go. All through my grad year he'd kept after me:

"What are you going to do when you graduate?"

"I dunno."

"Well, what do you want to do?"

"I wanted to be a Phys. Ed. teacher, but now I can't."

"Why not? You can be anything you want. You're coaching now,
aren't you?"

So I taught a few grade eleven and twelve math, geography and social studies classes, scared stiff at first, wondering how kids would respect and react to a teacher only a year older than they were, and in a
wheelchair to boot. But they were great, and it worked out fine.

That lasted one semester. If I was going to university, I'd need
money. So, in January 1976, I went to work. For a couple of months I
was the first male switchboard operator in Williams Lake. (Sometimes ladies would call and say, "I don't want to phone anyone; I just
want to listen to your voice.") Then I moved on to the Forest Service
as a radio dispatcher, standing by to take reports of forest fires.

My only action involved a brush fire in the Blue Lake area, where
the spotters called in to report that "Some idiot's set fire to the bank
underneath this A-frame cabin." It was our cabin. The idiot was
Brad. There was no damage. And I never did get to scramble the
water bombers.

In the fall of 1976, I enrolled at the University of British Columbia,
not in Phys. Ed., which is what I wanted, but in first year arts. It was
that or nothing. The admissions board obviously didn't like the
chances of a guy in a wheelchair trying for a Phys. Ed. degree. It had
never been done, so it couldn't be done. Maybe in second year we
could discuss it again if I was still interested.

But at least I was there, living in the Totem Park residences, still
fighting my personal dragons and plunging into a whole new world. I
joined Stan's basketball Cablecars, formed and was player-coach on
a volleyball team made up of the basketball guys plus other injured
athletes who couldn't take part in their regular sports at the time,
played some table tennis at community centres, and trained every
second day at a Nautilus centre with Burrell, who was no longer with
the national team and had enrolled at Douglas College. It was great. I
was on the move, training or competing three or four nights a week. I

didn't have to be a watcher anymore. School and sports let me push the *go* button on my life.

Outside of sports, I was still being a bit silly, holding on to that hangup about not letting people see my skinny legs. For the first six months I hardly ever used my chair outside the gym. I'd try to get between classes on my crutches and braces with a packsack on my back—ten minutes to go a mile, and me huffing and puffing down the road. The sensible thing would have been to wheel between buildings or classes with my crutches in my lap and leave the chair at the door. But in my mind that would have heightened the perception of my being disabled. So I did it the hard way, arriving in class out of breath and often late, until a heavier schedule and the sheer practicality of using the chair beat down my resistance.

The first year just flew by. I was playing or training all the time, getting stronger and stronger and more familiar with the fine points of a basketball game totally different from the one I'd played all my life. Meanwhile, I used the volleyball coaching techniques I'd developed with Redford, setting up offensive and defensive strategies, coaching and organizing so much I began to feel stifled because I wasn't getting enough time to develop as a player.

It was all crazy and exciting and wonderful. I didn't think life could get much better. Then, that summer, I met a guy called Terry Fox.

He wasn't a national hero then, he was just another innocent victim. All we knew was that he'd played junior varsity at Simon Fraser University, then lost his leg to cancer. I was almost afraid to make the call. What would he say? How about: "Hey, man, I've just lost my bleeping leg, but I don't have to sit in a wheelchair. Get lost!"?

What he actually said was, "Sounds great. I'll be there."

His parents brought him out that first night, skinny and weak from ongoing chemotherapy treatments. You could see he had great skills with the ball, but when he shot he could hardly reach the rim, and he was really slow manoeuvring the chair. But even then, the fire and determination were there. We trained together all summer. By fall and the start of the new season, he was playing first string—and beginning to dream his own special dream.

What a summer that was.

I stayed with Uncle John and Aunt Betty Jones, playing basketball, trying to get a volleyball league going, something aimed at the international level. I also had a summer job with B.C. Wheelchair Sports, helping co-ordinate programs and organize the B.C. Games for the Disabled. I did a lot of partying, got more into the social aspects of life, learning to inter-act with other people, slowly overcoming my shyness—all those things I should have been doing and learning in my mid-teens.

Suddenly, there weren't enough hours in the day. I met Tim Frick at an organizational meeting for the B.C. Games, discovered that he played volleyball, talked him into coming out and looking at our team—and finally into coaching it. More than anyone, Tim got me out and dealing with the public. We became close friends and socialized a lot together. He got me involved in staging clinics, and encouraged and assisted me in developing my athletic skills. As I grew more adept at moving and using the chair, we'd play exhibition games in schools, the two of us against the school team or a faculty team. It was great fun, and because we always won—Tim could really leap and spike, and I'd become pretty good at setting the ball for him—it became a great focus for the follow-up awareness talks when we'd tell the kids not just about the athletic opportunities open to the disabled, but about their potential in life and the problems and frustrations in pursuing it.

And I travelled. The kid from Williams Lake, B.C., found himself in Edmonton for the Canadian Wheelchair Games (where our basketball-turned-volleyball team won the volleyball title), then in Stoke-Mandeville, England, playing basketball at the World Games. We finished fifth, as we would the following year. The hay was coming off the shoes. I was growing more relaxed and comfortable in the outside world, accepting and beginning to understand who this Rick Hansen person really was, relishing the companionship as much as the competition. And while all that was going on, I was learning more about the sport that would really become my passion.

Actually, my affair with track and marathoning began when I first started playing basketball, watching Pete Colistro and Kevin Earl whip their chairs around as though they weighed nothing. Pete had won the Wheelchair Olympic Games 800 metres in 1976, and both attributed their extra strength to track-and-field training. So I began working that chair a lot off-court, first because I wanted to be stronger for basketball, then because I got curious and mad at the same time.

I'd go out and do a 1500-metre training session with Pete, and by the time I was on my third leg, he'd have lapped me and finished. It really griped me. How could he do that? So I'd watch him, looking for some reason why I was constantly getting my butt whipped. And I kicked my training into high. This nonsense had to stop.

By that time I was sharing an apartment with Glen about 10 kilometres down a hill from UBC. I started wheeling up that hill to school, every day. Before long I was working against the clock, trying to cover it faster each day than the day before. I found myself bulking up, gaining strength from the wheeling and continued work with weights.

And I still couldn't beat Pete.

Then, in second year university, I began learning more about body movement and efficiency, and found part of the answer.

Oh, yes, I was going to class, all right. UBC had let me into the Phys. Ed. faculty for second year, thanks mainly to the tireless efforts of my staff advisor, Bob Schutz. I was living off-campus in subsidized housing, and had a couple of scholarships and bursaries. I was getting by, all right. But athletics was my first priority, and when school got in the way of athletics, athletics won every time. I did the first two years toward my Bachelor of Phys. Ed. in regulation time, and spread the last two over a four-year period, fitting them in around competitions. Then I put it on hold. Truth is, I began my last project just before the Man in Motion tour, and graduated en route in April 1987, a month before we got home.

Anyway, about Pete. I discovered that because his disability was polio, Pete could generate power with his entire body and use more of the rim as he stroked. So, I started fooling around with chair designs, trying to build one that would be best suited to my abilities. And off we went to Newfoundland for the 1978 Canadian Games for the Physically Disabled—and another lesson.

Pete was both my friend and my hero, an Olympic champion, a guy I considered the best. And in Newfoundland, he was simply wiped out by Mel Fitzgerald, a long lean local guy who could stretch out his arms and pass for a 747. He was a polio victim, just like Pete, but he had an eight-litre vital lung capacity, which was unheard of anywhere, forget the disabled. Normal is about 5.4. Mine was 7.2. He could go on forever.

And he had this chair.

Until then, racing had been done in what amounted to standard wheelchairs with some modifications. There'd been some work done developing wheels, and the Americans had produced smaller push rims, thirteen to fifteen inches, but there was no such animal as a racing chair per se.

And here was Mel with this thing: aluminum conduit cut down to eliminate every unnecessary ounce, twelve-to-thirteen-inch push rims. It looked like a piece of junk. People stared at it and laughed, until Mel buried them with it.

For my money, Mel Fitzgerald is the father of modern-day wheelchair racing, the first man to bring together the small push rims, the bigger wheels, the lightweight alloy chair frame and the technique required to use them. After the races—I'd entered what I consider my first serious event, a leg in the 4x100 relay—I went into the dressing room where the Newfies were celebrating and introduced myself. Mel and I were to become good friends over the next few years, but right then I looked at him, looked at the chair and thought: "Okay, guy, I'll remember you."

I came home from Newfoundland and got down to it. Tim and I were already involved in preparing the world's first wheelchair marathon race, organized by Dennis Cherenko of the B.C. branch of the Canadian Wheelchair Sports Association and set for July of 1979. (A few Americans had entered, so we could call it international.) It was time to get serious about a new chair and new, more scientific training methods. If this was to be an equipment war, I didn't want to enter it unarmed.

We started by building the first set of training rollers I'd ever heard of. We set two steel rollers on bearings about eighteen inches apart across some 1x12s (the twelve-inch sides vertical), with a flywheel on the rear roller and two five-pound weights to give it momentum so the chair would glide as I stroked. The chair was set in so that the rear wheels touched both rollers and anchored by propping the front wheels against cement blocks. It wasn't exactly high tech: the whole thing cost us about $12 for parts, but it got the job done.

I pushed my chair on that thing all winter—mile after mile after mile, with a mirror in front of me so I could work on technique and a battery-powered metronome for accurate evalulation of my pace and stroke rate per minute. I became really strong. Now, when I wheeled to UBC, I also wheeled back. Meanwhile, I had a guy build me a new chair out of aluminum, based on Mel's with some of my own ideas added. When the Vancouver marathon came, I was going to be ready.

It came, and I finished third. Jim Martinson, a legless Vietnam vet from Puyallup, Washington, blew everyone away. He did the 26 miles, 385 yards around the roads and seawall of Stanley Park in two hours and twenty-four minutes. Ron Minor of Edmonton and I raced each other for second and third, and for me that made it special. A couple of months earlier I'd been playing in the world wheelchair basketball championships in Tampa, Florida. Ron had heard I was doing some track training.

"Hey, that's great," he said. "If you work real hard, by 1984 and the Olympic trials you'll be competitive."

"Okay, jerk," I thought. "Just wait."

Now there we were, neck and neck, shooting for second. He beat me out by inches, cutting me off at the end and almost driving me into a pool. We were both clocked at two hours and forty minutes—sixteen minutes behind Martinson. But I shook Minor up a little.

It was strange, the way things went from there. I went to Stoke-Mandeville, won a couple of bronze medals, came back to Vancouver for the Canadian Wheelchair Games, played on the winning volleyball and basketball teams, and won four out of seven track events, beating Minor each time. Then I went back to work on the rollers, getting ready for the 1980 world championship marathon at the Orange Bowl in Miami.

It was lonely work, and a bit puzzling. I had a new chair built for me by a man named Led Zmek who built motorbike racing frames. I knew I was stronger, knew my endurance was greater, my technique improved. But because I was on the rollers I had no idea how fast I could go. For me, Miami would be as much a revelation as a race.

All the big names in wheelchair racing were there including George Murray, an American who'd finished second the previous year, and people in Miami were bragging that this one was his.

My own plan was simple. Since I didn't know what I could do and really didn't expect to do well, I'd push to stay with them for the first 200 to 400 metres. When they bolted, I'd let them go and settle in and try for a good personal time.

The gun went off, and I jackrabbited out of there. After 400 metres I was still with the leaders. "What the heck," I thought, "might as well keep pushing and stay with them as long as I can."

We came to a steep hill. I kept pushing. Something was wrong here. They were leaving me, all right, but they were going the wrong way. "Migod!" I thought. "They're falling back! I can win this thing!" Then I thought again. "That couldn't be right." These guys were the best in the world! I must be doing something wrong, setting too fast a pace or something. They had the experience, and they were back there. Should I drop back with them, or just keep on pushing as hard as I could for as long as I could and pray I didn't fall apart? I decided to keep pushing and hope.

We were wheeling in eighty-five-degree heat. Any second now I figured I'd seize up. I wasn't looking back. I just visualized them, not away behind, but right there, breathing down my neck. I crossed the finish line pushing as though the hounds were at my heels. They arrived fourteen minutes later. I don't know which of us was more surprised.

I was clocked in two hours, eight minutes and thirty-four seconds, equalling the then-world record for runners set by Derek Clayton of Australia in 1969. Maybe that's why officials added thirty seconds to my time.

Nowadays, with wheelers regularly taking part in marathons along with the able-bodied, and the equipment and techniques so much improved, the top wheelers always come in first. In those days, when wheelers were let in almost as a concession and given a pat on the head by the organizers, it just wasn't supposed to happen. When it did, they weren't prepared to accept it.

But what did I care? I'd just entered my second marathon, and I was champion of the world. Score one for Tim and me, one for hard work—and one big one for the rollers. And for the next four years, the world was mine.

That victory was the first of nineteen straight. If you'll excuse the pun, I was on a roll. I wheeled track in Holland in 1980 at the Olympiad for the Physically Disabled, pretty much took a year off in 1981 for school and commitments to various Year of the Disabled functions, then really got moving in 1982. Because I was now among the wheelchair elite, there was funding from Sport Canada, plus athletic scholarships and bursaries from other sources if you were willing to pound the pavement and look. I had an additional break: a man named Cecil Walker, a polio victim who'd gone on to become a gymnast and a self-made millionaire. Cecil became my good friend and advisor, and my personal sponsor for five years.

I was on a world tour of a different kind from the one I'd take later, and loving every minute of it.

I won marathons all over the world. I won in Boston, two straight years in Oita, Japan, in Stoke-Mandeville, in Honolulu, in El Paso, and in Sydney, Australia. I won two more world titles at the Orange Bowl, in 1982 and 1983.

That was the year I shared the Lou Marsh Trophy with Wayne Gretzky as the country's outstanding male athlete, period.

Well, almost.

What I actually received was an "auxiliary" award, something the Marsh committee handed out on occasions when an outstanding athlete "didn't quite fit the category."

"Who does fit the category?" I asked.

Well, a male or female athlete, amateur or professional.

"I see. And what does that make me?"

It was tokenism. Throw something to the disabled athletes. Categorize them. At first I wasn't going to go. Then I was going to go, call a press conference and blow the whole thing out of the water. The kid from Williams Lake was back, ready to lash out in all directions. But I was learning: lashing out wasn't always the most effective way to get something accomplished.

Instead, I wrote a strong letter to the selection committee outlining my position. Then, when I accepted, I called it a step in the right direction and said that what the disabled were looking for was the day when there would be no need for separate awards, when we as athletes could be judged against our able-bodied peers as equals. The nice thing was that when Wayne accepted his award, he made a statement supporting and reaffirming my position. We must have made some kind of an impression: to my knowledge, not one media person—and there were a lot of them there covering the ceremony—ever referred to my award as "auxiliary." One more step on the uphill climb to equality.

Competitively, it seemed as though nothing could stop me.

On one of the trips to Stoke-Mandeville I left my passport in the glove compartment of my car. Stan told me to hide in the washroom on the plane until the customs officer came aboard to check us in a group, claimed one less in the group than we had, then hustled me out into the pack as we deplaned. By the time we were ready to leave, the passport had been shipped over. Fortunately, the customs people who stamped me out of England never noticed that, according to the passport, I'd never gone in.

When I won the Boston Marathon in 1982, I wasn't even supposed to be there. The Americans use Boston as the national marathon team trials, and all twenty-four spots were filled. But some of the top Americans hadn't come to Miami for the worlds, and I was determined to race against them.

On the Saturday night of marathon weekend I was in Ottawa, honoured as one of Canada's young achievers at a banquet attended by Queen Elizabeth II. On the Sunday another wheeler and friend named Lennie Marriott flew with me to Boston, where we checked the course as to terrain, possible wind conditions and any other factor we could think of as we laid out our race strategy. On Monday, race day, we simply showed up at the starting line and said we were there to race.

The officials were good about it. They could have told us to take a hike. Instead they agreed to let Lennie and me and an extra American wheeler compete unofficially—no entry number, nothing to indicate we even existed. And off we went.

At mile twenty-four I was so far out in front that when a policeman's horse shied and I wound up face down on a railroad track in swerving to avoid it, I was able to crawl to the chair, set it up, look back—and I still couldn't see anyone. It was decision time: be nice to the hosts and slow down—after all, these were their nationals and we weren't even supposed to be there—or smoke it?

I smoked it. I won in one hour, forty-eight minutes and twenty-two seconds, knocking more than six minutes off the course record. Lennie was tenth overall in two hours, three minutes, two seconds. I can still hear the guy on the public address system as I came down the chute in the final 100 metres:

"And here's the first wheelchair competitor about to cross the finish line . . . uh, we don't see an entry number . . . he doesn't seem to have a competitor's number . . . Ladies and gentlemen, this result cannot be official . . ."

I crossed the finish line, then rode off into the sunset like the Lone Ranger, reporters trailing after me, yelling, "Stop! Who are you? Where do you come from?"

"Canada!" I shouted. "If you want to talk to the winner, just wait!

He should be coming in a few minutes!"

I wasn't being smart. I had to move. I'd thought the race started early in the morning and booked our nonrefundable return tickets for 3 P.M. The race started at 11 A.M. There was just time to get back to the hotel, pack and throw everything into a cab. In fact, Lennie arrived just as we were pulling away from the hotel.

Everything I did seemed to work. Training for the 1982 Pan-American Games in Halifax, I got so disgusted with my brand-new chair and my inability to corner in it that one night I went into the garage, had a beer, stared at it for a moment, did a Hail Mary—and sawed the front end off. The chair was entirely of my own design, and the front-end extension was there for a reason. But the chair wasn't working, so I got mad and sawed it off. Suddenly, it cornered like a dream. Maybe it was afraid for its rear end—whatever. I won the 100, 200, 400, 800 and 10 000 metre events, was on the winning relay teams, and came home with nine gold medals.

How big a roll was I on? I actually finished fourth in my qualifying heat for the 100, but the Mexican who finished third was disqualified for going out of his lane. They bumped me to the third and last qualifying spot, and I went on to the gold from there.

There was a bit of a setback in the Honolulu marathon in 1982. I was trying new high-pressure tires, had three flats after 6 miles and had to pull out. The last tire blew just as I limped back over the starting line.

But there was a bright side. Five of us stayed on in Maui for eight weeks, training. (No laughter, please. We were serious.)

There was Lennie, Peter Brookes, Marshall Smith of B.C. Wheelchair Sports, who was there as a sort of overseer-coach, and me, plus Tim for a couple of weeks. Five of us, four with regular wheelchairs plus three racing chairs, spare wheels, spare tires, tools, gloves, weights, metronome, heart rate monitors and a blender, with the rollers set up on the lanai overlooking the pool and beach so we could at least stare down at the pretty girls while we sweat—all in a two-bedroom condo, two flights up.

After five weeks we had to change condos. The new one was even smaller, with two flights of stairs instead of an elevator, so Marshall moved in on the ground floor with some guy who looked like a hood or a drug dealer. We'd do the cooking and lower his meals out the window.

There were distractions, sure, and the beaches and weather were great, but we truly were there to work, and we did. I was going back to the Orange Bowl as defending champion, and I was determined to be in the best shape of my life. But when I went out and won it in under two hours, which everyone said was impossible, the drive to maintain high-level training slipped into neutral. After all, wasn't I winning everything?

Oh, I was big stuff, all right. So big that I forgot what it was that got me there. I almost mocked my sport. I hadn't lost a marathon since the first one in 1979. Hey, I was good! I worked out. But I used to *train.* Now I just trained.

I went to Boston in 1983 poorly prepared with my equipment not quite ready, and a guy named Jim Knaub of Long Beach, California, literally coasted away from me on the downhill. I was utterly humiliated. I hadn't just lost, I'd lost by two minutes, which is like losing a fight on the first punch.

There was a challenge there. I shrugged it off. Everybody has a bad race. Mine just took longer than anyone else's. I won a couple of short races and the Australian title to confirm my glowing opinion of myself. I went to Williams Lake that summer and took the rollers on a hunting trip with Brad and Dad, as I'd always done. I never touched them. Hey, I was on vacation, man.

I lost to Mel Fitzgerald in the last 100 metres in Montreal. In Boston I'd blamed equipment. This time I blamed strategy. I went back to Oita with a new chair and a semblance of the old determination, and lost by two seconds to a German named Gregor Golembek.

Now, finally, I was starting to ask myself questions. The Orange Bowl was coming up again. I'd won it each of the three times I'd entered, and set the world record. I had to go back. I was working on yet another chair. I was still in good enough shape to win. So I went, and I let George Murray psych me out as he did André Viger and a California wheeler named Marty Ball.

Let me explain a couple of things about wheelchair racing. It's just as competitive and similar in strategy to bicycle road racing. People stay in packs, work as teams, "drafting" behind the rest, letting them pull you along in their wake—then zipping out to take a turn at the lead. Throughout the race you're assessing the strengths and weaknesses of the others and altering your strategy to meet those assessments. Knowing when to draft and when to lead is an integral part of the race.

So here was George Murray, president of the International Wheelchair Road Racing Club and an accomplished racer across the U.S., telling us all before the race that he wasn't racing to win, that he just wanted to sit in the draft and pull in with a good time to make a good showing for his sponsor. He'd drop off the leaders after about 20 miles, he said.

So André, Marty and I let him stay back there, sucking wind in the draft as fourth man in the pack, taking it easy, conserving his strength. Meanwhile, I'd been evaluating the other two guys and knew I had the race tactically under control. But after 24 miles, George was still there with them. I surged a little just to see what he'd do. Sure enough, he surged himself from fourth place and tucked in behind me.

"George," I yelled. "What are you *doing?*"

"Don't worry," he said with a few phony huffs and puffs. "I'll drop off."

But he didn't. Instead, he began to take the lead once in a while. He was fresh. We could have dropped him at any point in the race. Instead, we'd let him stay in the draft and worried about each other. And in the last 300 metres he sprinted and nudged me at the finish.

I wheeled over to him, boiling mad, probably even more at myself than at George. I had let him do that to me because I'd fallen into a bad habit: I used to race to win. Now, after the losses, I was racing not to lose. In the winning days I'd never have believed him, never have let him pull that. It was my fault.

But I still had enough anger left for George.

"That was a rotten thing to do, George. A rotten thing."

I told the press George had won a race but lost a friend. It's one thing to go out and win at any cost, but to pull that kind of deception is pretty low. In a sense he proved that our sport had come a long way: we were just like the others now. Some of us would do anything to win.

For the year, I was now seven and four. I grabbed myself by the scruff of the neck and shook. "You got any pride left?" I asked. "You've been mocking your sport, you've been coasting, you've refused to take it seriously, and you've had your butt kicked four times in four different races. You want to race, or do you want to crawl?"

There was only one answer. Boston: I'd win in Boston, because that was where I'd lost the first time. I'd train like I never had before, and I'd get this thing turned around.

I never got the chance. I ran into a disaster, and then into a miracle—a miracle named Amanda . . .

It was four hours until my plane left for Boston. I'd trained hard and had a hot new chair built by Tony Hoar. But there was a worrisome hitch: it was too sensitive on the downhills, too difficult to control.

I decided to take it out for one last test run before heading for the airport. One more run, then decide whether to go with it or use an old chair with less speed but more control. Subconsciously I must have known it was a dumb move, because for the first and only time in my life I put on a helmet.

I guess I was doing about 30 miles an hour downhill when I ran into some turbulence. The wheels kicked sideways, the tie rods snapped, the wheels folded, I brought my left arm up to protect myself as I flew out of the chair—pow! My left arm was stretched under my head at a ridiculous angle. When I tried to pull it back, nothing happened. The shoulder had popped. My nose was swollen. I'd driven a tooth through my lip. So much for the helmet: I'd hurt everything it wasn't designed to protect.

All I could think of was, "I've got a plane to catch!"

The ambulance came and carted me off to hospital, where they gave me a Valium and Demerol cocktail—one hundred ccs. worth, because they forgot that my legs were down to spindles, and therefore I wasn't as big as I looked and would need less sedation. They popped the shoulder back into position. I didn't feel a thing. I was still higher than a kite when Stan and some of the boys came to take me home.

"Let's get going, guys," I said, all drug-cheerful. "There's still time to make the plane."

"Rick," Stan said gently. "How are you gonna race? You can't even put your pants on."

"Okay, don't worry about me for now. I'll just roll into bed."

"Yeah? And how are you going to get out?"

That's when it hit me. Boston was gone, and maybe my career along with it, not to mention a little round-the-world jaunt that was brewing in the back of my mind. The only place I was going was back to G. F. Strong for rehab. Somewhere, I'd seen this movie before.

I knew I was in trouble, but decided to make the best of it. "The only way I'll stay here," I told Dr. Sandy Pinkerton, "is if you get me your most qualified and best-looking physiotherapist."

"Okay, Ricky," he said. "Sure," I thought. "She'll probably be ninety years old." The first physio I saw as we came through the door was an elderly-type, rather plump lady. "Mine," I told myself. "She has to be mine." Then I looked around and went bolt upright.

"Wow! Look at that one! She's gorgeous."

"C'mon, Ricky," Sandy said. "I'll introduce you to your physio."

He started wheeling me toward this gorgeous creature. Naah! It couldn't be. Not the way my luck was riding. But it was.

"Ricky," Sandy said, "I'd like you to meet Amanda."

Bingo.

Amanda Blackmore (soon to return to her maiden name of Reid). Tall, freckle-faced, reddish-haired, beautiful, intelligent—and married. At least, that was what I'd been told. So one day I asked her. She said she was married but in the process of splitting up, and things weren't going well. I bit my tongue. How would it have looked, sitting

64

Top: The Hansens, circa 1967. Parents Joan and Marvin with (left to right) Cindy, Brad, Christine and Rick.

Bottom: At age ten, Rick (front row, second from left) joins the grads of badminton classes in Abbotsford.

Previous page: Sailor in Motion: Rick Hansen at fourteen months.

A few hours before the accident that would leave him paralyzed, Rick (right) and friends Randy Brink (left) and Don Alder (centre) display some of the day's catch.

Crossing this swaying bridge to go fishing was easy before the accident. Later, Hansen (front) did it the hard way—on braces and crutches.

New challenges on the horizon, Rick (right) and the gang leave Williams Lake for Vancouver and the University of British Columbia.

Logic said a disabled person couldn't get a degree in physical education. Hansen said: "Why not?"

Fighting off a challenge by California's Jim Knaub, Hansen (front) pushes to one of his nine gold medals at the 1982 Pan-American Games in Halifax.

The man who started it all —long-time friend and mentor Stan Stronge, whose encouragement led Hansen back to competitive sport.

Bill Cunningham

Top: With Terry Fox's parents, Rollie and Betty Fox (left), and B.C. Premier Bill Bennett looking on (centre), Hansen says good-bye on the tour start date, March 21, 1985.

Bottom: On the road at last, the Man in Motion tour heads for the Peace Arch and the first of many borders to cross in their 24,901.55-mile odyssey.

Facing page: The first set of mountains behind him, Hansen glides triumphantly across the Golden Gate Bridge into San Francisco.

Top: Take the chair apart, put it together, take it apart. In Oregon, the search for the perfect alignment goes on.

Bottom: Rick and Amanda roll through the Arizona desert.

there yelling, "All right! Hurray!"

From the start, Amanda was magic for me. Dr. Pinkerton hadn't just turned me over to a beautiful girl, he'd turned me over to a first-class physio who also happened to be a beautiful girl.

It was a tough time for me. There was both nerve and structural damage in the shoulder, and talk that they might have to put in a pin to stabilize it. I was also told I shouldn't train until September. The qualifying races for the 1500-metre exhibition race at the Los Angeles Olympics were coming up in June, then the worlds in Stoke-Mandeville, then the Olympics if I made the team. I had things to do.

"Sure," the doctor said. "You've also got the rest of your life. What happens when you're fifty or sixty if you damage it permanently now?"

There was one saving grace: Amanda was there to listen, and I could always talk to her. "There are no promises in life," she told me. "You fight for everything you get. We don't know you'll need surgery and a pin. We'll just keep working and wait and see."

We worked on that shoulder, and we talked about everything. She started coming in on weekends to give it extra treatment. She was a professional taking on extra responsibility for a patient—but I think we both knew there was something else.

That was the frustrating part. Marital problems or not, she was off limits. I had too much respect for her to put that sort of pressure on her. Besides, I knew by that time the world wheelchair tour was in the planning stage, if mostly in my head. I knew that somehow I was going to do it, and soon. There was no time for a solid relationship even if she was free. Forget it, Rick. Sure.

One day Amanda turned up after hours. She'd been at a meeting downstairs and just popped in to see how I was doing. Suddenly, my heart was doing flip-flops. She was standing there, smiling, and the words just popped out.

"Draw the curtain," I said.

She did, and I brought her over to the bed and kissed her. I told her I'd wanted to do that since the day I arrived three weeks earlier. I said I'd like to be able to go out with her some time and have dinner. And then she left.

I'm sure people could see something building between us. I had no permanent ambitions. My folks' marital problems had scared me off anything like that. I wasn't going to marry until I found the perfect girl for me. That was going to take a long time, and then it would be a one-time, lifetime commitment. There was no way in the world I was going to get romantically involved with anybody, especially at that point in my life.

We went out for dinner once in a while, keeping everything as casual as we could. But the attraction kept growing. By the time I was discharged, we'd built a solid base of mutual understanding and respect. We could talk to each other about everything or nothing. I could confide in her about my fears, about the tour, about anything that came into my head.

And then I was discharged and gone. I could move the arm again. I wasn't ready, but the Olympic trials were on in New York, moved up a week to the end of June, and there was no way I wasn't going to try.

I got a little bit lucky, got some great and generous tactical help from André Viger during a key heat—and made the team by one one-hundredth of a second. It just blew me away. My eyes were misted over. All I could think of was, Amanda should be here. She'd got me here with her expertise and quality of treatment, and with her understanding and encouragement. This was her win as much as mine. I'd let everything slip away. I'd been hurt and come back, and now I had another chance: a month to get ready for the worlds in Stoke-Mandeville, then a couple of weeks' break before the Olympic exhibition. Maybe I could put it back together, as Amanda had helped me rebuild the shoulder.

I went to Stoke-Mandeville, not ready physically or equipment-wise, but happy just to be there, and won the 1500 by one one-hundredth of a second on tactics over Peter Trotter of Australia, who came back to beat me in the 5000 metre by half a second. That left the marathon, featuring all the guys who'd beaten me: Knaub, Fitzgerald, Murray, Golembek. I wanted it badly, but more than that I wanted a good race for me, something that would tell us all that I was coming back, and with the right attitude.

It was a great race. Mel and I went out and dusted them all until it got down to the two of us—taking turns with the lead, staying far enough ahead to keep the others from drafting on us—right on into the stadium. People were screaming. It was Mel's turn to lead, and we were both bushed.

I hadn't trained for anything over 20 miles. After 18 miles the arm had started to drag. I didn't know whether the shoulder would hold. "Hang in," I told myself over and over again. "Hang in." Now we were down to it.

"Last 100 metres, we just push," I gasped.

"Right," he said, and that's the way it was: two close friends going at it hammer and tongs, me thinking about the way he'd edged me in Montreal. And this time, somehow, I beat him out at the wire.

I'd come all the way back, and I knew I'd never be silly enough to take my sport for granted again. It was the second-greatest thing that happened to me all year. Number three was Los Angeles, coming out of the dark tunnel into the sunlight and a stadium jammed with

80,000 people, and into history for disabled athletes: the first Olympic Games exhibition race. Some day, I thought, this will be for real, a real Olympic event. I hope I can be part of that, too.

But number one was back in Vancouver. I'd neglected her all summer, and in a few months I'd be going away again for a year and a half. The question haunted me all the way home:

What was I going to do about Amanda?

5

"You're going where? In a what?"

It had all seemed so simple at the start. Tough, sure, with no guarantee that it could be done, but basically just a series of wheelchair marathons strung together, and wasn't he the best marathoner in the world?

His friends didn't see it that way.

"When he first told me, the first word that came into my mind was 'straitjacket,'" Don Alder recalls. "I figured he'd definitely flipped out. But I thought about it, and I agreed to go along. Why? I dunno. I just knew Rick. If anybody could do it, it would be him."

Amanda Reid remembers the instant the subject first came up.

"He was lying on the bed at G. F. Strong, flat on his back with his arms flung out. We were doing the rehab on his shoulder, trying to get him ready for the Olympics.

" 'There's this other thing, too,' he said. 'I'm going to wheel around the world.' I just looked at him.

" 'That's nice,' " I said.

"What else was there to say? This nut didn't even know for sure he'd be ready to go to the Olympics, and he was planning to wheel around the world."

If he noticed the lack of enthusiasm, Hansen didn't let on. He had other things on his mind.

He'd been working on this since January of 1984, and here it was, March of 1985, the organization in near-shambles and with barely enough money to get the team to Los Angeles, let alone around the world. Every turn of the wheels would take him further away from an organizational hub in which he had little if any confidence. In a sense he was turning control of his life over to other people—people he wasn't sure of—not knowing whether they could pull things together or whether he might have to turn around in Los Angeles or San Francisco or somewhere in the sands of Arizona, financially hamstrung, the tour over almost before it had begun.

To an outsider there seemed no way the thing wouldn't fall flat. From the start, the Man in Motion tour was a camp divided, seemingly beyond unification because the trip began before the organization was anywhere near in place and neither side—one at home and one on the road—appeared to have any conception of what the other was going through.

It wasn't that Hansen hadn't thought about an organization. He knew there had to be sponsors, that the team had to be two-tiered: the group on the road and the group at home, not to mention the unknown army of support groups that would be needed in every city and community in each of the thirty-four countries through which he would wheel. But did it have to be this big? The bottom line was the wheelchair, the challenge and his ability to push it 24,901.55 miles. Why did things have to be so complicated?

Logistically it was a nightmare. What do you pack for five people who'll be away for nineteen months when everything has to fit in a motor home? What kind of safety gear, medical gear, training gear or clothing? What kind of food? How do you break down the wheeling days? Set up the support groups and accommodations along the way? Negotiate with city and state police down the West Coast and across the United States (Omigod, what about Europe and Asia?) to find out where the wheelchair could or couldn't go, and arrange for police escorts so the traffic wouldn't wipe Hansen and the chair off the road? What can you build in for R and R to keep them from throttling one another after two or three months?

Oh, yes—and while you're planning all this, find corporate sponsors who'll come up with about $750,000 in dollars or services so that you won't have to take money out of the Legacy Fund.

He could see disaster in the distance. His answer was to try to be everywhere at once, to squeeze in his training while playing Little Dutch Boy until he ran out of fingers and thumbs. It was a losing battle. The March 21 start date was rushing toward him and there was no way they could be ready. There wasn't enough money, time or preparation—but he'd had to postpone the start once already, and he was damned if he was going to do that again.

Looking back on the weeks and months of preparation, he sighed as he remembered how he'd explained it to a sportswriter in Vancouver in December of 1984 as he began to feel the tentacles of the organizational process tightening around him:

"We're committed to this thing! If it turns out that Tim and Don and I have to leave in a Volkswagen Beetle with three sleeping bags and the wheelchair in the back, then that's the way it will be. I'm going to wheel that chair around the world and that's all there is to it."

He knew better now. Boy, did he know better.

I didn't wake up one day and decide that I was going to wheel around the world. The Man in Motion project began as an itch in the back of my mind back in the days after I left G. F. Strong and headed back to Williams Lake. At that time it had nothing to do with awareness or fund raising and everything to do with pure, physical challenge.

At first it was one of those kid dreams where you lie on the grass staring up at the moon and imagining that you'll go there some day. Then, as I began to focus on marathoning and enjoyed some success, I realized I really was physically and emotionally strong enough to wheel around the world—if I wanted to. But so what?

Sure, we could do it with a tent and a trailer and set our own pace—but was it worth it to take three years out of my life? I was working on my Phys. Ed. degree and competing internationally in wheelchair sports. I didn't want to leave all that just so I could come home and say, "Well, I wheeled around the world." Big deal.

And then, in 1980, Terry Fox came along with his Marathon of Hope. He was going to run across Canada to focus attention on the horrors of cancer and to raise funds for cancer research. He wanted nothing for himself. He'd had cancer, it had taken his leg, and now he was going to fight back. That's what it was: a personal fight between one young man and this terrible *thing* that had attacked him. He would battle it one-on-one. He would show people it could be beaten, and in the course of the battle he would raise funds and inspire other people so that they would be better equipped to join the fight against cancer that would someday stamp it out for good.

I've heard and seen it written that cancer beat him. Not true. It only beat his body. It returned and raged through him this time, forcing a halt to his marathon after five months and finally taking his life. But it didn't win. In life and in death Terry did what he'd set out to do: he rallied Canadians to a common cause as never before. The money poured in and is still pouring in, because every year, in memorial walks and other fund raisers, people remember the fighter who wouldn't quit.

I'd often wheeled with Terry as we trained. He'd been my teammate and my friend. I knew something of what he'd gone through out there on the road. And, watching the people respond both before and after his death, knowing how much good had come out of his dream, I realized there was a factor in my own dream I'd somehow overlooked.

By that time I'd talked to many disabled persons in my travels, and discovered that we all faced the same barriers, physical and mental. Now I saw the impact Terry had had in raising the world's awareness. I'd always been active in fund raising. I enjoyed the giving. It made me feel good to know I was helping. That was one of the reasons I got into teaching, because I enjoyed working with kids, and there was a sense of giving there, too. What if I continued Terry's theme, made it the major focus of a wheelchair journey around the world in which I would be the catalyst or messenger, and as such help disabled people everywhere?

The potential impact was staggering. And as an afterthought—and that's all it was—maybe I could raise money for people disabled through spinal cord injuries for research, rehabilitation and wheelchair sport and recreation programs. Right then, the tour ceased being something I *could* do and became something I *had* to do. I had my physical challenge, my mountain to climb. Only now I had a better reason for climbing it.

Still, there was one missing piece to the puzzle. We needed a way to open doors and borders, the support and backing of a group or organization held in such regard that its very support would give us enough status to at least rate a hearing from governments of other countries as we tried to arrange the visas, the routing, the support groups from the disabled organizations, and the hundreds of other things to be done if this was to be more than just a push around the world in a chair. But for a chance meeting with Bill McIntosh of the Nike sports equipment company in December of 1983, we might never have found it.

I'd met Bill through marathon racing. He was a runner himself, and because of his Nike connection he was at a lot of the major events whether he was running or not. We became pretty good friends. When I began to win the big events, he steered me to a financial advisor, and he was always interested in my career. Now he'd been approached by a Vancouver Island tourism organization seeking Nike support for a Victoria runner named Al Howie in an attempted round-the-world run as the island's promotional tie-in with Vancouver's upcoming world's fair, Expo 86. Bill suggested I might be a more newsworthy candidate, but the group wanted Howie because of his Victoria connection, and the discussion ended.

"By the way," Bill said casually, "*Have* you ever considered wheeling around the world? I think you could do it, and maybe with Expo coming and it being a world's fair with a theme of transportation and communication, you could talk them into letting you be their worldwide representative. They've got the organization and the access to other countries you'd need, and they might come through with some money."

Bingo. We had the last piece of the puzzle.

Tim was involved almost from the time I spoke to McIntosh. We'd have long talks about how it could be done if a guy was really going to try it. What would it take in terms of training, physiotherapy en route, equipment and people? Could we find people crazy enough to go with us? We'd set out each potential problem, solve it—or so we thought—and move on to the next one. We'd get a motor home and sleep in that. Three guys ought to be enough: Don Alder to look after the equipment, Tim to handle the logistics, my brother Brad to do the cooking, and the three of them to share the driving and rotate the other jobs as we went along. Plus, an office staff to stay home and look after the rest. All I'd have to do was wheel.

Naive? You betcha! If we'd known then what we know now . . .

The first person I approached, in early January 1984, was Marshall Smith, at that time executive director of the B.C. Sports Hall of Fame and chairman of the B.C. Wheelchair Sports Association. Marshall phoned Doug Mowat, a member of the B.C. Legislature and head of the B.C. Paraplegic Association. They seemed logical choices: both men I knew and respected, both well connected, both active in many projects despite being confined to wheelchairs by spinal cord injuries, both heavily involved during the International Year of the Disabled. Tim and I were then introduced to Denny Veitch, a former star rugby player even though he'd lost his right arm as a youngster when he slipped while trying to hitch a ride on the back of a streetcar. He'd also been in charge of organizing the 1973 Canada Summer Games in Burnaby, B.C.

I brought in Dr. Bob Hindmarch of UBC, a veteran of years at the organizational and executive level of major international sports competitions. I wanted someone there I knew could make good decisions and do things on my behalf because the project was over my head in terms of my time, energy and contacts.

That was the first committee—Marshall, Doug, Denny, Bob, Tim and I. We held a lot of meetings, had a lot of good talks. After speaking to Marshall, I wrote to Expo asking if they were interested in getting involved in a world wheelchair tour. They said yes, and suddenly our tour had a name: the official theme slogan of Expo at that time: Man in Motion.

And so we set it up: Man in Motion would be a wholly owned subsidiary of the B.C. Paraplegic Foundation, with its own board of directors chaired by Mowat and including Smith, Hindmarch and Veitch—all long-time friends and sports associates—along with Dr. Sandy Pinkerton, Stan Stronge and Cecil Walker. We would get whatever volunteer help we could, keep the salaried staff as small as possible, and go on from there.

Tour expenses would be raised through corporate sponsorship in cash, goods and services. Unless otherwise specified by the donors, all donations once we began the fund-raising end of the project would go directly into a trust we set up called the Legacy Fund, and when we got home the annual interest from that fund would be distributed, in percentages to be decided later, to spinal cord research, awareness and rehabilitation programs, and wheelchair sports.

We began to assemble the office staff, the people who'd be running our home base as we got farther and farther from home.

One of the first people hired was Nancy Thompson, whom I knew through her work at Sport B.C. to be an experienced, well-organized and competent administrator. Patti Lueke was also on board. She'd virtually been my secretary through the latter part of my athletic career, handling all my correspondence as I tried for corporate sponsorship, and generally just being a friend. She was a natural for the project. She knew me and believed in what I was trying to do.

Marian Lay, a sports consultant who'd been in charge of the $1 million program to develop off-site activities for Expo 86—the program from which Expo was to provide its promised portion of our funding—had been working with us on a part-time, volunteer basis. One fine day, Expo dropped the hammer: the off-site activities program was cancelled, slashed out of existence as Expo sought ways to trim a soaring budget. Marian was now free to join us as our salaried director of operations, which meant she would run the Vancouver end of the tour. But financially, the Expo decision had left us high and dry.

But we'd come too far to quit now. I decided to put three years of my life into giving it my best shot. If it didn't work out, at least I'd know I'd tried.

Until the Expo news, I'd been feeling pretty good about the way things were falling into place. I was half right: they weren't falling into place. They were just falling.

From the beginning our biggest problem was one of time constraints. There was no time to put the tour in place legally or philosophically. My contract with Man in Motion was nowhere near ready—and when you're dealing in the kind of dollars the tour had the potential to generate, it was essential that there be one, for the protection of all concerned.

We had no cash, no nothing. Everyone was working on speculation. There was never one person in that office who understood what my vision of the tour was, what I wanted done or why I wanted it. We were all bobbing around on a sea of confusion, just trying to stay afloat.

I'd made up this tentative budget. I didn't have a clue about budgets, but I'd phoned airports, equipment people, and anyone else I thought could help. I didn't know about promotional costs and stuff like that, but I threw some money in for it anyway and came up with a project I said could be done for $750,000—end-to-end, us paying everything. Not enough, I was told. It probably will take at least twice that much—$1.5 million, or even $2 million in cash or value in goods and services.

That was in May of 1984. I'm now beginning to realize there are going to be problems. We didn't seem to be getting anywhere. We'd started in January 1984 and by June all we had was a few letters that had been sent out to no response. Marshall kept saying, "No problem! No problem! We'll do this thing!" Me, I started getting nervous. At the press conference to announce Expo's adoption of the tour, I sat there praying no one in the media would ask about our plans. We'd been saying, "Oh, yes, we're going to wheel around the world," and if anybody asked for details we were dead. Details? We didn't have a *plan*.

What we had was a soap opera.

Remember the $1.5 to $2 million we were going to need to finance the project? I came back from the Olympics, and we hadn't raised a sausage. Not a plugged nickel. All of a sudden it's "Well, it's not going to be all that easy. It's going to be a hard sell. Some of these corporations we're talking to are international. Maybe it's because you're Canadian."

Does all this sound like I was getting confused and ticked off and afraid this whole project might sink before it was launched? That's close enough. The more I thought about it the more I recalled the words of a friend named Dale Shumka, who worked for Osaga Canada, a sports and athletic wear firm, when it was one of my athletic sponsors. From the beginning he said:

"There's only one person who's going to get this project done, and that's you. Like it or not, you're going to have to do it. You're going to have to watch to be sure it stays streamlined. You're going to have to keep it lean and mean until it can walk, and then until it can run, and finally until it can race. If it tries to run first there'll be nothing but chaos all the way through. There is no easy way."

While all this was going on, the would-be road crew had been proceeding on the assumption of a March 1 start date. Our preparations were a combination of scientific approach and comedy amidst the chaos.

Tim, Don and my cousin Lee Gibson from Port Alberni moved in with me in my one-bedroom apartment to simulate crowded conditions in the motor home—Tim in October 1984, Don since the following January, Lee a bit later. Lee replaced Brad, who'd planned to go but decided engagement and marriage had more to offer than nineteen months with three guys in a motor home.

The apartment was a great testing ground because, as Tim put it, "If we can live there, we can live anywhere." He was just picking on me because one day he looked in my closet and found mummified bananas and pears.

Well, it was a bachelor apartment, and I'd never been the world's best housekeeper. When I went away for a meet, whatever was in there stayed where it was dropped until I got back. Once Tim came in while I was away and did four loads of my laundry. While he was sitting there waiting for it to dry, he started counting the number of wheelchair wheels strewn around the living room. There were nineteen. It was so messy we always met first-time guests in the lobby of the apartment block. If they looked like people who wouldn't mind the sight of the iron that had burned through the wall-to-wall carpet and stuck there as the fibres fused around it, they were invited in.

Those were the quarters shared by me and my new roomies. I slept on my waterbed, Lee on a mattress between my bed and the closet, Don on a couch in the living room and Tim on a strip of foam on the floor. Sometimes it got a little hectic, particularly when the smoke alarm started screaming every time we turned on the oven. But we unscrewed the top, stuffed a towel in to muffle the sound, and cooked on. Motor home? Piece of cake.

Brad's decision kind of put me off at first, because his early December wedding was set for the day I was leaving for Hawaii on vacation, and he wanted me in Williams Lake to be best man. But Tim and I decided to make the best of it: we'd drive up, and while we were there we'd speak to a meeting of city council and other local businessmen and try to drum up a base of local interest in the tour.

We spent the drive asking each other questions we figured we'd be getting from the council briefing and from the media once the tour started—serious questions, stupid questions (not as stupid as some we'd wind up getting on the road, but close), ludicrous questions that had us doubled up laughing. And for every question, we'd frame an answer. I mean, we were ready.

We went to the council meeting, and found my Uncle Herman Hansen.

Uncle Herman was sitting in the audience as we made our pitch. He'd come to the meeting with my dad, and it seemed he'd gotten an early start on the wedding festivities. He didn't pay much attention to the proceedings. At times he looked as though he might be dozing off. But when we asked for questions from the floor, his hand went up like a shot.

I ignored him.

Other people got great service. I was grateful for any hand that showed. Sooner or later, Uncle Herman would get tired of waiting and put his hand down.

He out-waited me. I looked at Tim, who rolled his eyes. There was no way out.

"Yes, Uncle Herman?"

"Ricky," he said, "I just wanna know one thing: who's skimming it off the top?"

This was my uncle. He's on my side.

"Uh, I beg your pardon?"

"I mean, what's in it for you," he said. "Who's skimming it off the top?"

So I explained: there'd be an honorarium for the crew members, and some salaried help. As for me, I wasn't taking anything out of it.

"Okay," he said, settling back.

Everybody had a good laugh, and we actually came out looking better for the question. But we said our thank yous and got out. We had a wedding to attend. And besides, Uncle Herman might have another question.

We tried to plan for everything. We brought in a psychologist named Dave Cox to talk to us about the best mental approach to the stresses of the tour itself as well as to the constant togetherness, and spoke to a consultant who gave us some tips and written material on the art of public speaking.

Now, when you're planning a trip around the world, it's kind of essential that you know where you're going before you start, particularly when the guy out front will be in a wheelchair. Tim and I went down to the basement of my apartment block, armed with Automobile Association road maps and bicycle tour road atlases, and began laying out possible routes. It took us three weeks—one route per week.

The first one was 65,000 miles long. Great, if I wanted to be out there for seven years. I was committed, but there's a limit. We decided we'd best try again.

The second was 30,000. Better, but still too long. The third was 24,000, including zigzags to compensate for oceans that got in the way.

Well, the circumference of the earth was 24,901.55 miles. That seemed an appropriate target and a good natural tie-in. With that as our guide we finalized a route based on political, geographical and climatic conditions to cover as many countries as possible.

Meanwhile, there was the small matter of raising the money we needed before we could go anywhere.

Well, the office fund raisers weren't having any luck. Tim and I looked at each other. What the heck, we'd take a shot at it ourselves. We had no choice. I was the ticket. The only people who were supporting us were those who knew me or knew of me.

Tim bought some books on how to make presentations and lay out financial packages. We studied up, put on our best suits and hit the bankers.

The first place we tried was the Royal Bank. We were halfway through our spiel before we realized that our would-be fund raisers had already been there. Hey, the books hadn't mentioned anything like this! We did a hasty backtrack. ("We know that you've been approached by our organization before. We just wanted to keep in touch and to remind you that we're still proceeding, full speed ahead.") Ha ha. Shuffle shuffle. Exit.

Enthusiasm considerably dampened, we headed for the Bank of B.C. and an appointment with president Edgar Kaiser. What if the same thing happened? What if he wasn't interested? I mean, how many banks are there?

We didn't get a commitment from the Bank of B.C. that day, either. But Mr. Kaiser himself gave us $50,000 (U.S.) from the family's Kaiser Foundation — $25,000 in each of the two years we'd be away!

We thanked him, and walked out of the bank as though we'd been doing this sort of thing all our lives. When we hit the sidewalk we turned to grin at one another, yelled *"Aw-right!"* and gave each other the high five. Not too bankerish, maybe, but it was a big, big day.

We weren't to have many. Corporate sponsorships just weren't materializing as we'd hoped they would. Some came through — like McDonald's restaurants, who were to prove a godsend from start to finish. They gave each member of the tour a gold card good for free food at any McDonald's in the world, and many's the time they saved our necks. Or, at least, our stomachs. Nike was in, and Air Canada, and Esso. But mostly the corporates shied away. In some cases, corporations were reluctant to take on an association with a project involving disabled people. That attitude was beginning to change, but not quickly enough to help us at that point.

It forced a change in my thinking. My original idea that all donated funds would go into the Legacy Fund unless otherwise specified had been based on the assumption that corporate money and goods would be there to handle our expenses. Now we'd have to use some of the donated funds, or we wouldn't get out of the parking lot. The big responsibility now was to keep the total expenses at or below ten per cent of the money raised, which is the ground rule figure of most fund raisers.

It made me wonder: did we really have the public behind us?

The kids believed, particularly the kids of a Vancouver school project called QUEST, which placed a heavy emphasis on community involvement. They came in after school, made salads, cleaned the apartment, did the laundry and helped take the load off when we were really swamped. I got a lot out of just being with them, and looked forward to their arrival every Friday. No matter how depressing things might get, they could always find a reason to laugh. It was a perspective I badly needed.

But they were working for the cause, not the means of financing it. The media got solidly behind it, but were they there because they thought I could make it, or because it was a good story at the moment?

Expo? It provided a room for an organizational meeting, an Expo flag we carried with us all around the world, and two hundred Expo pins to distribute. All we had to do in exchange was make sure the wheel was over in October of 1986 so we could have the big finish at Expo. But the world's fair provided something else worth more than money. Through Expo—and Amanda—I got the aid, assistance, advice and friendship of Patrick Reid.

Patrick was commissioner-general of Expo, former president of the Bureau of International Expositions and a man with an extensive government background in diplomatic and external affairs. I first met him when we were co-chairmen of the B.C. Wheelchair Games in the summer of 1984, just a few months after I'd met his daughter, Amanda. His diplomatic experience and contacts opened doors around the world and got us the hearings we needed. (Later, I was to draw Patrick into the Man in Motion fire. I wanted him to stay on as chairman of the board, but when Expo ended he was posted to San Francisco as Canadian consul general.)

Governments? Well, I had a congratulatory telegram from Prime Minister Brian Mulroney and, through the efforts of provincial secretary Jim Chabot, lottery money from the B.C. government, plus $43,000 in federal works grants to help pay three office and support group employees for ten months. A trip to Vancouver city hall on Rick Hansen Day brought me a scroll, best wishes—and $100 that Mayor Mike Harcourt pulled from his own wallet. Later the city came through with some funding, but at the time it was tough keeping a straight face when I said thank you.

But when you think about it, it makes a kind of sense. Terry got much the same response when he first came up with the idea of a Marathon of Hope.

Talking about doing something is one thing. Doing it is another. No one had ever tried anything like this before. Not at that kind of distance. The public perception of a man in a wheelchair was a man who was helpless or at least severely limited. I was being blocked by the very misunderstandings I was going out to correct.

Awareness is such a vague term. I couldn't promote it to the public from Vancouver. I had to go out there, to see and feel it happening, and thus be better able to communicate it to others. Essentially what we were doing was starting out with a brave front and hoping the sponsorships or some other form of miracle would come along before we ran out of money. That's all we had: high hopes, a few bucks and the knowledge that we might soon be washing dishes to raise the money to get home. But we had office space. Boy, did we have office space.

Our first office was in the basement of the B.C. headquarters of the Canadian Paraplegic Association with barely enough room to hold the volunteers who were licking the stamps. Then the Cominco company donated about 4,000 square feet of offices they weren't using on the twenty-first floor of the Guinness Tower in downtown Vancouver. Unfortunately we had nothing to put in it but a few boxes, some posters and a small staff that rattled around trying to work with little or no office supplies. But the ones who were there were resourceful and dedicated—you might say to a fault.

It seems that in the early days we just didn't have enough of the basic office supplies. What we did have was an offer from Jimmy Pattison, the head of the Neonex conglomerate and of Expo 86, to come down to his offices on the sixteenth floor and use the company photocopier as often as we wanted. The girls who went down to do the photocopying couldn't help but notice the enormous piles of office supplies down there compared to the tiny amount (in some cases read "zero") upstairs. Not big, expensive things. Little notepads, those yellow sheets with the sticky part on top you stick to letters that come off without damaging the original, that sort of thing.

In a matter of days the girls had a new dress style, a style that included deep pockets. I am afraid, Mr. Pattison, that a few of your notepads and the occasional box of paper clips went south—or, rather, five floors up—until our own organization was in place.

Not that it was all joy in the office. Before we left, Tim and Don and I had to put down a revolt. The office staff wanted us to delay the start. They wanted all the i's dotted and all the t's crossed before we left. They wanted more time to get organized, which was a great idea if you've got $1 million in the bank to keep you running. We didn't have enough to last more than a couple of months. We'd exhausted all our local options from people who were supporting a gutsy idea they thought would fail. The only way to get additional financial support was to leave and prove we could do it.

They gave us an ultimatum: delay until April 1 and preferably until August—and they wouldn't guarantee they'd be with us after April 1 in any case.

We excused ourselves and talked it over. We knew we had to delay a little. For one thing, I still wasn't totally over my injuries. But the longer the delay, the less chance we had of finishing during Expo, and the more chance we had of missing the good weather seasons around the world upon which the schedule had been based. Besides, we didn't want them dictating terms, or they might ask for another delay later on.

We picked a day—March 21—and told them that was it, there would be no further delays. We thanked them for their efforts to date and told them to establish their priorities. A few quit. A couple came back.

This was the time. If we waited until everything was perfect, we'd never start. My confidence would be shot. The organization would dwindle, the interest would lag, and Man in Motion would be that thing that was a pretty good idea, but they never got it together. We went now, or we went never.

I know a lot of effort by a lot of people went into getting the show on the road. Maybe, in a year or so, we'll be able to sit down together, look back and laugh at how green we all were and the silly things we all did. But at the time I felt squeezed in on all sides with everything spinning faster and faster around me. And I meant it with all my heart that last night in my apartment, with the reporters and the crew and the confusion spilling over me, when I looked at a friend and said: "Tomorrow the easy part starts. Tomorrow, all I have to do is wheel . . ."

We were actually on the road. I couldn't believe it. We'd waved a final good-bye to the crowds at the Oakridge shopping mall, survived our first accident and my first fit of temper, and we were on the highway that would take us to the first border crossing and into our first foreign country, the United States of America.

We had our motor home, donated by Vanguard Trailers Ltd., and specially modified by them for my convenience and privacy. What they did was cut away the bedroom side wall of the bathroom, so I could slide off the bed and go directly in without having to come out into the kitchen/living area and go through the regular door.

We wanted a lift to get me in and out of the van, but it was too expensive. Besides, we didn't have time to have it installed. We fooled around with ramps, and at one point we were even thinking about getting a tiny little wheelchair that would stay inside the van and allow me to get from the door to the bedroom. What we ended up with was a towel. We'd spread it over the door sill and I'd lift myself butt-first out of the chair and on to the floor, then bum-hitch my way down the narrow aisle between the fridge and sink to the bedroom. It may not sound like much, but when you're doing it six or seven times a day four or five days a week, it's no picnic, particularly when you're already beat from wheeling.

We had one (1) chair in which I'd do the actual wheeling. We had the Canadian Paraplegic Association's Variety Club van as our escort vehicle, loaded with spare wheelchair parts, tires, one spare chair frame and anything else we could think of to keep me on the road. But how do you decide what's needed and what's not when you're packing for a minimum five people over nineteen months, and when everything has to be stored in one motor home and an escort van?

We made lists and took off in all directions on what looked for all the world like a scavenger hunt. Take a peek at some of the things on those lists:

Eighty pair of deerskin curling gloves.
Dress clothes.
Roofing tar.
Tools.
Kitchen appliances (blender).
Fifteen bottles, Shur-Grip.
Stick 'n' Sew.
Bicycles.
Communal socks and underwear.

There were good and logical reasons for every item. I'd used curling gloves to wheel for a long time, and figured I'd average a pair a week. Doing 70 miles required eighty strokes per minute for ten hours per day, which worked out to 48,000 strokes every wheeling day. Eighty pair seemed a good guess. The roofing tar was to spread on the gloves for a better grip on the push rims.

Nike was supplying our tour clothing: twelve sets for me—I'd be in and out a lot and if the weather got bad I'd have to change at each rest break—and four sets apiece for the others. But we'd need dress gear for banquets, official meetings and such. Stick 'n' Sew to put the sponsorship patches on my clothes. Bicycles for the crew members who'd be riding beside me. The blender for food preparation in the motor home. Tools, of course.

The underwear didn't start out as communal property. At first, all the guys had their own. Then, as the tour pace got more frantic, it got mixed on laundry runs and wound up in one big sack to be drawn upon as needed. That worked until I started getting careless with the roofing tar, at which point anything with tar on it was mine and the boys shared the rest. Eventually, I had tar over everything, and we were back to communal undies.

The road crew had grown and changed. Now it was me, Tim, Don and Lee, plus Nancy Thompson and a girl named Sheila O'Gorman, who had done public relations in the political field in Ottawa and would be in charge of media relations and publicity along the road. (Sheila had already set one Man in Motion record. We'd sent her to Woodward's department store to pick up what special clothing she'd need, and she came back with about $3,000 worth. I guess it's easy to get carried away on a shopping spree. The majority of which went back even faster than it arrived.)

Lee would be the cook. We needed one, because diet was going to all-important if I was to stay in the physical condition I'd need to keep going. Nancy was our advance person, travelling ahead of us to set up the route and accommodations and assist local groups in setting up their rallies or special events. She was supposed to leave after two or three days, but it soon became obvious that we'd need someone full time, so she sent home for some clothes and stayed on.

And we had $90,000 in operational funds—$50,000 from the B.C. Lottery Foundation and $40,000 from the tour patrons—plus goods and services: free motels en route, free gas, that sort of thing. Just enough, I figured, to wind up in Texas, dead broke.

So off we went, armed only with our optimism. And we almost didn't make it out of the parking lot at Oakridge.

As the pile of equipment grew, Don and Tim realized there simply wouldn't be room for it in the escort van. Their solution was a large box fixed to the top of the motor home. Unfortunately, getting out of Oakridge required going through a narrow, twisting tunnel.

The crew was impatient, because I was already away and they wanted to catch up quickly. They eyed the height of the box, eyed the tunnel, and figured it was a go if they could just lift those silly chains dangling from the tunnel's roof. Lee lifted them—and Don gunned the van. The box hit the roof. The chains were there to indicate maximum passage height. Everything came crashing down into the tunnel, including the only extra wheelchair frame we had, which now resembled a saucer.

I missed that part of it, but we made national TV. "Here it is, folks: from Vancouver, the beginning of wheelchair athlete Rick Hansen's round-the-world tour." Smash! Great start. Wonderful.

I was wheeling, and operating on fumes and nerve ends. The send-off had been emotionally overwhelming: hundreds of people swarming around the chair, lured there by a morning fund-raising blitz involving all the major radio stations in town. Disabled persons in wheelchairs of all types. Some disabled, who couldn't wheel and depended on operating the joystick of a motorized chair, were accompanied by parents and friends. They wanted to be a part of it. They wanted to see me off.

One little boy in a battery-powered chair he ran with a joystick grew impatient at the man in front of him who was blocking his view of the take-off. Gently, he rolled the chair forward until it touched the backs of the man's legs. No response. The boy reversed, then tried it again. Still nothing. So he rolled the chair even further back, got up a head of steam and bashed into the legs.

"Got him!" he crowed.

The man turned, saw the problem and stepped aside. It was Bill Bennett, the premier of B.C.

I guess I looked a little bit scared. Certainly Jim Taylor thought so. He worked his way through the crowd, leaned over the chair and offered one final, encouraging word:

"Don't forget," he said cheerfully, "a book called *Almost Around the World by Wheelchair* won't sell shit."

All this time I'd assumed Amanda was in the motor home. She'd been in this thing from the beginning, helping me in innumerable ways to make it happen. She wasn't making the tour, but she was supposed to come with us until we hit the border, then come back with my dad and Brad. Now I'm scanning the crowd as we wheel out, and I see a familiar face. It's Amanda. She's about 30 feet away, standing with her mother, all tearful and red-faced. There'd been some confusion. She thought she'd already said good-bye. Her mother was there to take her for a long, consoling lunch. I saw her just as we began to roll, waving pitifully with the tears starting to gush.

I wasn't exactly touched. I was boiling mad. Couldn't *anybody* get *anything* straight?

"Get in the motor home!" I yelled.

For a minute she just stood there, stunned. Then she hugged her mom and leaped in. Good thing, too. If I hadn't seen her then, if she hadn't gotten into that motor home, I might never have seen her again. I was that mad. I certainly wouldn't have gone looking for her when I got home.

I tell her that now and she just grins.

"Bluff," she says. "Big bluff. We'd have found each other."

As it turned out, we found each other a lot sooner than either of us expected.

6

"Don't any of these hills go down?"

*T*he first tape Rick Hansen shipped home for what would eventually be-come this book was full of excitement and optimism laced with grimness as the size of his task grew more apparent — plus an emotion none of his team at home had taken into consideration: loneliness.

Loneliness? In the first week? Ridiculous. Claustrophobia, okay. Six people in a motor home day after day with no place to hide is bound to make a guy a little claustrophobic. Depression, maybe. Those hills were going to be hell. But loneliness? When does he have time to be lonely?

But it was there on the tape in asides voiced on the road as he wheeled or in the hotel late at night when, so tired his voice had a slur to it, he would mutter something that almost sounded like a cry for help.

"Boy, I sure miss Amanda . . ."

"Amanda's my girl. Did I mention that? Well, she is, and I miss her a lot . . ."

For his co-author, the tape presented a king-sized conundrum. Ob-viously, there was a problem out there, a problem that perhaps only one person could solve. But Hansen had agreed to do the tapes under one condition. "I'll tell you everything. But no one hears the tapes but you, no one hears the information but you. If I'm going to spill my guts, I don't want a bunch of girls at a business school giggling over them as they transcribe."

So: stick his nose in and tell someone what Rick was feeling, or keep the lip zipped?

What if Amanda didn't feel the same way? She had a full-time job as a physiotherapist at G. F. Strong. If the relationship meant more to Rick than to her, she'd be crazy to quit work — just drop everything and go — to join an eighteen-month ordeal like this one. If someone told her and she didn't go, she'd be upset, and Hansen would be furious that she'd been told in the first place.

Nope, stay out of it. Cupids have been known to have their wings torn off. Let Rick handle it. Que sera, sera, and all that. Hell, he'd get over it. They hadn't known each other that long. Absence makes the heart go wander.

But the tape gave the lie to that. It carried a sense of feelings deeply entrenched and settled in for the lifetime haul. He made himself a silent bet: if something wonderful didn't happen to resolve this, the Man in Motion tour wouldn't make it much past California.

Something wonderful did happen. The Man in Motion wrecked his wrist.

That first day was such an emotional mishmash. The sendoff, people lining the streets, my family there with me—mom, dad, sisters, brother, aunts, uncles, both grandmothers—and Rollie and Betty Fox, Terry's parents. A couple of weeks earlier, Mrs. Fox had given me a statue of Terry. We wired it to the wall inside the van before we left. Terry wasn't able to finish his own journey, but he'd be with us in spirit every mile of this one.

There was a real temptation to pinch myself in case it was all a dream and I'd wake up in the middle of the night in a cold sweat, back in the apartment on Second and Cypress with a million things to do and the tour nowhere near ready to open.

And then there was Amanda. What was I going to do about that? She'd been there for the first day as team physio, which was good because she'd be able to visualize what it would be like out there, what we'd be going through. But she wasn't there now. She'd gone home, and I felt like my stomach had a hole in it.

I wasn't the type of guy who got serious with a girl, but this one had snuck up on me so quickly I had no control. Such a beautiful person I just wanted to be with her, and now she was gone. Would the feelings we have stand up to an eighteen-month separation? Would she be there when I came back? Was it fair to ask?

I tucked her safely away in a corner of my mind. She wouldn't stay there. I was to learn she never would.

We made some bad mistakes that first wheeling day. So did some other people, particularly the guy driving toward Vancouver just after we came through the Massey Tunnel heading for the border. The police had cleared one lane for us, and the guy slowed down to have a look. Unfortunately, the blonde in the car behind him was looking, too, and she rear-ended him doing about 55 miles per hour.

The police escorting us said it was just a fender-bender with no one hurt. Then I couldn't help but laugh. Minutes before, Tim had lost his bearings and crashed his bike into the tunnel wall. By now I knew about the box being scraped off the top of the motor home back at Oakridge. Ten miles on the road, and the accident box score was already at Man in Motion 2, Spectators 1. At that rate we'd return home leading 553 accidents to 276, and people would be afraid to line the streets in case we hit them.

I was ticked off already, and I knew I'd have to watch that if this tour was to survive. I've always been hard on myself, and some of that attitude flows off onto what I expect from other people. So, even knowing that they were all working hard, all putting their lives into the project as I was, I still had this inclination to go to the whip when things didn't go the way I thought they should.

To me, timing was everything. We had to stick to our schedule. We'd do it as though we were a machine: wheel around the world, get to Expo on the day we said we would, and that was that. If we said we'd be there at a certain time, we had to make it. I'd drilled that into everyone. Yet we were late for the sendoff party because of last-minute packing that hadn't been done when it should have been. That had a domino effect, forcing us to cut short TV and radio interviews. We'd be looking for publicity everywhere we went. Barely out of the shopping centre and already we'd learned a hard truth: the schedule had to be a lot more flexible than we'd thought.

I wasn't in the best of moods anyway. If we'd started off March 1 as we were supposed to, we'd have begun in good weather with winds at our backs so strong they'd have blown us halfway to San Diego. But there'd been the delays, and now we were starting with rotten, rainy weather and the winds blowing from the south and working on my face like sandpaper.

Worse yet, we'd seriously miscalculated the mileages for the first day.

All my training had been aimed at 23-mile wheeling sessions. Physically and psychologically that was what I'd programmed myself to do: three of those per day with regular short breaks during each wheel, and two-hour rest periods between sessions. Sticking to that schedule might not sound all that important, but if you've ever competed in any sort of endurance event you'll understand: to keep yourself going you have to establish goals-within-goals, carrots dangling out there in front of you to break the ordeal into mental and physical segments. And here we were, lousing it up on the first try.

We'd planned on a 60-mile day for openers: 20 miles, rest period; 10 miles to the border, stop for ceremonies and a press conference, push on another 10 miles to the rest break; then 20 more miles to our overnight stop in Bellingham, Washington. Even that was too long a haul, considering the 40-mile-an-hour head winds.

Then we were told that the distance from Vancouver to the border was only 20 miles, not 30. So then we decided to switch from three wheeling sessions to two: do the 20 miles to the border, take the rest break and do the press conference; then do the 30 miles to Bellingham. There was only one problem. We'd been right in the first place. It wasn't 20 miles to the border, it was 30. Instead of easing into the tour, we wound up doing two 30-mile sessions. Oh, yes, we also took one wrong turn, the alternator on the motor home went dead, and the hotel at the end of the day was perched on top of a hill that looked like something out of "Streets of San Francisco."

Don't get me wrong. It wasn't all bad. Not with the memories of the reception, and the people on the streets and the highway, honking horns and yelling encouragement, and my family and Amanda and friends like Tony Hoar, who'd built the chair, and Pete Turnau, who'd built my training gear back in the marathon days, and Stan Stronge, yelling "Take care!" as he and my wheelchair basketball team passed us on the way to Eugene, Oregon, for the Pacific Northwest sectionals of the the National Wheelchair Basketball Association championships. But late that night, after the massage and the shower and something to eat, I drifted off to sleep with one final thought about Day One of the rest of my life:

"Just think, Rick. Tomorrow, you get to do it all over again . . ."

Don't look down the road, I told myself. You might scare yourself spitless. Just wheel one session at a time, three hours and 23 miles per session, three sessions per day. Don't think about 24,901.55 miles, think about 23. Slice this thing into realistic, manageable sections or you'll go nuts. Plug along. You want to worry about something, worry about body parts falling off.

Cheerful thought, that. But in the two months prior to sendoff I'd had nothing but trouble with my body. My elbows, my back and now my wrists seemed to be turning on me, just when I needed them most. I'd been wheeling in pain, but I could endure that. It was the wondering that was killing me. Was there a point where the pain went away? Or a point where the body said to heck with it and quit? Or a point years down the road when my body would say, "It's payback time, boy," and my shoulders and wrists would forecast the weather a week in advance?

Just thinking that way can be be psychologically devastating, and I knew from the start this tour would be a mental battle as much as a physical one. I resolved to put it out of my mind, but it was like playing that kid's game, when you tell yourself you're not going to think about elephants, elephants, elephants, elephants . . .

One day into the tour, and I had a pain in my left wrist, the palm of that hand was sore and I was gnashing my teeth in frustration because I knew the problem wasn't physical or mental, it was technical, and no matter how hard Don and the boys worked on the chair we couldn't seem to sort it out.

Maybe I'd better explain about my chair. It's not your average wheel-down-the-road or hospital-corridor-variety chair. My chair is to those what a hot rod is to an eight-passenger Cadillac: stripped down, built for efficiency, not for looks. If there was a beauty contest for wheelchairs, mine would be the one in charge of cleaning the gym when it was over.

The basic Everest Jennings home and hospital model weighs from thirty-seven to forty pounds with footrests. A racing chair weighs fifteen to seventeen pounds. The chair I left Vancouver in weighed twenty-seven pounds. Most chair body frames are rectangular with two small wheels in front and two big ones in back. Mine was shaped more like an I, with one long centre shaft down the middle and one axle shaft front and back. It had kingpin steering, with the front wheels joined together by a tie rod. The front part of the centre shaft pivoted and acted as a a crude suspension system. The centre steering handle came up at the front centre of the chair, with a brake lever that applied tension to both rear wheels.

The rear crossbar supported the seat, which was really a bucket that looked as though someone had sliced the top off a hard-boiled egg and emptied it. I'd stick my rump in the bucket, which effectively tucked my knees up against my chest, and strap my feet in stirrups more or less level with the frame. No, it didn't look like much, but looks are deceiving. A lot of planning went into that chair and the ones that would follow it. In each case, what counted was what you didn't see.

Aside from the brake lever, which we'd need for control on the long downhill slopes coming off the mountains, it was essentially the same chair I'd won the world title with in England the previous year. That was the problem: I wasn't wheeling a 26-mile 385-yard marathon, I was wheeling around the world.

For this type of wheeling, it was essential to be able to adjust wheel positions—not just for efficiency to deal with changing terrain but to take care of the old bod. Changing wheel positions forces you to bring different muscle groups into play. If one group was sore in, say, the back of my shoulder, we needed to be able to adjust the chair until the stress was taken off that particular area and other muscles were brought into heavier use.

Before I left I knew I should change the design to something more adjustable and easier to maintain than the bucket, something with a seat made of upholstery (known as a "cage") with adjustments you could make by tightening or loosening laces at the back. The chair I was using, the one built for me by Tony Hoar, had no convenient adjustability. But I'd been using the bucket since 1980, and old habits die hard.

Besides, I still had this silly idea that all I had to do was find the elusive perfect position, the same one I'd used in winning all those races. What I didn't realize was that it no longer existed.

Structurally, I was changing. I had a rotation in my back: the vertebrae above and below the point of the break were losing their ability to stay stabilized, and twisting top and bottom. I also had a minor injury to my right shoulder and the major dislocation in my left shoulder in April of 1984 while getting ready for the Boston Marathon, not to mention the second injury to the right shoulder I sustained while preparing for the Olympics three months later. The combination of injuries had literally changed the structure of my body. For my new body, the old position just wasn't there anymore. But in my mind I wasn't prepared to accept that. I felt strong and healthy. There was no pain in my shoulder. All that was really bothering me was the ongoing problem with my wrists and elbow. I'd had an irritation of the right elbow before and cured it with a minor change in the position of the seat. It was natural to assume the same thing had cropped up again, and try to treat it the same way. Find the position, dummy, and everything will be fine.

Well, I'd been trying for six months, and at 2 A.M. the day we left I was up drilling holes in the bucket and getting it to where I thought it should be and guessing wrong like everyone else. Worse yet, Tim had bet me I'd be working on the chair after midnight on the last day. I wasn't just working, I was a hundred bucks down.

Let me describe the bucket change routine. The bucket was held to the frame by six bolts—two in back, two in the front and two through the bottom. They were the extra-long type, which meant three nuts per bolt.

The bucket didn't just move side to side and backward and forward. It also tilted up and down and rotated clockwise and counterclockwise to allow me to square myself with the axles. To make a change, you had to measure for new bolt positions taking in all four factors, remove the nuts, pull the bolts, and drill new holes where you thought they should be. Naturally, the constant changing wore away at the bolts. As the threads stripped, the bolts became more and more difficult to remove. And because we were drilling so many holes so close together, eventually a couple of them would overlap, leaving us with one huge hole. You could get by with the big hole by using washers if you absolutely had to, but the bolt would shift and your precise change wasn't precise anymore.

Talk about frustration. Drill a hole to compensate for a tilt problem, and you created a side-to-side problem. Drill another to compensate for that, and the bucket would have to be slid forward. Drill to fix that, and you threw the original tilt adjustment out of kilter. And you did all this knowing that an error as tiny as one-eighth of an inch in any one plane could cost you as much as a kilometre an hour if you were in a race or, worse yet, blow out a muscle if you were out there doing 70 miles per day. Someone in a chair for two hours might not even notice the difference. Someone pushing hard for seven to eight hours could literally be in agony or put out of commission. When I say Don and Tim worked on the chair, they worked on the chair— hour after hour, sometimes into the night, adjusting, discussing, looking for just the right combination out of a hundred possibilities.

And we just weren't getting it. We were getting closer. I could feel it. But it still wasn't right. Each time I climbed into that chair I hurt myself even more and heightened the risk that my body would end the tour because the tour wrecked my body. What idiot thought up this tour, anyway?

The next three days, which took us from Bellingham to Olympia, Washington, were reruns of the first, with variations. We'd start late, arrive late and apologize for being late. We spent about five hours looking for one reception at a McDonald's restaurant, arriving at 9:15 P.M. instead of 4 P.M. We had our first flat tire. The wind refused to get out of my face, the rain refused to stop.

It was demolition derby time. Sheila backed into Nancy's Camaro with the lead van and sprung the hood. Nancy turned beet red, smiled, and didn't say much at all. That became her approach as the tour progressed. Something would go wrong or someone would make some impossible demand, and she'd just look at him with those big blue eyes, flash that big smile and say, "Gee, I'm sorry. We just can't schedule that." Then she'd turn away, and they never heard her final word on the subject: "Jerk!"

Jim Martinson, an old friend from racing days who lived in nearby Puyallup, came out to wheel with me, and boy, that meant a lot. He'd just gotten over the flu and felt rotten, but there he was, the first wheeler to come out there and push with me.

Jim lost his legs in Vietnam the day he made sergeant. Someone next to him stepped on a land mine, and Jim had his legs blown off. He'd been an outstanding, multisport athlete. When he was shipped home he turned to wheelchair athletics, won the Boston Marathon in 1981 and today is involved with a company called Magic in Motion, which manufactures racing chairs and other sports equipment.

Now here he was, wheeling just in front of me. Next to him on a bicycle was a guy named Harry Fraser, who was there representing a vitamin supplement firm that wanted me to use its products. We were zipping down a hill at about 28 miles per hour when Jim hit the bump at the bottom.

It got a little hairy. Jim hit the bump square on and bounced into the air, but was able to stay with the chair. Harry missed it, but with the two of them so close in front of me, I had no time to do anything but attempt a swerve. It didn't work. I went flying, too—except that because I hadn't hit the bump squarely, I also twisted. I just had time to think, "Oh-oh, here goes another shoulder," before I made one of those kidney-crunching, bone-jarring landings. But I managed to keep control, get the chair righted, and we just kept on rolling.

It was the old story. We'd been bucking strong head winds. When we got going down a hill, it was such a welcome relief we more or less turned loose and flew, and wound up losing control. I knew better. I had a 25-miles-per-hour red line that I never exceeded—well, hardly ever. That time we got away with it. Next time we might not be as lucky. So there couldn't be a next time for me. Not if I planned on finishing the tour.

But the derby wasn't over. One of the girls from the office who was cycling with us took a spill. Then Jim bounced over some railroad tracks, and when Harry reached out to steady him, he crashed himself. At this rate, the motor home might roll into Oregon empty.

We were averaging about 62 miles per day. The money was coming in slowly, $600 one day, $55 the next. Somehow we had to develop a better system for letting people know we were coming far enough in advance so they could plan their own events and receptions if they chose. We had to get maps to the media with our stops clearly marked. We had to get signs for the sides of the motor home and the escort vehicle, saying that we took donations right there. Some people didn't know we did, and unless they stopped to talk to us and take one of our brochures they didn't know where to send a donation, either.

You know that "wave" cheer that fans stage at football and baseball games? It starts with people in one section, the people in the one next to it join in, and pretty soon you've got it getting stronger and stronger as it roars around and around the stadium. That's how I saw the tour response developing. Vancouver was the first section, and everyone was standing up and waving. Washington was the next section. So far, the people were sitting on their hands because they didn't know what was going on. We had to get them jumping, or Vancouver would get tired of the whole business and sit down—and there would go our wave.

In those early days the only way we could measure success and the impact of the tour was in dollars and cents. We had no way of knowing how or if the awareness would grow. We had to see it happen and see how it developed. The people weren't flooding us with money, but they were showing their support in a lot of wonderful ways.

It started with a member of our police escort, riding along beside me on his motorcycle and saying, "My wife and kids and I will be praying for you every day."

As I wheeled along, a lady reached out and thrust some money in my hand. "This is for my daughter," she said. "She's in a wheelchair, too." A man and woman in their sixties heard about us on the car radio, turned their beat-up old car and spent an hour looking for us so they could give us some money. "We're Hansens, too," he explained.

Then there was the young boy who said he was just getting started in wheelchair marathoning. Jim Martinson knew him, in fact had built a chair for him. We talked a while about training, racing techniques, things like that. He said he wheeled quite a bit, but not as long as usual the previous day because it had been raining. His parents looked at him, then looked pointedly at me, sitting there wet and wind-blown. He sat silent for a second, then grinned and said, "Well, I guess that excuse doesn't go anymore."

All sorts of people in chairs showed up to say hello and offer encouragement, including my old basketball team and the Edmonton Northern Lights, both on their way home from the tournament in Eugene. My guys had lost in the early rounds, but the Lights had won the whole thing and became the first Canadian team ever to qualify for the final four. They deserved it, but while I was hoping they did well I was also hoping they didn't win it. We used to beat those guys regularly. I wanted us to be the first Canadian team to win the whole thing. We'd come so close so many times. Maybe a couple of years down the road when I could play and we could get some new recruits, we could go all the way—if not for us, for Stan Stronge, who'd brought us all together.

We were getting all sorts of gifts—T-shirts, pins, walkie-talkies, cards, hats, cakes, cookies, religious tracts and even some clothing. It was good, because at a time of great stress it tended to jerk us back to reality and remind us that there really is no end to the goodwill of people. You get locked in your own narrow environment and sometimes you remember only the rotten things that happen. Then a little girl would hand me a card she'd made in school, saying something like "We're with you, Rick!" and all the good things would snap back into focus.

What we were going through back then were growing pains. We'd expected them, even tried to plan for them. But how do you do that when you don't know what they're going to be?

Tim was under tremendous pressure. As road manager, he had a lot of decisions to make on a daily basis, and it was getting to him. He was getting snappy with the media, which we really can't afford no matter how much some of them deserve it. These are the people who'll make or break it for us. Without them we're just another bunch of nuts on some wacky world tour. He was worried about Sheila, already asking himself—and me—if he should send her home. She was wrapped up in the tour and she really wanted to do well, but it was beginning to look as though the media skills she'd developed in the political world in Ottawa weren't going to help her much in the world of the road.

Well, I thought, maybe that was because she was out ahead of us by herself so much. We'd have to make a special effort to make her feel part of the project, give her some time to fit in and us some time to work with her. Her position was critical. We had to get more publicity. We'd virtually slid past Seattle unnoticed. Where were they? We'd wheeled right past the local ABC-TV affiliate, and they didn't even look out the window.

Don and Lee seemed to be settling into the routine, getting more comfortable with each other and with the lifestyle we'd have to adopt, even though we were all fouling up on a more-or-less daily basis. But Tim . . . I don't know, maybe it was that he'd been with the project so long, fought so many of the preparation fights, that he didn't have enough left to tackle the tour. Maybe a couple of days' worth of sleep would do it.

And yet, at the end of the third day he'd hugged me and said how happy he was to have them behind us. It was as if he thought the whole thing would get easier once we got on the road. Judging from the first four days, that was as big a dream as the tour itself.

Yes, we were all screwing up. And no one was doing a better job of it than the guy in the wheelchair.

Nobody knew my body as well as me. I'd trained it. I knew what it could do. I knew the danger signs and what to do when I saw them. And at a critical moment, I decided I could out-think it.

We were still struggling with the bucket. I was still convinced that the cause of my physical problems was of a mechanical nature, that if we could just figure out the proper position and alignment for the chair to take the stress off, my body would look after the rest. On the second day the left hand quit bothering me, but the back of the right wrist was a little sore. So we dropped the bucket one-sixteenth of an inch and moved it forward one-eighth. That took care of the stress on the right wrist, but now the left wrist developed the same problem. It was Newton's Law, or maybe Murphy's: every positive action triggered an equal and opposite reaction somewhere else.

I was convinced that my hand was coming down too low and I was forcing the extensor muscles on the back of the hand. We raised the seat back up one-eighth of an inch. That didn't work either. Now I was getting severe pains in the long tendons of the fingers on both hands. We were trying everything. Harry Fraser jumped right in, helping to massage my arms and pack them in ice. I was getting major league pitcher treatment, ice packs on the hands, wrists and elbows after every wheel, hoping to slow or stop whatever my body was doing to me.

I was a mental and physical wreck. The rain and the head winds were beating on me, and I was sure I'd ruptured a tendon on the third finger of my right hand: the first knuckle was red, swollen and throbbing. And we still didn't have the ultrasound unit I'd been asking for. Here I was, my body feeling great except for these stupid tendons, which could only end the entire tour if we didn't get the problem solved, and I didn't have any ultrasound equipment!

Okay. I'd go where the equipment was. We drove to a hospital, and I talked my way into the physiotherapy department.

The physio on duty didn't want to do it. He said it might do more harm than good.

"Don't worry," I said airily. "We do it all the time. I can handle it."

That was me talking: Rick Hansen, the no-magic, no-short-cuts kid, suddenly looking for the quick fix. So he did it, and by Sunday night the right hand felt worse than ever. There was only one thing to do.

I phoned Amanda.

Okay, so it wasn't just to talk about my wrist. By that time I knew I loved her. I could talk to her the way I couldn't talk to anyone else. With Amanda I could just pour it all out. Besides, I felt better just hearing her voice.

I told her about the wrist and finger problems. I told her we still didn't have anywhere near an efficient organization, that so much of what was happening was almost counterproductive, that the boys were working their heads off with the chair and everything else that needed to be done, but by 10:30 P.M. it wasn't ready. I had to help them with it. We had to be up and wheeling at 5:30 A.M. to make it into Olympia to meet the state governor at 8 A.M., it had hailed and rained all day, and the weather forecast for the next day said "variable rain and snow, heavy wind."

She listened and asked one question.

"Do you want me to come down?"

Did I want her to come down? Did I want the pain in my wrists and hands to go away? Did I want the wind to die down and the rain to stop and the hills to flatten out? Did I want to see her again?

"I think you'd better," I said.

Three days later she was there, joining us outside of Portland. What she saw really scared her.

I'd just finished the day's wheel, and I was wiped. She checked out the wrists and found extensor tendonitis (those are the tendons on the back of the wrist) extending down into the finger extensors. There were also signs of nerve irritation in the wrists because of the swelling. And she really wasn't sure what she could do about it.

Treating injuries like that when the patient is resting the wrists is one thing. Treating a patient when he's aggravating the injury by wheeling every day is something else entirely. And we both knew that if the wrists didn't improve at least a bit and we weren't able to eliminate or at least control the injury problem, the tour might have to be scrapped or postponed before we hit California.

I knew one thing, though: just having Amanda there made me feel a lot better. She'd taken her holidays and would stay two weeks—just long enough, as it turned out, to see me through the climb that almost did the tour in.

We did 70 miles in each of the next three days—three days of endless rain and wind in my face, and each day ending in a question mark. Should we take a break until the injury situation was licked, or shouldn't we?

I don't mind admitting we were all pretty scared. Going on was an hour-to-hour thing. There were times after a break when I wanted to go out again but was almost afraid to, because if I tried and couldn't finish, it might signal the end of everything. Once I just sat there and cried like a baby. Failure itself didn't frighten me. If the job was too big and we gave it our best shot and couldn't do it, that was one thing. What frightened me was the thought of beating myself and failing because I didn't make sensible decisions. Had the office staff been right? Should I have waited?

We were still playing the guessing game with the chair. On the third of the three 70-mile days before the break, Tim and I had decided to switch from the eleven and one-half inch push rims to the thirteen-inch, which is like going down to a lower gear ratio. We figured it would ease the pressure on the wrists going into the head winds, and besides, I should get used to using them before tackling the really steep hills up ahead. We forgot that because they were bigger, the rims would be higher, which would affect my wheeling stroke. When we did think of it, like a couple of bozos we decided to try it anyway. We did 24 miles, all uphill into a head wind. It took about four hours, and when we finished my wrists were gone.

We did some more fiddling with the bucket and actually came up with a position that was pretty comfortable for the bigger rims, but the cost in pain and injury had been almost unbearably high.

Amanda had the wrists up to fifty per cent of what I felt they should be. That made it bearable. But there was another problem lurking in the background, a problem that is the fear of every disabled person. I had a pressure sore on my butt.

I know, it sounds funny: *pain in ass stops Man in Motion tour.* But it wasn't. Disabled people have been hospitalized for a year and longer, lying flat on their stomachs, waiting for pressure sores to heal. They can result in horrible infections, even in death. Before the tour started, Dr. Pinkerton said he felt that pressure sores were the thing that would stop me. And I had one right on my rear end, which I planned to plunk into a wheelchair bucket for the next eighteen months.

It had started, as most do, as an abrasion. We'd put some supports on the bottom of the bucket, and a bolt had worked its way through the upholstery the way a tack comes up through the bottom of your shoe. By the time I noticed, the abrasion had turned into a welt. Then we tilted the bucket a little farther back to ease the pressure on the wrists, which created a bit of a ridge at the front of the seat in just the spot where the welt would rub back and forth across it as I wheeled. The timing was perfect: we'd made the change just as we hit the rough roads and bumpy pavement.

Like a donkey, I tried to hide it from Amanda. I figured she had enough to worry about with the wrists. I'd ask her for a band-aid and put it on when she wasn't watching. Finally, she asked what the band-aids were for.

"A little welt on my butt," I said.

She took one look, said "Omigod!" and I knew the jig was up. She couldn't do much to treat it. One method was exposure to the sunshine and ultraviolet light, and we weren't getting much of that. All she could do for the moment was cover the sore with protective material and add more padding to the seat of the bucket. But she talked me into two days' rest in Roseburg, Oregon, after those three brutal 70-mile days. I just lay on my stomach and thought about the road we'd covered—and mostly about the road ahead.

More than anything, though, I lay there and thought about the hills we'd face over the next four days. Three of them stood between us and the town of Grant's Pass, 70 miles to the south: the climb to Canyon Creek Pass (el. 2,020 feet), then down into the valley and up again to Stage Road Pass (el. 1,727 feet), down again and finally up over the

Sexton Mountain Pass (el. 1,956 feet). And up ahead, standing even higher, like a watchdog between us and California: Siskiyou Summit, 7 miles on a continuous six per cent grade which started at 2,000 feet and finished at 4,310.

It was a crucial part of the tour. Get through those mountains and we were into California. Were we ready to tackle the hills, or weren't we?

We did the 70 miles and three hills to Grant's Pass in one day. Don't ask me how. It was push, adjust the bucket, push, change the wheels, take a break, ice the wrists, push, and change the bucket again. After a while it just blurred.

People were yelling, horns were honking. Two guys in fire hats screeched their car to a stop and jumped out, waving madly. "Crazy Americans," I thought foggily. But no, they were crazy Canadians: Fred Cawsey and Pat Bell of the CBC, there to film for an eventual documentary. A man about seventy limped up on his cane. Said he'd been injured in a mine explosion years ago and told he'd never walk again. "I screamed and fought and worked and I showed those buggers!" he yelled. "You do it! You show 'em, too! You're gonna go all the way!" I kept wheeling. If I couldn't get over these, how would I get over the Siskiyou? Push!

We hit the Sexton Pass Summit at 8:30 P.M. It was pitch black, but we had our runway. The local ham radio operators, who'd come out to form our communication link with the road ahead and the people back home, had parked their cars on both sides of the road, headlights pointed in like beacons, guiding me in.

Maybe it was an omen. Maybe there was a light at the end of the tunnel that wasn't a freight train coming my way. My wrists felt good. For the first time in a long time I felt like I could apply force instead of wheeling along like a wimp. We were getting into the warmer weather. The chair still wasn't right, but it was closer than it had been in a long time. The guys had changed and drilled and changed until they could do it in their sleep. Sometimes I think they did. But they hadn't complained, they'd just kept working. Please, I pleaded silently, just let it hold until I get over the mountain. Please, just get me to California. Get me over that stupid mountain . . .

The next night we wheeled into the town of Ashland, Oregon, about 8:30 P.M. Before long the crew and the CBC boys were having a bit of a party on the floor below. I could hear it from the bedroom where I was trying to grab some rest. All at once I felt a twinge of frustration—okay, and jealousy.

Amanda was down there getting some ice to do my arms and shoulders, there was laughter and the sounds of people having fun—and I couldn't be down there with her.

In retrospect it was a little bit silly. In my state of mind at that moment I found myself thinking, "Why isn't she up here with that ice? We're not here to party. I can't party." From Amanda's perspective, she'd simply gone downstairs for ice. She couldn't have been gone for more than twenty minutes. Why all the fuss?

And inside, we both knew what was wrong. She'd be going home in a few days when we reached Sacramento—and I didn't know what to do.

I wanted her to stay with us for the entire tour, but it wasn't that simple. First, I didn't know if she wanted to or would even consider it. Second, I didn't want her there if it was going to endanger any chance at a long-term relationship. Every day so far had been great—but how about every day for eighteen months in a climate of continual stress and pressure? Could she handle it? Could I? She was the best thing ever to happen to me. Tour or no tour, I couldn't let that slip away. I didn't want her to go, but maybe I couldn't afford to let her stay.

Maybe I'd been right the first time. Maybe the easiest part of this whole thing was the wheeling.

Next morning, we attacked Siskiyou.

School kids lined the road out of Ashland. The CBC boys were there and—my goodness!—NBC. Maybe the word was getting around, at that. A construction crew had stopped work to yell and to tease a little.

"Wait till you see the next hill! It's even worse!"

"Keep on truckin'!"

Truck drivers honked their horns and waved as they passed. More than anyone, they knew that hill and what the climb entailed. But I was pumped up. We climbed for two and one-half miles, then stopped to adjust the bucket. I was pushing my guts out. The weather had turned, giving us one of those southern Oregon spring hot spells that had the temperature in the mid-seventies by noon. After all that rain and cold, I simply wasn't ready for the change. I could feel the sunburn coming. The boys took turns on the bikes, spraying me with water as I wheeled. At every break, Amanda would smear me with zinc oxide.

Two miles, stop. Two miles, stop.

I was blocking the world out, concentrating on the one task at hand, repeating one "power word" over and over again:

"Push! . . . Push! . . . Push!"

There's nothing mystical about it. It's just a way of focussing on one thing so the mind can lock itself totally into the job at hand. I've had people laugh and say if it's so effective, why didn't I use a more sensible power word? Like "cab" or "car." Let 'em laugh. It works for me, and it was working now.

Two miles.

"Push . . . !"

Two more miles.

"Push . . . !"

Nothing mattered but the road and the hill and beating both of them. At times I was almost overcome with emotion. I was burning hot, but there were goose bumps on my arms. I didn't want rest periods, I wanted to keep going, do it all in one swoop, get it over. No hill was going to beat me. We'd worked too long and too hard, all of us.

"Push . . . !"

And suddenly, we were on the summit.

The TV cameras were there, and the newspaper and radio people, and the photographers and Tim and Don and Lee and Amanda. Lee was scrambling up the pole of a sign that read Siskiyou Summit. People were trying to shake my hand. Everyone was talking at once.

Tim wanted to discuss the rest of the wheel, the glide down into California.

"Not now," I said. "Not now."

Now was for looking back at the clouds over Oregon and thinking about the rain and the wind and everything we'd been through together, and for looking ahead to California and the sun. Now was for thinking "We did it," and for being so proud of the whole team, because there were so many places and so many reasons to quit, and we didn't.

I sat for a bit and savoured the moment. Then I got into the motor home, pulled the drapes, lay down on the bed, and cried my eyes out.

7

"St. Elmo's Fire"

Almost always, there was The Song.

It was never intended to be a symbol of the Man in Motion tour. Certainly David Foster, who wrote the music, and John Parr, who wrote the lyrics, never thought it would become a worldwide anthem for the disabled. It was a movie theme, nothing more, the title song of a movie called St. Elmo's Fire.

Except . . .

David Foster, the self-styled "little guy from Victoria, B.C.," was in the process of becoming one of the biggest names in pop music that day in 1985 when a Vancouver radio and TV host named Terry David Mulligan asked him to write a song for this guy named Rick Hansen, who was going to wheelchair around the world. Foster had already shared a Grammy Award with Lionel Ritchie. And now someone wanted him to write an extra song?

"I told him I didn't have time," Foster says. "But right about then I needed something triumphant for a particular point in St. Elmo's *where a guy was driving through the mountains, and I was thinking about Rick, you know, pushing his way up those hills? And I came up with this little, two-minute piece of music.*

"I'd never met Rick until I played that little piece for him when he got to California, and I'd never met John Parr. But there were the two of us, working on the music for this movie about a bunch of young people trying to come to grips with what they were doing and where they were going—and John was having trouble with the lyrics for the particular song that was going to be the main theme. And I said, 'I know a guy like that . . .' Then I showed him a video of Rick wheeling, and the lyrics just spilled out of him."

John Parr, a virtually unknown British songwriter and performer getting his first big break, remembers the moment vividly. "I met David the day before we were to write the song. I had a real block on it, and he said if I needed inspiration, he'd met this guy Rick Hansen, who was trying to push a wheelchair around the world. And it just fell into place."

They were, Foster admits, almost blatant about it, altering the words to fit Hansen's situation more than that of the movie characters the song was supposed to represent. "Listen to the words," he chortles. "You broke the boy, but you won't break the man . . . Gonna be a man in motion. All I need is a pair of wheels . . . Hell, there isn't a wheelchair in the whole movie!

"Then, to make it perfect, the producer hears the theme and says, 'You know that little piece you did for the mountain scene? Why don't you stick it on the front of this one as an intro?' It was like it was just meant to be."

In a matter of weeks after its release, the "little piece of music," now "Theme From St. Elmo's Fire," was number one on hit parades all over the world. Everywhere they went to publicize the movie and the song, Foster and Parr told the story of the inspiration of the man in the wheelchair—so much so that it presented a problem: they could be jeopardizing their chances for an Academy Award. To qualify for nomination, a song must be written exclusively for the movie. But was it?

John Parr had an interesting answer for that.

"I'm not going to stop telling the story," he said. "I've been down myself. I never got much of a break in this business until I was thirty. I'd love the nomination. I'd love the Oscar. But this is more important. If it costs us, that's the way it is."

There was no Oscar nomination for "Theme From St. Elmo's Fire." But on roads and streets and highways in thirty-four countries, Rick Hansen would hear it, smile, and dig a little deeper in the well. Rick Hansen, whom John Parr had never met . . .

"Where the *hell* do you think you're going in that thing? Pull it over, get off, and get into that motor home *right now!*"

They were the first words I heard in the State of California. The man doing the yelling was a member of the California Highway Patrol. He did not look happy. Gee, they were always friendly on "CHiPS."

Besides, what were they doing there? We knew we didn't have permission to wheel on the I-5 once we crossed the state line and were to stop immediately. But the line was at the bottom of this long, lovely, steep hill I could glide down for a couple of miles from the top of Siskiyou. It said so, right there on our route plan.

Wrong again. The border was just on the California side of the peak. I'd done about half the glide, even stopped to change a flat. Now here I was, surrounded by about sixteen Smokies.

"You got a permit for that thing?" one of them asked.

"I dunno," I said. "Ask the coach." I wasn't being smart, although probably that's the way it sounded. I was just going where the crew told me to go. But in the eyes of the highway patrol I was just another foul-up—a pedestrian on a freeway.

That's what I said—pedestrian. In California they don't have a precise legal definition of a wheelchair and refuse to consider it as a form of bicycle because it doesn't have a chain or gears. A wheelchair is driven by pushing. So, if my chair wasn't a cycle and there was no definition of a wheelchair on the books—what was this guy who was *sitting* in it?

Why, of course! I was a *pedestrian*. So get off the highway, buddy, and get off *now!* We never got back on the main highway till we left California.

The highway exit was at the bottom of the hill. If they'd let me wheel to it, I could have had an extra 1,000 feet of gliding. But oh, no. I had to get into that motor home *right now*. We drove down and onto the side road, where Tim decided we'd pull off into one of those rest areas for the break and resume wheeling from there. Another dumb mistake. Had we driven 2 or 3 miles up that road we'd have been back at the the top of a plateau. But because we started at the bottom, I had to wheel another 2,000 feet uphill just to break even.

We wheeled into Mount Shasta that night—a warm, peaceful, beautiful evening with a big, gorgeous moon, and stayed the night celebrating getting over that bleeping hill.

We moved on to Redding the next morning and took the entire day off. Amanda insisted. She put me flat on the pool deck and rolled back my trunks to bare the area of the pressure sore, ultraviolet light being one of the better treatments. I lay there and seethed while I rested.

There was a danger in stopping. This time it was legitimate, and there'd be a lot of other things—sickness, injuries, equipment problems—that would force us to stop again. But we had to be careful: the more reasons we found to take a day off, the easier it would be to do it again, to turn over in bed in the morning and go back to sleep. That's why I'd promised myself from the beginning never to make that decision anywhere but in the chair. No matter how badly I felt, I'd get up and begin wheeling, even if it was only a kilometre before I had to quit. Otherwise, we'd never get home.

I still had major worries about the crew. To a certain extent, Tim was coming to grips with the pressure, but Don said he was still concerned about him. Me, I was concerned about Don. It worried me that he might be wondering if he'd done the right thing by coming, but feeling compelled to continue out of commitment, loyalty and pride, rather than doing the best thing for himself. He's such a quiet guy that he slips into the background so easily. He spent most of his time around the motor home, sleeping there, almost living there while the rest of us welcomed the chance to be in a hotel.

Even the thought of losing him bothered me, because he's a great guy and was a great benefit to the tour. But first he's my friend, and I was worried on that basis. I took him aside and more or less told him to make up his mind. I said there was no shame in leaving if that's what he had to do to be happy, and there was no sense sticking it out if it meant being unhappy for eighteen months. He assured me he wanted to stay, and I think the talk helped to clear the air.

But I couldn't stay mad for long. The weather was gorgeous, we'd received word that David Foster had written a song about Man in Motion—and Amanda was staying. She'd leave when we got to Sacramento, but she was coming back to join us for keeps in Arizona.

After all my worrying, that part of it was easy. She'd wanted to stay all along, just as I'd wanted her to stay. Once we got that established, it was simply a matter of talking to the crew to see how they felt. If having her there was going to generate any resentment, we could have a big problem. But Amanda had pitched in so quickly and taken so much of the load off them that there wasn't the slightest hesitation. To the crew, the only unfortunate thing about it was that she was going away at all.

And we were off to San Francisco, the Golden Gate Bridge, Hollywood—and a date with David Foster to hear our song. "Wouldn't it be nice," I thought, "if it could turn out to be some kind of hit . . . ?"

California was sunshine every day, the usual body and chair problems, the usual crew mistakes—mine and theirs—and the inevitable head winds. One day I'd have kindergarten children serenading me and bringing me drawings and gifts and donations, giving them rides on my lap and popping their eyes when I did a wheelie. The next day, ticked off by the delay we caused in traffic, a lady was reaching out the window to give us the finger. Wheeling past a school outside of Sacramento behind a police escort, I heard some kids cheering and felt really good, until a little fat kid darted out onto the road, looked at my wheelchair, and yelled:

"My soapbox is better than that piece of shit!"

I just bit my tongue and smiled. Even then, I was learning to do a lot of that.

The road into Sacramento taught me something else. The head winds were so bad that when I looked over at Tim on the bike beside me, he seemed to be riding at a forty-five-degree angle, pumping as hard as he could, but barely moving. I was cut to 6 miles per hour in-

stead of the usual 9, my elbow and shoulder were giving me problems
—but we had an event scheduled up ahead, and we wanted to be on
time. So, for the first and only time on the tour, I let myself fall back
and tuck in behind the motor home to take advantage of the draught.

I stayed there for about 8 miles. With the motor home shielding me
from the wind and pulling me along in the draught, my speed went
back up to 9 miles per hour, we got to the event on time—and I felt
like a cheater. There was only one way to straighten it out. I knocked
one-third of the 8 miles off my mileage total to cancel out the advantage I'd gained. My conscience still bothered me. I was there to
wheel around the world, not get sucked around it. From now on, the
wheeling came first, the events second. We'd do our best to arrive on
time, but not if it meant compromising or endangering the tour in
any way. And I'd never go behind that motor home again.

We were getting the odd civic reception now, such as the one in
Sacramento when we were greeted at the state capitol. That generated more media coverage—which heaven knows we needed—and
sent me to school again. We had to learn to be as co-operative as possible, how to say no while smiling, and how to create situations that
would trigger the kind of publicity we wanted.

That's right, I said "create."

I learned that lesson from a veteran wire service reporter the day
we crossed the Golden Gate Bridge. We'd come across at 10:30 A.M.
on April 11 after a 23-mile morning over hills that only a billy goat
could love. For some reason I hadn't been told where to stop, so I
rocketed right on past a group of radio, newspaper and TV people that
materialized as I turned a corner. When they caught up with me,
they had me go back and rewheel the last 100 yards or so off the
bridge—twice—until everyone had the shot. The wire guy took me
aside when it was over and gave me the word:

"Every time you see media, particularly media with TV cameras,
you *slow down*. Fake something if you have to, but slow down and
give them something to shoot. They're only going to try once, and if
they miss the shot they've got nothing—and neither have you!"

Fake something? You mean, everything we see on TV isn't spontaneous and live? Another illusion crumples.

But we learned to play the game. Take, for instance, the photo opportunities—or, as we came to call them on our schedule, the "photo
opps."

Photographers staying with the tour would get plenty of chances to
take any shot they wanted. But a lot of newspapers and TV stations
would send a guy out to park by the side of the road and get one quick
shot as we went by. Most of them shot while I was gliding by on a

downhill, maybe even smiling and waving. The public would see it and think, "Hey! He's not even *working*. He's just gliding along. Big deal!"

So I developed my "media stroke," also known as "the PR Shuffle." If I was on a downhill glide when the cameras showed up, I'd fan my wheels as though I was stroking furiously. The photographers never noticed the difference, and we got a shot that was a more accurate picture of the work that was going into the wheel. My conscience was clear. Nobody knew better than I how tough it really was.

We were still getting in the 70 miles most days, although sometimes the winds would get brutal, the temperature would drop, and all we could do was 35 or 40. Every day brought a new set of frustrations. I'd get annoyed with the crew—as I'm sure they'd get annoyed with me. Sometimes we'd all go to bed at night mad at each other and wondering how long we could keep going.

We were averaging $1 per mile in donations. Keep that up and we'd finish with $25,000. At that rate, why bother? Tim had his own way of trying to combat that. I'd hear him during rest breaks, talking to the media people: "Yeah, it's still only $1 a mile. I just don't know how to break it to Rick. It's so discouraging for him. Here he is, busting his butt to make this thing a success, wheeling 70 miles a day—70 miles a day!—and people aren't responding. How can I tell him? How?"

That night or the next day in the papers, there was a good chance that the story would centre around the disappointment and frustrations of the Man in Motion tour. It was a good story, and a legitimate story. But without a little timely prompting, it might never have been written or broadcast. Obviously, I didn't have a patent on the PR Shuffle.

No matter what, we kept moving. A 24,901.55-mile tour was too unnerving to contemplate. But a 23-mile wheel I could handle. So that's what I did, one after another, until we got to Los Angeles. Along the way, on the move with little time to shop, we'd gather lemons, oranges, grapes, nuts, cauliflower, lettuce, broccoli and all sorts of other fruits and veggies right out of the fields. I kept wondering when the boys would get caught and imagining what the media would do if they did:

MAN IN MOTION CREW MEMBER SHOT STEALING ORANGES.

I couldn't have that. If anyone was going to shoot one of them, it was going to be me. Unless they got me first.

We'd been debating whether or not Sheila was going to be able to handle the PR job. More and more it was looking like a case of a good, capable person in the wrong position. It was a tough assignment, alone out there in front of the tour, constantly talking to strangers and promoting an event most of them weren't all that interested in. But it had to be done. I'd told Tim: "Look, if she's been given her job description beyond a shadow of a doubt and isn't doing it, replace her now. Don't even wait until tomorrow."

We decided to give her one last chance. She would go on ahead to Los Angeles and set up the David Foster event.

The mere fact that Foster was writing a song for us was something of a miracle, and more proof that wishes don't have to die if you're willing to take a shot at making them come true. Away back in the planning days, I'd asked myself what we could use to bring the tour to mass public attention. The answer I kept getting was, "How about a hit record, a number one single with a rock video?"

The first person I asked to write one was Don. He was a musician. He'd played in bands and done studio work. Why not? When he said he didn't feel he could, I said, "Okay, let's go for a big star. Who's the biggest in Canada?"

"David Foster."

"Oh," I said. Then: "Who's he?"

"He's the greatest songwriter in Canada and one of the best in the world."

"Good. Let's get him to do it."

There were all kinds of reasons it was stupid even to think about it. But in this life you've got to take a shot. At a benefit dance I asked Terry David Mulligan, a national TV and radio personality, if he knew this David Foster guy.

"Of course," he said.

"Well, how about getting him to write us a song for the tour?"

"Uh, leave it with me," he said.

Mulligan didn't forget. Foster did write a song. We were going to meet him and hear it at this press conference. It had to go just right.

Now, there were certain basics. David was going to be there. He'd have to be properly introduced. He was going to present the song. That had to be properly displayed. The media was going to be there because David was there. Someone would have to arrange a "scrum session": one mass interview with me rather than a series of individual interviews, because otherwise I'd be there all night and I had to get up the next morning to wheel.

We get there, and all Sheila announces is: "I'd like to introduce David Foster. He would like to play a musical composition for the Man in Motion tour."

I'm dying! This guy is *big*, and we're treating him like some *hick*.

David gets up and says, "For those of you who don't know who David Foster is, I'm a music producer who just won a Grammy

Award with Lionel Ritchie. I happen to have this demo tape of a piece of music that was inspired by Rick Hansen. I'd like to play it for you."

He puts the tape on, and the machine doesn't work.

People scramble around for a while, testing various other equipment. Finally, David digs out this little Sony Walkman he happened to have, with the two tiny little speakers. He sets it up on the table, and that's how we heard "St. Elmo's Fire" for the first time — hunched over a table with the composer and seven or eight media members, trying to hear this wonderful piece of music.

To cap it off, the media has me pinned, everybody pushing forward, asking for individual interviews. What happened to the scrum session? Who knows? Back to the wall, I turned to Tim and said, "This isn't Sheila's kind of job. Fire her. Fire her now!"

You know what the upshot was? This star of the music business, about the hottest guy around, this guy we'd never met who'd been good enough to come out to a press conference that turned into a shambles, invited us to his recording studio that night to watch them record the background tracks for a record by Vikki Moss (Wayne Gretzky's girlfriend, as it turned out), and wrote us a personal cheque for $1,000.

Without telling me, he'd also arranged for me to receive a call at the studio.

"Hi, babe," said this voice on the phone.

"Who's this?" I asked brightly.

"Lionel Ritchie. Listen, man. I think it's a great thing you're doing, and if there's any way I can help, you just tell David."

Me, David Foster and Lionel Ritchie! Wow! It had been such a great evening. I wanted to give David something as a small measure of thanks. One of our tour track suits would be nice, but we didn't have a fresh one handy. So, as we sat there in the car, I stripped off the one I'd wheeled in that day, and presented it to him. He seemed really pleased.

David has a better version of the story. "After the session was over, Rick took me out to the car and began taking off his clothes. He said he wanted me to have them. I said no, but he insisted. This guy I'd met only that night takes me to his car, strips down to his shorts and hands me his clothes! I thought, 'Whoa, there! What's with this guy?' "

But he'd written this piece of music, this gorgeous piece of music, and given a lyricist named John Parr the inspiration for the words. We didn't know it then, but leaning over that table, hearing it for the first time, we were listening to a song that would become number one on the charts in North America and a smash all over the world.

David and John had their hit — and the Man in Motion tour had its marching song.

We had a police escort all through Los Angeles, did some interviews both live and on the phone, switched into the new chair Peter Brookes had built, which seemed to work a lot better for me, and pushed on down the coast to San Diego along some of the most beautiful beach in the world. And one morning, just outside of San Diego, we did something I'd been waiting to do for weeks.

We hung a left, and headed east.

If we had a dollar for every person who honked, waved or cheered us across the United States, we'd be richer than Arab oil sheiks. But they were cheers instead of money. The average donation was a lot higher than it had been, but donations were relatively few and far between. "Awareness," I kept telling myself. "You are creating awareness. Listen to the cheers, look at the faces, and remember that." True enough. But awareness *and* money wouldn't have been hard to take, either.

We had a new and distant target, a new goal hanging out there waiting, the two of us separated only by the width of a continent: Miami, Florida, the last stop on phase one of the dream. Reach Miami and the doubters and wait-and-sees would have to admit we had a chance to make the whole thing happen. Vancouver to San Diego and across the United States to Miami. If we could do that, we wouldn't be a bunch of people trying to do the impossible. We'd be an expedition in serious pursuit of an incredible goal.

So we gritted our teeth and put our backs into it. California, Arizona, New Mexico, Texas, Louisiana, Mississippi, Alabama, Florida— one by one we chewed away at them and finally through them, seeing America as few Americans see it, and learning a lot about ourselves along the way.

It was never easy. Settling into a daily routine was tough enough. Maintaining it once we had something workable was even tougher. Tim, Don, Lee, Amanda (from Phoenix on) and me in the van, Nancy darting ahead doing reccy and helping get media and receptions organized before we got there. We fought weather, we fought the wheelchair and my body, and sometimes we fought one another. And over everything hung the crushing sense of sameness. Was that Arizona out there, or New Mexico? After a while, we barely knew the difference, or cared.

Get up in the darkness. Load the motor home and drive to the start point. Wheel 24 miles with small breaks at 8 and 16 miles. Take a two-hour break. Wheel another 24 with two small breaks. Take another two-hour break. Wheel another 23. Flop out on the bed in the motor home during each break while Amanda iced down my shoulders and elbows so I'd be in shape to do it again. Handle the media sessions. Keep smiling.

Check into the hotel or motel. Make the phone calls home, trying to keep a finger on what was happening back at the office. Eat—room service or something planned and nutritional the boys have prepared in the motor home, or another in a string of Big Macs, Chicken McNuggets, pizzas and cardboard boxes of Chinese food that by themselves would make a chain across the country.

Get to sleep (by midnight, if I was lucky). Get up at 5 A.M. and do it again . . . and again . . . and again . . .

That was my end of it. The crew had their own drill.

Their day actually started the night before, after dinner, when we'd decide what to do as far as altering the chairs, based on how I'd felt wheeling that day. It wasn't unusual for those chair alterations to take until 2:30 in the morning. But they'd still be up half an hour before me, packing equipment or getting breakfast or the ice we'd need for my shoulders that day. The two in the motor home would try to catch up on their sleep during the wheel, one driving, one snoozing. But the snoozer had to be ready with the food and water for my breaks, because every little delay tacked on to the other little delays added up to less time to do what had to be done that night, and less sleep to prepare us for the day after.

Eight hours' sleep? What's that? Would you believe five or six?

We had a manual, a Standard Operating Procedures manual prepared back at the office with every little detail and contingency theoretically planned and accounted for. It was as big as the world's phone book, and essentially useless because it was written *there* and we were *out here*.

By now we had charts and lists for everything: the route, climbing rate, terrain conditions, weather conditions, chairs used, repairs and changes to chairs, elevation changes, medical charts (how I felt before, during and after each wheel, broken down into areas of concern and potential treatment), media schedule, names of people to thank at the stops ahead (all written out on file cards in advance so I could have them ready during my thank you speeches), how to act at school stops and border crossings, lists of volunteers ("I'd like to thank the Telephone Pioneers, Fire Department and Chief Blank of the Blank County Police for their wonderful co-operation"), logging of gifts—and a homemade white box with a piggy-bank slit in the lid for donations that were trickling in from the roadside.

But all the lists in the world, all the planning and foresight, couldn't have plotted anything close to what it really was.

For instance, who could have anticipated the need for a Designated Flipper?

We were horribly short of rain gear, and when the weather was cold and miserable I was taking breaks every 7 or 8 miles. Each time I came in, I had to get into dry clothes. We just didn't have enough to swing it, and we were in a moving motor home without washer or dryer. But—aha!—the motor home did have a heater. We'd string wet gloves, socks and tuques across the dash, turn on the heater, and dry them that way. The person in the passenger seat was in charge of flipping them over so that both sides would get dried, and replacing the dry ones with wet.

What with the stuff on the dash, and the other clothing hanging from so many lines you had to part the legs of sweatpants to get from one end of the motor home to the other, there was this constant odour of steaming sweat. We'd have the windows down even though it was cold outside. Otherwise, with the heater on so high the motor home was like a greenhouse, and the windows would steam up. And there was dirt everywhere.

Funny, I couldn't find anything in the manual covering that.

Or how about the driving? I'm afraid I put the drivers through hell. Their job was tough enough, staying close enough to me so that a passing car couldn't swing in front of the motor home and wipe out both me and the chair, yet far enough back so that the motor home wouldn't accomplish the same thing should I decide on an unscheduled stop. Amanda says I was like a conductor out there, waving them closer or waving them back, glancing back over one shoulder or the other and giving signals they couldn't understand. They also had to keep track of the route and stay aware of the mileage between us and the next rest break so we didn't pass it. And throughout that, there was the numbing tedium of driving across the continent at 7 or 8 miles an hour.

Besides, no plan ever quite worked out. There were too many variables. Angry policemen who could and did pull us over for delaying traffic. Well-meaning friends who wanted us to stop and talk. A spontaneous event (or a planned one no one told us about) would send us flying out with pins and brochures. Weather, terrain, injuries, sickness—any one of a dozen other things could throw the schedule out of whack. So we planned as much as we could, and played every day as it was dealt.

We came away with a view of America broken down into little scenes like movie clips, so many of them that we'd argue sometimes about just where each one happened. Was the Suicidal Armadillo in Texas or Louisiana? The bikers—remember the bikers? The day the baby mountain lion got into the van—was that the same day the tarantula attacked Lee's bicycle? Or how about the time Lee and Don thought they were going to spend their lives in a Mexican jail? And the Dogbusters. Where did they pop up, anyway . . . ?

Does everyone in America have a dog? It sure seemed that way. And none of them seemed to have a leash. We'd be wheeling down back roads or through residential sections, and some dog would come boiling out of a yard taking after the man in the funny car with the great big wheels. I was going at just the right speed to invite the chase. At times in the country I was chased by *cows*.

The crew tried various ways to scare off the dogs. At first they honked the horn, or swerved the vehicle toward them. Later they tried sirens and shouting through the microphone we used for crowd control. Nothing worked. One day we even bought a tin of Mace. When Nancy tried to use it, the nozzle fell off. Disgusted, she threw the whole thing at the dog. That didn't work, either.

There was only one answer: brute force. We kept a big stick handy in the motor home. Whenever a dog came after me, someone would grab the stick, leap out, and charge the dog, waving madly and screaming.

And we got a dog. Stopped him dead in his tracks. Lee had seen it coming up from behind, heading for the chair. He grabbed the stick, threw open the door and leaped out. Now, there is a trick to doing that. You're supposed to jump out in the direction the van is travelling. But the dog was still slightly behind the van, so Lee jumped in the other direction, and fell flat on his face. Luckily, he wasn't badly hurt, merely skinned and bruised. It looked so ludicrous, the crew just broke up. The dog stopped, looked down at the fallen Lee, then turned and slowly walked away.

When the wheel was over and I climbed back into the van, they were all wearing badges—pictures of dogs with a circle around them and a line drawn through the circle.

"*Dogbusters!*" they yelled.

The heat. It had to be the heat.

Heat got blamed for a lot of things as we crossed the sands of Arizona and New Mexico and worked our way into Texas. For instance, I don't normally talk to buzzards. But I can remember sweltering on a desert road in Arizona, thirsty and tired, sore-eyed from the glare, looking ahead and seeing nothing but road and sand, looking up and seeing two buzzards circling. I watched them for a few seconds, then shook my fist at them and yelled:

"You haven't got me yet! And you're not going to get me, either!"

Now, there was a motor home 20 feet behind me, with food and water and comfort and friends. All I had to do was signal, and someone would be there to give me a drink or spray water on my shoulders. But for just a second there, it was me and the desert and the buzzards. It was personal, and I wasn't going to let them win.

It was Daniel Boone, I think, who said he'd never been lost in his life, but once or twice he'd been confused for a couple of weeks. Well, we got confused, too. A lot.

Because there was never enough time after a wheeling day to do the routine things that make up daily living—shopping, laundry, banking, mail, shipping home souvenirs and crates of plaques and hats and poems and scrolls and such we'd been given along the way—the motor home was constantly leapfrogging ahead or staying behind and catching up later. I'd be on the road in the middle of nowhere with no one around but one crew member on a bike, trusting that the motor home would be back in time for the rest or water or bathroom break. Mostly, it was. But not always.

They lost me twice before we left Arizona. The first time, Lee and Don had leapfrogged ahead. They had the water for my break and there was no sign of them. The temperature was about one hundred degrees. We were supposed to do 12 miles, then break. They showed up just as we hit 18. Did they have a reasonable excuse? Certainly. They were making a video with a cactus.

Clyde Smith, the physio who had come down to substitute for Amanda until we hit Phoenix, was asleep in the motor home when he awoke to the sound of giggling. He peered out the window and there they were, Don and Lee, out in the sand in front of this cactus with the videocamera facing them on a rock so they'd both be in the picture. Lee had taken a slice out of the cactus and was handing it to Don, explaining that the tour had just folded, we were out of money and food, and this was dinner.

Clyde yelled at them and pointed to his watch. If it was possible to turn white in the middle of the Arizona desert, they did it. They were having so much fun they lost all sense of time. Or maybe just all sense, period. Somehow, when they caught up with me, the story didn't sound funny at all. I guess you had to be there.

Sometimes it was fate, like the time outside of Sierra Vista, Arizona, when Tim, Amanda and Don drove ahead in the escort vehicle, then waited for me on the assigned route. I never showed up. They drove the road in both directions, then flipped a coin to see who'd phone the police to report misplacing a guy pushing a wheelchair. Tim lost.

"Uh, excuse me, but we're part of the support group for a guy wheeling around the world in a wheelchair and, well, we've kind of lost him . . . He's out on the highway somewhere and we were wondering . . ."

There was a simple explanation for that one. A few days before we got there, the Highways Department put in a new bypass. We were taken that way. They took the original route. But I was furious. In fact, when they finally caught up, I wouldn't even speak to them.

112

When I wanted something, I'd signal. In the motor home, they were killing themselves laughing, but I had a good steam on and wasn't going to let go that easily. So I signalled for a sweat jacket, Lee brought it, and as I wheeled I put it on—backwards. If I could have, I'd have thrown up my hands and surrendered. But first, I had to get them out of the sleeves.

I'm told I was on a bit of a hair trigger out there sometimes. Tim swore that he and Nancy developed a system for dealing with problems at the beginning of the day: they'd figure out the best alternative, then give me four others. I'd reject the four on principle and in most cases suggest the one they wanted to use in the first place. Well, maybe. But there were days, boy. There were days . . .

We kept thinking that the next town or the next state was going to be better. We wheeled and wheeled and listened to the stories about how good it was going to be down the road, and it never happened. Remember that story about the little boy who was so optimistic that when he found his front room full of manure he just started in digging, because he knew that with all that manure around there had to be a pony in there somewhere? I was the little boy—and I was getting awfully tired of shovelling.

El Paso, Texas, was a good example. We'd heard these great stories about the reception being laid on at city hall, the brass band (there was always going to be a brass band), a guest appearance by the famous sports mascot and comic, the San Diego Chicken, and thousands of people. Once again, we let ourselves hope. We made the effort and got there. It wasn't at city hall, it was in a parking lot. The Chicken never showed. Neither did the thousands of people. Instead of a band we had the American national anthem on cassette deck. Total crowd? About fifteen people, mostly organizers.

But I'm glad we went. Out of that visit came one of the more satisfying moments in America.

A boy named José Mendez was there in a wreck of a wheelchair, determined that he was going to wheel the first mile with me. I mean, his chair was junk. We had a folding chair in the van, an Everest and Jennings that I wasn't using anymore. We used to kid around about selling it because we were so broke. I asked Tim to bring it out, and presented it to José.

I thought he was going to jump out of the chair and hug me. His mother started crying. José couldn't speak much English, but the look on his face said it all. He wheeled the mile with me in his old chair because the new one needed some minor adjustments to fit him. When he and his mother left, I looked around at the crew. Who needed a band when we had a memory like that?

We kept going, dealing with the crises as they came and laughing every chance we could. Given the make-up of this particular crew, there was no shortage of opportunities.

Don and Lee took the escort van and made a run into Mexico for a little relaxation. It wasn't until they were about to recross the border that something occurred to them: all our medical supplies were in the vehicle with them. They were coming out of Mexico with enough drugs to land them in serious trouble.

Every story they'd heard about Mexican jails flashed before their eyes. When they got to the checkpoint and the woman began the routine questioning, Lee started babbling about the tour and handing out brochures as fast as he could. She stepped into the van for a quick look, but waved them on without searching. Much later they laughed about it. Once they'd stopped twitching.

There was something about our crew—I'm not sure what, but it was definitely something—that attracted animals, snakes, insects and creatures living and dead. And we were in the right stretch of country for it. You couldn't wheel 10 miles without finding at least one dead armadillo or rabbit or snake squashed in the middle of the road by a passing car. After the buzzards had finished with them and they'd been rotting for a few days in hundred-degree heat, I could barely wheel past without heaving from the stench in my nostrils. Once, just as he passed me, some Sunday driver squished one that had been frying for about a week, and there I was with armadillo guts splattered all over me. Nice country.

Lee was fascinated by anything that moved. Once he rode his bike up to a snake that was coiled and ready to strike, and started teasing it with the front wheel. It struck, all right. Fanged his front tire. At which point one of the policemen in our escort opened the trunk of his squad car—revealing enough armoury to put down a revolution, looked at Lee and asked conversationally: "Which one would y'all like me to use t'kill it?"

Or how about the tarantula? There it was, a hairy thing about the size of a fist, skittering up the middle of the road as though it owned it, heading for the spot where a dozen of his buddies were working over the remains of a dead rabbit. Well, Lee had to see a spider that big. He went after it, teasing and poking at it with the antenna of his walkie-talkie. I swear, it reared up and jumped at him.

That was enough for Lee. He reached over and dropped the tool bag on it. The thing was stuck on the bottom and still wouldn't die. So Lee waited until Don was about to reach into the tool bag, then screamed: "Don! There's a tarantula in there!" Don dropped it like a hot rock, which finally finished it off. But migod, it was big. Later we saw what looked like an army of them, some squished on the road.

"They start marchin' 'cross the road," a local guy said, "means we're gonna get rain."

That's nice. You want to plan your picnic weekend, look for dead tarantulas. Me, I'll stick with a barometer.

The crew still laugh about the time in Texas when they borrowed a lady's pet baby wildcat, tossed it into the motor home where I was flopped out on the bed, and closed the door. They were still giggling over what would happen once I saw it, when the woman said, "By the way, you do know, don't you, that the cat has never been declawed?"

They jumped into the motor home, and there was the playful little baby wildcat on my back, sinking its playful little claws into my neck. (Sudden thought: "Amanda loves cats. She'll probably want one when we get home. We may have to discuss that.")

My favourite tour animal story, though, involved the Suicidal Armadillo.

We were about to cross a small bridge in Florida. Lee was riding beside me as I wheeled. And there, in the middle of the bridge, was an armadillo. Naturally, Lee had to go charging up for a closer look.

The armadillo watched him coming and hopped up onto the bridge railing. It looked back, and Lee was even closer. It looked down into the water about 20 feet below, looked back at Lee, looked back down at the water—and jumped.

We waited there on the bridge for a couple of minutes, peering over the railing, waiting for the armadillo to surface. It never did.

"Never mind, Lee," we consoled him. "You'll find a date sooner or later."

And then one day—June 24, 1985, around 4,700 miles from the B.C.-Washington border, we wheeled into Miami. The band played—yes, we finally had our first band—the people cheered, and I could sit back and reflect on the successes and failures of Phase One.

We'd scrapped and fought—the country and each other. We'd battled enough pain and injuries to fill another book. We'd done without sleep and, but for the unfailing and constant aid of the Telephone Pioneers of America, without much in the way of outside help. There'd been weeks when the crew had worked together like a Swiss watch, and days that were strictly cuckoo clock.

But we'd made it this far.

Okay, we'd crossed one of the biggest and most powerful and wealthy nations in the world and put only $6,000 in the Legacy Fund. But we'd started from scratch without knowing a thing about how to get the word ahead that we were coming, without knowing how to generate attention, without knowing anything, really, except how to push the wheelchair. Even at that, the publicity and media attention were growing. We were starting to get a fair amount of local coverage and the occasional network shot, probably because we knew now what they wanted and tried to make sure they got it.

We were learning—but the cost in personal relationships was threatening to get terribly high.

Some of the board back in Vancouver were jerking me around on my contract, which wasn't ready to be signed before I left and now had turned up full of changes. I wouldn't sign that version, either, and tempers were rising at both ends of the argument. The office was complaining that we weren't filling out all the daily progress forms they wanted, which would have taken all of one crew member's time every day. Our expense money was held back. At one point, Tim had to get an advance on his Visa card to live. They told us to live off donations we took in and keep track until things got straightened around, which was totally contrary to everything we'd told the public before we left.

And the relationship between myself and Tim had stretched almost to the breaking point.

His heart wasn't in the tour anymore. In a way it never had been. He'd said it many times: "I'm not out here for the cause; I'm here because of Rick." He'd started out because he was my friend. We'd been together for eight years, travelled all over for wheelchair sports events. We'd almost been like brothers. It was only *natural* that he come with me on this one.

But he'd been thrust into a management position for which he wasn't suited. He was too good a guy; he wanted to be a buddy to everyone in the crew. You can't do that and run it, too. The pressures piled up on him. He kept telling himself that it was going to get easier. Instead, it got harder, which created more pressure and increased the tension between the two of us.

In a situation like that, little things become gigantic. For instance: Lee liked to do a lot of the cycling with me, which beat being in the motor home. I wanted it shared and, in particular, once Amanda rejoined us, I wanted her to get her fair share of bike time. I asked Tim to tell Lee that Amanda would do the first 23-mile segment the next morning. I got up, and Lee was ready to bike. Tim hadn't told him. So I called Tim aside and asked him to straighten it out. His method was to call out to Lee in front of everyone: "Lee, you're not on the bike. Rick wants Amanda to do it."

Now I had Tim mad at me, Lee mad at me, and Amanda, who was fighting for acceptance as part of the team, was caught in the middle.

I did the wheel, came back, and blew my top at Tim— which shows you how the strain was getting to me.

I should have handled it long before we reached Miami. I should have found other duties for him and pushed to bring someone else in as tour manager. But, as our friendship influenced his original decision to come on the tour, it now got in the way of the two of us making a regretful but logical decision for him to go home.

What a mess. And there we were in Miami, and not a solution in sight.

But I had a sackful of memories, some scary, some maddening, but mostly good, because no matter how bad the day I always had the sense that the people understood, that when we passed through a town we left some of them with an understanding that would stick, and that their numbers would grow if we just kept trying.

So many memories . . .

Amanda, so strong and competent in any situation, frightened by the thunder and the lightning when we hit the storms . . . the stormy day coming out of Tallahassee, Florida, when she was riding with one hand on the rearview mirror on the driver's side of the motor home, leaning in to look at the map, and suddenly I heard this sickening, crunching sound. I looked back, my heart in my mouth, and there was the bike under the wheels and Amanda rolling and bouncing across the line into the oncoming lane of traffic. We were so lucky —no cars coming, and somehow she hadn't gone under the motor home with the bike. A few cuts, a few bruises, and five people scared spitless. Somebody was looking after us that day . . .

The ghost towns killed by freeways that sprang up overnight and passed them by . . . The man and wife with their beautiful five-year-old daughter, bicycling just outside of Tucson. They'd been doing it for three years, crossing their country as we were, looking for a place they could really call home . . . The nostalgic rush when the freight train roared past us near Whitman, Arizona, and I saw two flatcars of lumber from the two mills I'd worked for in Williams Lake. God, we were a long way from home . . .

Visiting the Alamo in Texas, wheeling through the southern states that looked in some places as they must have looked before the Civil War—and getting the feeling that in some minds and hearts, neither battle was over . . . Wheeling along by the Mississippi River, feeling like Tom Sawyer or Huck Finn . . . Sitting in a lovely hotel room in New Orleans, wading our way through a pile of Cajun shrimp and crawfish that all but buckled the table . . . Fishing off a bridge in the Florida Everglades, hooking into a garfish, watching Lee lean out over the edge with Don holding one arm, trying to scoop it in with a bucket because we had no net. He had it part way into the bucket on the third try, but swinging it the rest of the way might have meant a fall into the river. "Crocodiles," he thought, "there might be crocodiles in there," and let my fish and the bucket both fall into the water and disappear . . .

The incredible rush of good feeling that swept over me on an unscheduled stop at the Freeport Chemical Company in St. James Parish, Louisiana, where employees came flocking out, cheering and reaching into their pockets for donations. One man had read about us, spread the word at the plant and flagged us down. So there I sat with my lap full of money—almost $400 in bills—with all these people congratulating and encouraging me. It was the first and only spontaneous fund raiser we'd had in the entire trip across the United States. "Maybe now," I thought. "Maybe now it's starting to happen . . ."

The bikers in a place called Stone Cabin, California—one gas station, one cabin (not stone) and miles of desert—tough-looking dudes and a girl with a cigarette dangling from the corner of her mouth, taking our picture and saying, "Go for it, buddy. *Awright!*" They'd already talked to the crew, and had their donation ready . . . The day in California when I sent Lee out to scrounge some lumber to make shims so we could raise the bucket to various heights and planes, and he came back with five fence pickets, all new lumber. I didn't ask . . .

Sitting in front of a TV in Monterey, New Mexico, watching George Murray win the 1985 Boston Marathon, and feeling lousy because I couldn't be there. In the early days of planning, I'd figured I could break from the tour wherever it was, fly to Boston and race, then fly back and start wheeling again. Ha! I wouldn't have had the strength to get to the airport . . .

And, finally, sprawled in the chair one Sunday evening on a lousy back road in Arizona, with Tim on the bike next to me, a tough wheel in 110-degree heat just completed, when a car pulls up so the driver's window is right next to us. The window hisses down, a woman looks out and says, "This is the stupidest thing I've ever seen." The window hisses back up, and she's gone.

You know, some days out there it was easy to believe she was right. But here I was, sitting in a hotel room in Miami, Florida, with about 4,700 miles in the bank, sipping a little champagne and watching the sunset with the girl I knew I loved.

Lady, it can't get any better than that.

118

8

"If I'm sick, it must be England."

*T*he Man in Motion tour didn't so much roll into Europe as it heaved in. From the day they landed in England until the day they left for France, Hansen and Amanda Reid were so sick the tour flag should have been a barf bag.

Months later, as Amanda recalled those days in painstaking detail, you could almost see the weariness creep back into her eyes . . .

"We should have just said, 'That's it, we're not moving until Rick gets better.' I should have insisted. We both had the flu. Rick's had sunk into his chest. There was no way he should have been on the road. He should have been in bed. But we were so tired, so mentally, physically and emotionally wiped, that we were in no condition to make the right decisions, and consequently we made a lot of wrong ones. The group dynamics, the personal relationships, the lack of organization — the whole thing was a continuing nightmare. We were two days off our own continent, we were sick, and the tour was literally falling apart.

"It's amazing that we survived. I really do not know how we did it. The tension between Tim and Rick was getting worse by the day. Nancy was back home doing some work at the office. Don had lost his passport the first day in London and had to stay there while we did Ireland and Scotland, which meant we were two bodies short and with two others sick. When he rejoined us he obviously felt badly about missing that part of the trip and, in his mind, letting us down. Tim was even further stressed out than he'd been in Miami, trying to juggle the situation on the road with the commitments that were being made for us up ahead.

"Me? I was still struggling with an alienation problem, sensitive about being Rick's girl and his physio, worried about his health, too sick myself and too busy doing the office stuff in the back of the van to be available to do the other things that might have given me more of a sense of fitting into the team. I had to deal with that sense of alienation every day.

"Oh, we were a cheerful little group. I doubt there were a half-dozen good laughs between the landing in London and the crossing to France three and one-half weeks later. It wasn't until we got over there that, out of desperation as much as anything else, we set up group discussions. It was a question of clear the air or risk the explosion.

"They were marginally successful. Everyone had a different approach. Don would arrive with a list of points he wanted to make. You could never spring a meeting on him; he wanted time to prepare so he could get it just right. Lee dealt superficially: 'I'd like to say, I like the way Don's fixing the chair.' Okay, but how did he feel about Don? Tim's approach was always, 'I'm doing the best I can. I know I'm not doing a great job, but I'm doing the best I can.' I was the one who always started crying, because I tend not to hold things back.

"The meetings helped, I think, because at least they made us all aware of the main problem: through circumstance we were spending a lot of time together in close quarters and in an atmosphere conducive to stress. It wasn't likely to change over the next year or so. We had to learn to adjust to that. If we didn't, we were doomed."

There was one other adjustment that had to be made, something in direct conflict with the tour plan as Hansen had originally envisioned it. From the beginning he'd said, "All I want to do is wheel and do the public relations end of it. Attend the events, meet the people and create the awareness. The planning that leads to that should be handled by the crew."

"It could never be that way," Amanda says. "No one person in the office at home knew him well enough to make decisions with any confidence that was the way he'd want them made. On the road, if something was done that he hadn't known about and it didn't turn out quite right, then he'd be angry and we were working at cross-purposes. The best way was to look at a situation, get ready to make a decision, then clear it with Rick. It wasn't fair; it certainly put more stress on him, but in the end, it had to be."

Amanda Reid made one other telling observation about the situation in Europe.

"People didn't understand what the tour was about yet, even those of us who were on it. Rick was off in right field with his reality, which was the pursuit and the preservation of the dream. We were in left field with our reality, the day-to-day grind of working in the outside world to make it as easy as possible for him to do that—and somehow we all had to get together in the centre.

"We were so green, so inexperienced. People would say, 'I don't know how you do it!' I'd smile brightly and say, 'Well, we communicate.' Then

I'd stop and think: 'Do we?' Maybe we survive because we don't always communicate. We do for a while, then we pull back and do our own jobs. We could be in the same motor home, but miles apart. But when we needed to, when we really got down to the bottom, we were there together.

"There were moments when the tour all came together—flashes in the pan, sure, and not often—when an event would come off just right. Rick felt better, Don had the chair working really well, Lee had good meals planned, everything worked. And it was the best feeling. The best."

We'd spent forty-five minutes at the baggage carousel at London's Heathrow airport, looking in vain for a suitcase to match our one remaining tag, before I realized the piece we were looking for was my wheelchair, in which I'd been sitting all the time we searched. Maybe someone was trying to tell me something.

In rapid sucession we found out that our rest day was cancelled because someone had scheduled an event (no media, no dignitaries, and the school kids were late); Don had lost his passport and visas for Europe (which meant he had to stay in London for two weeks straightening out the mess); and our advance person, Wendy Robertson, had some sort of flu or virus that had made it impossible for her to perform all the duties she'd been assigned. (When we shook hands, I could almost feel the germs leaving her and hopping over to me.) That put more load on Tim, who looked as though he'd aged five years. Nancy was back in Vancouver doing some work at the office, Tim, Lee and Wendy were off to Ireland to do additional reccy and advance work, and Amanda and I were sicker than dogs. Boy, England was going to be fun.

It lived up to all its promise.

Maybe if we hadn't been so sick, if there'd been time to catch our breath between leaving Miami and arriving in London, it might have worked out better. But there was never a moment.

We flew from Miami to Toronto. (By skipping the wheel up the east coast then, we hoped to arrive in Europe and Asia at a time when local weather and climatic conditions would be best for wheeling. When we returned to North America, we'd begin the wheel in Miami, come up the coast into Newfoundland, then hang a left and head for Vancouver.) We did a full media day in Toronto, then flew to Ottawa for another full day there, including a reception on Parliament Hill hosted by the Speaker of the House, at which I was given the opportunity to address many of the country's leaders. Then we rushed to catch our plane back to Toronto, where we had a few things to do the next day.

It started with national TV at 6 A.M. and ended at 1 A.M. with an appearance via satellite on a Man in Motion telethon out of CKVU-TV in Vancouver that raised $76,000. (Amanda's mom, Alison, donated $500. I recognized her voice. It was all I could do to keep from shouting, "Thanks, Alison!") In between there was a luncheon at Ontario Place with Jocelyn Lovell, the former champion cyclist who was left a quadriplegic when he was struck by a dump truck while on a training wheel in 1983; and a fast drive out to Brantford, Ontario, to attend the banquet for Wayne Gretzky's annual celebrity tennis tournament, at which he raises funds for the blind. I was at the head table with people like Jamie Farr (Klinger on "M.A.S.H.") and ex-National Hockey League referee Bruce Hood. Amanda was at a floor-level table, and I couldn't make eyes at her because the Stanley Cup blocked my view.

The Lovell luncheon was a bit disturbing, because he obviously felt that life in a wheelchair was the most terrible thing in the world, and he was going to be bitter and angry until he found a way out of it. He worked for an organization called the Spinal Cord Society, whose motto was "Cure, Not Care," its logo a circle containing a stylized drawing of an individual in a wheelchair with a line slashed at an angle across it like you see in those No Smoking signs. I found it depressing that the line seemed to eliminate the person as well as the chair.

I also had a lot of trouble with the "cure, not care" philosophy, which basically says that the hopes, dreams, time and energy of spinal cord injured people should be totally devoted to finding a cure. My question is, what about the quality of life in the meantime?

The day before we left, the boys informed me there was a girl hanging around asking whether I was married. Said she knows two of the New York Mets. Pretty funny—right, Amanda? Amanda . . . ?

I guess not.

All in all, I was in a garbage mood by the time we hit London. It didn't get any better. Amanda and I had a day's rest to get even sicker than we were. We also discovered that all of our medical supplies, Amanda's medical books and one of her logbooks had been left in Miami, and the ultrasound unit had blown again. The van we'd ordered for Europe must have been custom-built for the Seven Dwarfs —16 feet from dashboard to tailpipe. We had to devise a racking system on the back to haul the chairs. We must have looked like a circus train.

But off we went to Ireland. Our chauffeur on the six-hour ride to the ferry was a delightful old guy named Stan from the Stoke-Mandeville organizing committee who was determined to tell us about his city as we drove. So there I was in the back seat, answering Stan with occasional grunts and periodically moaning "I'm gonna be sick" at Amanda, who's trying to keep Stan occupied with small talk of her own, except that she's sick, too, only a day behind me. Oh, well, Stan had a lot of fun.

Ireland was one reception, two 51-mile wheeling days on the "wrong" side of narrow roads jammed with cars driven by crazy people obviously born without fear (for total donations of $20 in the entire country), thirty-six hours in bed and a visit from a doctor who pumped us full of antibiotics. Scotland was more of the same. It was such a shame: we were wheeling through some of the most beautiful country on earth, with its historic old castles and landmarks, and we were too sick to enjoy it. Mind you, even if we'd been healthy we probably wouldn't have had much time to see it properly anyway.

The people were nice, though, and understanding. Just outside of Edinburgh we stayed overnight at a holiday camp for the disabled, an old mansion, almost a castle, like something out of *Jane Eyre*.

"I'm sure you'd like a room off by yourself after the long wheel," said the elderly lady who ran it as she bustled and fussed over me. When I explained that I'd need two beds, one for me and one for my physiotherapist, she just said "Oh!"

Nancy joined us in Scotland for a few days before jumping ahead to do the reccy, and in the time she was there we practically planned the rest of the tour. Tim and Lee had been great while the others were away, taking on the added work, trying their best to look after us at the same time. But it was obvious we were down to two choices: get better organized, and/or bring in more people.

As a concession to illness, we'd dropped our mileage target down to 52 per day. But in our determination to make a good showing and establish credibility as we began the journey across Europe, we made two basic mistakes: we should have stopped until I got healthy, and we didn't. And we made the scheduled events a top priority. Instead of saying, "Okay, that's 52," and packing it in, we would then drive anywhere from 20 to 40 miles to a scheduled event up ahead where we'd originally planned to stop. So we weren't wheeling the full distance—but we weren't getting the rest we needed, either.

And so we crawled across the face of England and over the Pennines, the largest mountains in the country—strong head winds, tough hills, wet, miserable weather. When we got to the top, I went into the motor home. Tim and Lee went into the pub. Didn't it do anything in this country but rain? Now I knew why my grandparents had left that sodden hunk of rock for Canada: they were looking for somewhere to dry out.

We had other problems.

I had scalded the big toe of my left foot when the water came into the tub on instant boil. It was three months, with dressings changed three and four times a day, before we had it under control.

We came into Stoke-Mandeville with another emotional crisis building. It's the home and origin of wheelchair sports and, eventually, all sports for the disabled, a rehab hospital with an athletic complex on the same property, located outside London.

"An evil place," Amanda calls it. To this day she says there are evil spirits there. Stoke was difficult for Amanda because of the circumstances. I had the memories of competition. Stoke had been a magical time for me, a time when some of my biggest dreams were being realized. I could look out on the track and bring it all back. Amanda could see only what was there: the cold, the wetness, the gloom. The problem was, we were both feeling the strain that the tour was putting on our personal relationship. We were together twenty-four hours per day, with little if any time just to be alone—either together or by ourselves—to forget the tour for a few hours and just relax and unwind. We needed those quiet times, and we weren't getting them.

And one morning, after a particularly tough day and a lot of talk that had turned into heavy argument the night before, the dam broke.

Amanda was emotionally upset to the point where I was really worried about her. I did the only thing I could think of. I took her for a walk out to the track, to the finish line of the marathon course where I'd won the year before. I sat her in my lap and told her about the race, trying to help her to visualize it and to understand what it had meant, how special it had been for me, and how she'd made it all possible with her support and her treatment of my shoulder back in 1984. We talked about how difficult it was on the road for each and for both of us. We wrapped ourselves in a time capsule and went back to the days before the tour, and ahead to all the days we'd have together when it was over.

After a while she began to relax and cry, and so did I. The setting was unusual. Picture an open track with a big infield, the evening mist settling in over the grass. And off in a corner, a guy sitting in a wheelchair with a girl in his lap, the wind blowing her hair as they sit there, just crying and holding each other. But it was special, and good, and right.

And how's this for suave? We're invited to a special event in London at which we're to meet the Canadian high commissioner, the commissioner general for Expo 86 and other dignitaries. I'm sitting in the motor home trying to dress for the big day, which is difficult, because my head is between my knees and I'm throwing up. Amanda helps me, and we take off in the motor home. Stan gets lost and the trip in from Stoke takes us two hours—two hours of bouncing over the roads with me vomiting, dry heaving, feeling so miserable I'm afraid I might live. But we get there. Before we step out onto the parking lot, I know I'm going to be sick again. Someone grabs the only available receptacle. It's the food blender. How you you want your eggnog tomorrow, Rick?

But we make it, boy, and there I am, standing at the door with this sickly smile somehow pasted over my face, being greeted by the high commissioner. It's a really big moment. And only one thought is flashing through my mind:

"Please, God, don't let me throw up on his shoes!"

We left Stoke and somehow managed to wind up wheeling on the freeway and were pulled over by the police and told to get off. The day we wheeled into London, there was another mixup. We gave the police the wrong meeting place and ended up—unescorted and nerves jangling—wheeling into the heart of the city in rush hour traffic.

It got so frustrating we just gave up. If we couldn't find the police, we'd let the police find us. We deliberately parked the car in a "definitely no parking" area at Hyde Park corner and waited. Embarrassing, but it worked like a charm. The police escort wheeled up, and quickly converted the whole mess into one of the high points in Great Britain.

It turned out they'd honoured us with the Queen's own motorcycle escort. They actually blocked off traffic both ways on London Bridge —at the height of rush hour—to allow us to go the the centre of the span to take photos, then make a U-turn and come back.

Now we were heading for the coastal town of Folkestone,18 snivelling, snorting, barfing miles into the rain. What was I doing here? I was killing myself. I threw my arms into the air and yelled: "That's it! I'm finished! Take me to a hotel! We are checking in, and we are not moving until I get better!" We were put up for virtually nothing in a hotel overlooking a golf course. Amanda and I ordered a bunch of french fries and Heinz ketchup (a fix that was to become traditional in times of depression) along with tea and hot chocolate, had a good dinner a bit later, and went to sleep.

The next day, July 20, 1985, we said good-bye to the British Isles, piled our wheelchairs, motor home, supplies and assorted viruses aboard a ferry, and headed for France. What's French, I wondered, for upchuck?

There are all kinds of songs about Paris in the spring, Paris is for lovers, Paris is this, Paris is that. Let me tell you something: when you're sick, Paris is the pits.

We'd spent an extra day in Folkestone. Following our landing in Dieppe and a stop at a nearby cemetery to honour Canadian soldiers who'd died there during the Normandy Invasion, we'd cancelled every function between there and Paris and driven all the way. We'd decided to scrap the schedule up ahead and take three days off in the city of lovers. We'd seen a new doctor, tried his new antibiotics. We were going to whip this thing once and for all.

Nothing worked, and that didn't make sense. I'd been on the outside, wheeling. Amanda was in the motor home, working on the books and resting. Yet we were both continually nauseous, light-headed, drowsy and just plain sick.

Something wasn't right. Now I remembered that on the wheel to Paris, taking my rest break inside the motor home with no traffic around, I'd still smelled what seemed like exhaust fumes.

"Check the motor home," I told the boys. "Something's screwy here."

They found it. The exhaust pipe ran directly under the back of the van beneath our bed. There were three holes worn in it. I'd been getting the carbon monoxide in small doses on the road from the traffic, then coming in and taking concentrated doses of it as I lay down for my rest breaks. Amanda had been working back there as we drove, or resting on the bed for an hour at a time. In our efforts to get rid of the flu, we'd been unknowingly and systematically poisoning ourselves.

Considerably cheered by the word that carbon monoxide had been removed from our diet, Amanda and I tried to enjoy Paris in the brief time we had. But the fates seemed to be lined up against us.

Amanda's birthday was coming up soon in Belgium—but we were in Paris. Why, she asked, couldn't we go out on the town and celebrate now? Well, somehow the night on the town was spent in the hotel room eating from room service again. She wasn't too thrilled about that, or about the message slipped under the door from a female friend of mine who happened to be in Paris and said she'd love to get together. We discussed—at some length—the probability of notes from ex-girlfriends in Norway, Australia, New Zealand, etc.

Finally, we went for a stroll. We tried to find the Champs Elysées, got lost and somehow wound up on Boulevard St. Michel in the Greek end of Paris. We had a beer, got driven back by a crazy cabbie who swore at anything that drove, walked, cycled or honked, and ordered chocolate crepes from a stand by the hotel. As a trip it wasn't much, but we'd tried. We'd attempted something normal. As Amanda said, it was a question of sanity.

By this time the organizational groups up ahead were getting antsy, afraid we wouldn't make Belgium on time. We looked at it, and grudgingly made a decision: if we drove 275 miles to the Belgian border we'd be back on schedule—but it would mean that the wheeling miles skipped would then total 500 plus. It had to stop. Keep it up, and we'd become the Rick Hansen Speaking Tour. This would be the last time we'd drive over scheduled wheeling territory to keep appointments for events. I was here to wheel 24,901.55 miles, not drive them.

We drove, then resumed wheeling in the village of Seclin, France, across the border through Binche, and on to Tournai, one of the oldest cities in Belgium. It was my first real taste of cobblestone streets—beautiful, though unbelievably hard to wheel over.

But the reception in Belgium made it worthwhile. All through the south, despite the rain and the high winds and miserable weather, we had cheering crowds, marching bands, and disabled wheelers joining us on the road. There was a federal reception. Obviously these people had been told in plenty of time who we were, when we were coming and what we stood for. And they just jumped in and became a part of it.

The first day's wheeling ended in the village of Binche. It was Amanda's birthday, so I had Tim rush out and buy roses, a card and champagne. I couldn't have much because I was wheeling the next day, so Amanda drank most of the bottle. It took about ten minutes to work, at which point she talked. And talked. And talked. And talked. Then she barfed. And barfed. And barfed. Good thing she has only one birthday per year.

We wheeled into Brussels and stayed at the Brudeman Spinal Cord Rehabilitation Centre, Amanda and I occupying a model apartment where the injured train to go back into a normal lifestyle. It had a single bed. All the beds in Europe seem to be single beds. No wonder the world is in trouble.

The next day, between Brussels and Bruges, I laid a wreath in a special reception at the military cemetery at Agadem, where 25,000 soldiers are buried—the majority, I was told, Canadians. I looked at the headstones, and at the ages: nineteen, eighteen, twenty-two, twenty-four, eighteen . . . Kids. Just kids. I spoke to the people about how the Canadians had come here to fight for a dream of freedom, and how in a sense we were doing the same thing in a different way, fighting to free disabled people.

A World War II veteran gave me a bottle of wine and a loaf of bread. "We used to break bread and drink wine, the Canadians and us," he said. "I look in your eyes now and see the same fire and enthusiasm."

As he spoke, I remembered a man we'd met as we entered Belgium. He was ninety-six years old, a veteran of two wars. He talked to me about the bond between Canadians and Belgians, and how sad he was that he'd lost track of a wartime friend, now living in Victoria, B.C., with whom he'd exchanged letters for better than forty years.

I could feel my eyes filling up. Chances are, his friend in Victoria was dead. But he had his memories and his lifelong friendship with Canadians, and as we shared the moment, the years between simply slipped away.

We crossed each border suspended between trepidation and hope, never knowing whether we'd be mobbed or ignored. Through 150 wheeling miles in Belgium and 250 more in the Netherlands, the organizers were so enthusiastic and had scheduled so many events that they'd left little time for wheeling. We had to cancel a few appearances or extend our time in those countries—and we didn't have the extra time. In West Germany, we ran into faces as stony as the architecture. A lot of it was our fault. We arrived at the border with no interpreter, no phrase book, no idea where we were supposed to stay, who we were supposed to meet or what we were expected to do. We'd done a poor job of letting them know in advance how the tour worked and the time frame we worked under. In their place, I'd probably have been a bit stone-faced myself.

Oh, did I mention that it was still raining? If I ever come back to Europe, I'm coming as a duck.

Two quick memories of that part of the tour:

In Belgium, surrounded by wheelers, one little guy wheeling along in an ordinary chair, unable to stay with the pack for more than a short stretch. Every time he started to fall back, I'd reach out and give him a shove and shoot him ahead. He'd look back, give me a big grin, sticking his tongue out at the big guys as he went by. Obviously, he'd trailed in every wheel. Now he was getting his chance out front, and enjoying every minute of it . . .

Hamburg, the morning after a shopping and relaxation day with Amanda, flopping into the pool and having a little old lady bustle out screaming, "No diving!" She saw my legs, caught herself, and apologized. But when Amanda asked her if we could use the sauna, she snapped "Fifteen marks extra!" then looked at my legs and said, "And please put your towel on!"

Meanwhile, we fought our own wars in private. Wendy Robertson had ended her temporary stint as advance person in Europe and was

Hansen gets a taste of London traffic—on one of the few days it didn't rain.

The kid from Williams Lake, B.C., in Moscow's Red Square with St. Basil's Cathedral in the background—and 7,000 miles behind him.

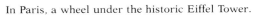

In Paris, a wheel under the historic Eiffel Tower.

In Portugal, as in many countries, Hansen's wheelchair draws curious looks from passers-by.

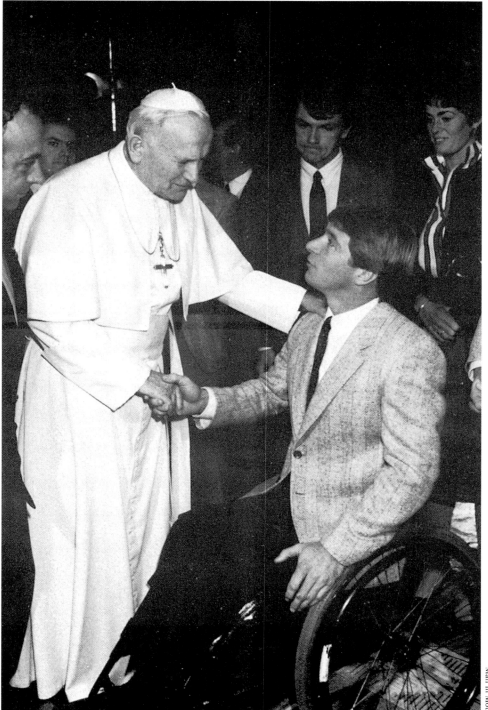

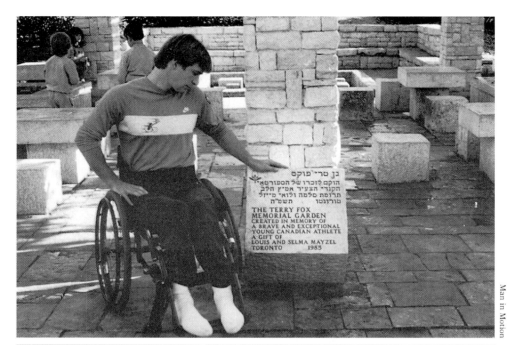

Top: Memories of a friend. A quiet moment at the Terry Fox memorial in Israel.

Bottom: The sign belies the picturesque look as Hansen crosses the Allenby Bridge separating Jordan and Israel.

Facing page: "May you accomplish all your hopes and dreams and arrive home safely." In Rome, Hansen is received by Pope John Paul II.

Top: No brass bands, no speeches. Just a paper banner and a line drawn with whipping cream as Hansen breaks the 12,000-mile barrier in Australia.

Bottom: "Never be afraid to dream . . ." Hansen passes on the Man in Motion message to enthralled school kids in Australia.

Marking the end of Man in Motion's visit to Japan, Rick greets a fan in the city of Toyota.

Top: Every muscle straining, Hansen presses onward living a long-time dream—wheeling his chair along the Great Wall of China.

Bottom: Where stairs make wheeling impossible, Hansen gets help from white-shirted team members as the Great Wall assault continues.

heading home. We were going to be short-handed again. The old tensions were building on the crew. So, in Arnhem, Holland, I called a staff meeting.

After four months, we were still making the same mistakes. Nobody expects perfection, but you do expect improvement, not only in daily chores but in terms of following the rules and regulations of conduct I'd established:

—Communicate honestly with me and with each other. Under our living conditions, we couldn't have it any other way.
—Get your sleep. Look after your body first, because if you're not at your best, I can't be at mine.
—Take particular care in your conduct with the volunteers and associations involved with the tour wherever we are.
—Alcohol in moderation only.
—Do your job in as efficient and professional a manner as possible and try to improve.

From my perception, they were hedging on the rules.

Tim didn't like going ahead and doing the needed advance work. He wanted to be with the boys. But he was too protective of them and wouldn't delegate responsibility to them. He tried to do too many things himself. Lee was walking a fine line between being friendly and being too friendly with some of our female supporters. His other challenge was to learn more about nutrition and to become better at scheduling my meals and their content. Don was withdrawing, becoming even more introverted than usual. A rift had developed between him and Lee. Most of all, he wasn't managing his time efficiently or getting enough rest. None of them were. They were burning the candle at both ends.

Their environment was controllable. They could schedule their work and rest according to the events of the day. My routine was constant. No matter what, Rick had to wheel. I was wrecking myself on the road, dealing with all the off-road issues—my contract, the office, the hand-shaking and speaking responsibilities wherever we went. Why should I have to watch them and stay on them all the time to make sure they did their jobs the way they were supposed to be done? But the more I tried to assert myself, the more they banded together. It was developing into a Them vs Me, and something had to give.

It was a heavy session. I loved those guys like brothers. Otherwise, the simplest and most effective thing for me to do when things got uncomfortable would have been to send them all home, move in a new crew and run the whole thing like a business, changing personnel until I got what I wanted. Our feelings for each other were very strong. Before it was over we were all crying, and the individual sessions I had with them afterward didn't get any easier. I felt guilty that the world had to revolve around Rick Hansen, but to do what we had to do, that was the way it had to be.

I told them the tour would grow and we all had to grow with it. It wasn't going to get any easier ahead. More likely it would get tougher and tougher until it was over. Friendship, I said, had nothing to do with it. We were friends when we started, and we would struggle to be friends when it ended. But in between, I'd do whatever I had to do. If that included sending them home, so be it.

Smiles! We were getting smiles. We'd crossed the bridge into Denmark, the weather was good enough for me to wear a tank top for the first time in Europe, we could pick plums and apples from trees along the roadside as we wheeled, and people were waving and smiling.

We did 70 miles in Denmark, finishing up at the Canadian ambassador's residence in Copenhagen. One lady asked me if my family was from Denmark. My conscience got the better of me and I said Norway. But there are Hansens everywhere. From then on, unless really pinned down, I was Scandinavian. Except when we were in Norway.

The countries flew by.

Sweden: lovely and peaceful, except for the odd truck driver making throat-slitting motions as he passed when we delayed traffic. We hit the quarter-pole for Man in Motion—6,228.25 miles. Must have seen about five thousand Beware of Moose signs, but nary a moose. Did see one badger. Maybe they should change signs to Beware of Badger.

Oh, yes: Amanda and I were falling deeper and deeper in love. The thought of marriage was starting to pop up, although I didn't want to think about it a lot until after the tour ended. I already considered myself as good as married, anyway.

Norway: reindeer meat with cream sauce. Great stuff. Reminded me that Brad and the boys at home were probably on the second day of the annual hunt. First time in a dozen years I wasn't with them. I sure missed it—not just the hunting, but the peace and quiet and the solitude.

Finland: hit the 7,000-mile mark and celebrated my twenty-eighth birthday. Popped champagne with the crew and reinforced some decisions. No more driving, no more letting the schedule compromise us.

We were still laughing over our aborted fishing stop. We'd come to this bridge, looked down and saw these beautiful, plump fish. Lots of them. We had the gear out in a flash, threw some cheese on the hooks and got at it. Lee and I caught one right away and gutted it, looking for roe to use as bait. Amanda had another on the hook when this Finnish guy who was walking by started yelling at us.

"No feeshing! No feeshing!"

Amanda got nervous. Lee went down the bank, unhooked her fish and let it go. Just as well. It turned out these were special fish grown in a restricted lake, an enormously expensive delicacy. And we were going at it as though they were salmon in the Fraser River.

In the United States, it had been animals and insects; in Europe, we were constantly in a fuss over fish. A few weeks later in Czechoslovakia, when we told our guide, Frankie, that we'd love to fish, he nodded his head and disappeared. Two miles later there he was, surrounded by a crowd of people from a nearby fish farm, who presented us with a large carp that was still alive and squirming. "Fish," Frankie said proudly. "Fish!"

I wondered what they were thinking at home, holding a birthday party for me there, too, with the corporate sponsors all watching me on the video we'd made a few weeks earlier. "Look happy," they'd said. I wasn't happy. I was tired, injured, miserable and frustrated. Smile, Rick. It took about twenty tries to get the thing done, and even then it wasn't great.

Well, to heck with it. After much red tape cutting, Amanda and I were going on a side trip. While the rest of the crew went in various directions, for holidays, reccy or what have you, we were taking the Man in Motion show on the road by ourselves. To Moscow.

Nobody will ever be able to say we didn't make a spectacular entrance into the Soviet Union.

There were stairs from the deplaning level to customs in the Moscow airport. I figured I could just hold onto the railing and bounce my way down in the chair. The rail was too wide at the top, so I grabbed the circular rail along the bottom. It wasn't a rail. It was a single fluorescent light tube, running underneath the hand rail the length of the stairs. It came out in my hands, smashed as I dropped it to maintain my balance, and I bounced all the way down to land in front of an armed soldier at customs.

They let us through. Maybe they thought if they kept me there I'd break something else. We were driven into the city, past the monument marking the spot where Hitler had been turned back, his dream of entering Moscow crushed forever like those of the Germans in World War I and Napoleon before them, and settled in for a brief stay that was interesting but in many ways discouraging.

This was a country that was rumoured to lead the world in spinal cord research, yet when our hosts took us on tours of hospital and rehab facilities, we saw mostly amputees. In the labs, the demonstrations involved their work with artificial limbs in which so many marvellous strides have been made. We even met Lou Yashin, the legendary former Moscow Dynamo goalie, who was being fitted with a new leg after losing his because of a vascular problem.

It was interesting, but when I asked about wheelchair sport I was told the Soviets weren't involved with it and wouldn't be for quite some time. It was a question of priorities. So where were the wheelchair-bound people of Moscow? What were they doing? We never saw them.

The next day we went to Red Square and posed with St. Basil's Cathedral as a backdrop. It was wet and cold, but there I was, having my picture taken in T-shirts representing sixteen different corporate sponsors. Take a picture, change my shirt, take another picture, change my shirt. It drew some puzzled looks, I'll tell you. The Russians must have thought we were crazy.

Amanda and I did the tourist bit from the square, me wheeling and drawing stares, almost as though they'd never seen a person in a wheelchair before. I could have been from outer space. When we saw some people eating ice cream cones, we backtracked them by the amount of ice cream in the cones they were holding. The bigger the scoop, the closer we were to the vendor. We found him, too—just as he sold the last one. So we hung around until another showed up, Amanda watched some other people paying so she'd know how many Russian coins to give him, and we slurped our way back to the hotel.

And that was pretty much Moscow: no organized wheeling, no sign of anyone in wheelchairs, no signs of any concentration on rehabilitation for spinal cord injured persons.

Once again, we'd done a poor job of advance communication. Given more information and time, the Russians might have let us wheel in Moscow or visit some of their spinal cord disabled. Still, I wasn't sorry to leave.

We flew from Moscow to Helsinki and into Gdansk, Poland. As it turned out, we had the easy route. The boys had taken the ferry from Helsinki, figuring to do some repair work on the motor home en route. The trip was so choppy they spent all their time being seasick.

But there we all were, ready to put the Man back into Motion. The question was, in what form? At our current rate, we weren't going to be home in time to finish at Expo 86. So: did we make that a priority, which would mean skipping Greece, Yugoslavia and the Middle East, or press on with a more realistic finish date, like sometime in November?

Racing on our original route to try to keep a date with Expo was out of the question. And that really browned me off.

In my heart I knew that had I not had the dislocated shoulder and received the injury to my bicep tendon on my right shoulder, I would have been able to do it, do it with style, 70 miles per day and finishing fit and strong. I knew the arms weren't hurting just because of the 70 miles per day. The left shoulder was hurting because of the right shoulder. The right shoulder was hurting because the injury had been there from the beginning.

If I'd been able to start in 1980 or 1981 when I originally got the idea, I'd have been stronger, psychologically relaxed because I wouldn't have had to concentrate on every stroke lest I aggravated something (we figured I'd done about four million strokes to that point).

The next part, from Poland to Greece, was going to be tough. I could feel it; we all could. We talked about it a lot. "Get to Greece," we told each other. "If we can make it to Greece, the end of the European section, then nothing can stop us."

Okay, Hansen, snap out of it. That's a loser's attitude. You're here. You've got 7,000 miles in the bank. You know you're going to finish this thing, no matter how long it takes. So get at it, kid. Think Greece.

One day in Poland and I was asking myself who started the Polish jokes, and why? The country was oppressive, the black market raged on unchecked (thank goodness, or Lee never would have found us the propane we needed the night the tanks went dry), but the people couldn't have been friendlier. The entire reception in one community had been arranged by a man of about fifty, a double amputee who got around on what amounted to a skateboard, and he'd done us and himself proud. There were crowds everywhere. People threw roses in my path. The disabled who wheeled with us were obviously proud to be a part of the tour, because of the way they were now being perceived by the people in the area.

Yet, I have mixed memories of Poland. It was also the place where the motor home caught fire. I was sitting in the bathroom and smelled smoke. The boys threw open the closet door, and the stuff just billowed out. They dragged me out of there so quickly I was outside before I had a chance to pull my pants up.

And Poland was the place where Tim and I finally decided it was time for him to leave.

He'd just returned from a week-long break that obviously hadn't done him much good. The stresses of the tour, the pressures of the decisions he had to make on a daily basis after long hours with little rest were still with him, with no end in sight. It wasn't working for him, and it wasn't working for us.

I suggested three options: (a) rest in Europe and then rejoin us, or stay on now, but not in any position of authority or stress; (b) go home and work at the Man in Motion offices as a liaison with the road crew—as the only person who'd actually been on the tour and knew what it was like on the road, he'd be invaluable; or (c) go home, period. Tim's added option—joining Nancy in New Zealand and Australia to help with the reccy—I rejected. They'd developed a relationship on the road. If he wanted to go there on his own, I certainly had no right to stop him. But if he went down, I wanted it to have nothing to do with the tour.

We spent a lot of time on it. He was my friend. He'd been part of this thing from the beginning. I'd promised him we'd start together and finish together, and I still meant it. Maybe something could be worked out about rejoining us near the end. But we couldn't go on like this.

He thought it over while he continued with the books and advance work through Czechoslovakia and Austria. When we reached Switzerland, Nancy took off for New Zealand and Tim took off for a holiday and home. All things considered, he'd decided it was best if he left the tour.

I'd lost my coach and the biggest contributor in nursing the dream through its early stages. I just hoped I hadn't lost my friend.

Somehow, we bounced our way through Europe, pinballing from crisis to crisis. "Greece," we said over and over again. "If we can make it to Greece." But there were days when I wouldn't have taken bets.

Austria had been fog banks and steeper hills. The Alps were the Siskiyous all over again, only worse. At one point we climbed 2,700 feet on 11 and 14 per cent grades. It took us 12 hours to do 50 miles to St. Antoine summit. Somewhere in there, Lee climbed into a spare chair and tried to wheel with me. I knew he wouldn't last— but no matter how hard I pushed, I could still hear his voice behind me. Finally, I turned around. He was walking behind his chair, pushing it like a baby carriage.

With Tim and Nancy gone, Don and Lee took on more responsibilities. Still, Amanda was slowly pulling herself to pieces. We were two people short, and she tried to do their logistical jobs, too.

I kept telling her she'd get swamped, and to establish some priorities, but she was determined to do it all. I was prepared to cancel everything until Greece and just wheel. It was a vicious circle for her: too much to do, not enough time to do it, and therefore more to do tomorrow. She was spinning faster and faster, but she wouldn't listen.

I had no choice. I did what any concerned man would do in those circumstances for the woman he loved. I slipped her a mickey.

We were leaving Switzerland for another dart into France. During the first morning break I sent her outside on some errand or another. Then, with Don watching in amazement, I swiped two sleeping pills from her medical kit, checked the fridge for juice, found enough for two glasses of orange and one of grape, and crushed the pills in the bottom of one of the two glasses of orange.

"A toast to new beginnings," I said as Amanda jumped back into the motor home, handing her the loaded juice and Don the glass of grape.

"I don't want orange. I'd like the grape," Amanda said.

"Okay," said Don.

I could have killed him.

"I'm proposing a toast!" I snapped. "Drink your orange juice!"

She gave me a look that suggested I'd gone nuts, and drank it in about three gulps.

I went out and began wheeling. Twenty minutes later I looked back at Don in the driver's seat. He gave me the thumbs-down sign. Amanda was out like a light. I wheeled for three or four hours straight so the next break wouldn't awaken her. Finally, she woke up, smiled sleepily and said, "Gee, I must have been more tired than I thought."

Mistakes and mini-disasters continued to haunt us.

In France, we had another motor home fire, this time while we were in a gas station filling up. At least this time I had my pants on when the boys dragged me out. I kept screaming at them to get the van out of there. One spark and the whole gas station might have gone up, and us with it. But no, once they found a fire extinguisher that worked, they rushed in and out, taking turns to avoid asphyxiation from the fumes of the burning synthetics in our clothes, and put out the fire without too much damage.

The next day one of the chairs fell off the roof of the motor home. We drove several blocks without noticing until a guy pulled up beside us and began pointing up at the roof and then backwards. That same day, Amanda almost took an Esso sign with us as she somehow caught it on the corner of the motor home.

Don backed the van into a tree and crushed the seat of one of the wheelchairs. He and Lee pulled into a service station to gas up the vehicles, and accidentally filled them with diesel fuel.

We couldn't go on like that. Finally, after innumerable panic calls to the office, and threats to shut down everything else and just wheel, we finally got our relief help—Trish Smith (Marshall's daughter) and later the two Davids, Holtzman and Archibald. They helped a lot, but went away shaking their heads, wondering how we'd existed this way for that long. We just kept smiling glassily and saying, "Greece. Once we get to Greece . . ."

In Spain we found we'd been booked overnight in a juvenile detention centre. The supervisor who welcomed us looked drunk and slapped our translator. It took us until 3 A.M. to find a motel.

In Portugal we passed the 9,000-mile mark. South of Lisbon we came upon a gypsy encampment at 5 A.M. and stepped into a world of campfires and wagons and big-eyed kids running out to stare in wonder as we passed. In a tiny Portuguese fishing village, a dozen old ladies, dark-robed, their faces covered by shawls, tried to press money into my hands. We weren't fund raising in that area. Obviously, these people were poor. But some of them were weeping and insisted that we take the money for the cause. I had a flashback to all the days in the U.S. and Europe, when the big expensive cars roared past us, and we couldn't raise a nickel. Suddenly there was a big lump in my throat. Must have been that darned flu.

We crossed the border into Italy looking like survivors from a lost battalion. Up ahead we had a date with the Pope. Good. Maybe we'd make it in time for last rites.

Now we were battling horrendous rain, wind and cold. Once we arrived in a community for a scheduled event so late most of the guests had left and the rest wanted us to stay and party. Sorry, we said. We have to wheel tomorrow.

"You people are crazy!" someone said.

"You're right, sir," I thought. "We probably are."

The schedule called for us to wheel, then come back and stay there overnight. The weather was still miserable. Amanda and I had a bit of a spat, and she was out running off the anger. We got lost and climbed an unnecessary hill, which made me so mad I just hung a right and bounced down the side, heading back to the hotel. Amanda got lost, but found her way back. We got into our room, and it was so cold that we turned on every hot water faucet in the place and huddled around the steam.

I couldn't feel it, of course, but the night before we reached Rome my legs were so ice cold they had to be massaged or I could have been in serious trouble. I'd had stomach problems since Spain, but it was Friday night and I was thinking of all the things we could have been doing at home. I grabbed a beer. The last 13 miles were the longest in history. Reminded myself never to be that dumb again.

There was a mix-up over bookings at the Sheraton Roma. We thought they'd been paid for, half by the hotel and half by the Italian disabled sports group. They weren't. By that time we were too tired to move. Tour policy was that any extras, anything beyond basic accommodation, were paid by the individual crew members. Amanda and I splurged and paid $100 for one night, flopped on the bed and ordered from room service: two cheesebugers with fries and two Cokes. The food arrived, and the bill was $75. At that, the guy had the nerve to ask for a tip.

The next day we were out of there before breakfast, leaving Lee and Dave Archibald in Rome to do inventory and clean the motor home while we flew to Yugoslavia for a three-day wheel from Split to Dubrovnik. We got a tremendous reception everywhere we went in Yugoslavia, overall the best we'd received in any country to date, with music and dancing in the streets. At one point, climbing a steep hill, I was followed until dark by about one hundred young children. I felt like the Pied Piper.

From there we rushed back to Rome. Amanda's parents met us there, partially for a visit and partially to see how their daughter was faring. "Fine," she said, but she didn't fool her father. The nervous smile was too bright and too quick, the cheeks too drawn, the eyes too wide. For the first time, he really understood how tough it was out there, and what we'd been going through on a daily basis.

"I've seen this in the war," he told me. "What you have here is battle fatigue, and if you don't do something about it, you're going to be in serious trouble."

We tried. We had our audience with Pope John Paul, a warm and gracious man who spoke about the tour and about sport for the disabled, then gently shook my hand and said, "Bless you, my son. May you and your team accomplish all your hopes and dreams and arrive home safely."

I left Amanda in Rome for three days to shop and relax with her mother while we wheeled south almost to Naples, then drove to the coast. By now we were wheeling about one-third of every day in darkness, putting in 70 miles per day over cobblestone roads, trying to ignore some of the world's rudest drivers and getting virtually no support anywhere.

But we didn't care. We were getting on a ferry—and when we landed, we'd be in Greece.

Remember Greece? The target? The goal? Good old once-we-get-there-we'll-be-fine Greece? We got there, all right, and I had the scare of my life.

I was already nervous. There'd been a hijacking incident involving an Egyptian airliner just before we arrived, and a separate terrorist incident in which a man in a wheelchair was killed. What if the tour really caught on there and I became a public figure? Would I be a logical target?

We'd checked into a hotel in the first village after landing, figuring on a quiet rest day before we headed for Athens. I was towelling myself off after a shower when I felt a strange flush creeping over my body. My sensory level was changing. I was numb higher up my back, and suddenly my heart was pumping like crazy. Jeez! I was going to pass out!

I'd been having some severe stomach cramps, some suspected intestinal bleeding, nothing but grief. So I lay down, hoping this thing would go away. When it didn't, when I began to worry about slipping into unconsciousness, I called the boys.

They didn't waste time. One look and they simply grabbed all four corners of the blanket under me and hauled me down the stairs to the hospital. On the way down we passed a lady carrying flowers. She was from the Greek ministry of health, coming to welcome me to her country.

You can imagine the look on her face, and on the faces of the three guys in wheelchairs waiting outside the hotel. According to our hosts, Greece had the most pressing need in Europe for a program to make the people aware of their problems and potential. The disabled there were treated like third-class citizens. And here was this Rick Hansen guy who was going to be their hero and their leader in the awareness battle, being helped down the stairs in a blanket.

To this day I don't know what the problem was. The doctors examined me and said I was okay. For an old guy standing there screaming at me, this was the last straw. I'd come barging in, I'd taken his place in the lineup—and I wasn't even sick? Worse yet, I was disabled—which, in that country was worse than being a woman. "How would he feel," I wondered, "if I was a disabled woman who happened to be black?" I probably ruined his whole day.

The next day we were back on the road, wheeling into Athens through rush hour traffic. We'd done it! London to Athens! There wasn't much time to celebrate. I did a video for the office—which caused no end of trouble, because I did it standing on my braces on the balcony. I'd done it for a purpose, to tell everyone back there that you can't stereotype the disabled. But the CBC ran it, and the switchboard got flooded by people yelling, "Hey! What is this? He's in a wheelchair, and he's standing up!"

But we popped a bottle of champagne, and we couldn't keep the grins off our faces. We'd beaten Europe. We'd made it to Greece. Everything would be all right now. We'd be fine.

Sure, we would.

9

"You're going home? Fine!"

*R*ick Hansen's dissatisfaction with the performance of his crew was by no means a one-way street. There were times when, individually and collectively, they were tempted to tell him to shove his tour up his nose.

Never was the temptation greater than in the days spent in New Zealand and Australia. "In one month he changed from my cousin to a hard-ass I didn't know and didn't particularly like," says Lee Gibson. "He was Jekyll and Hyde, and we never knew which side we were going to get. He was so grouchy that sometimes he wouldn't talk to me for days. Once he pulled the curtain across the back of the motor home, and I'd have to reach around it to pass him his food.

"When things weren't just right, just the way he wanted them, he'd be on Don and me. Mike was just in. He was the new guy, and he was Amanda's brother. That left Don and me, so we were on his hit list. There were times when I wanted to grab him and shake him. Don and I were scapegoats, and I resented it. I resented it very much."

So did Don Alder, but from a softer perspective. The problem, Don suggested, was that for all that the project was Rick's, for all that he attempted to keep his finger on the pulse of every phase of the operation, when it came to what the crew was doing, he just didn't know what was going on.

"He was totally involved in the wheeling," Don explains. "He'd wheel, come in exhausted, and go to his room to take care of the phone calls and all the other things he had to do. Somewhere in there he'd try to get some rest, which was never enough. But with his time filled that way, he was never aware of the difficulties presented by some of his demands for the following day. He'd just make them, and when he woke up at 5 A.M. and they hadn't been met, he'd be furious.

"For instance: say we got in at 8 or 9 P.M., which wasn't unusual. He and Amanda would disappear because they had all their work to do. But *they'd just* assume *we'd have the vehicles gassed up and ready, and the ice for his arms, and the chairs repositioned for the type of terrain we'd be facing the next day or the type of injury he had at the moment. That was our* job, *so do it. If everything went right, we could. But when you're in a strange town in a strange country, where do you get ice at 10 or 11* P.M.? *How do you get propane to fill the tanks? Which stations are open?*

"*All those things took time, and if there was a delay in one, it meant we had less time to do the others. It became a nightly gamble: tell him at night that everything might not get done and watch him explode, or gamble that somehow you would get it all done and risk having to tell him in the morning when he'd* really blow up."

Getting it all done inevitably meant that Alder would be drilling holes in the wheelchair bucket anywhere from midnight to 3 A.M. When other hotel guests complained about the noise, he'd plug in the extension cord and move out into the hall until the manager came and demanded he stop.

"*At that time of the morning it was easy to get careless," he admits. "I'd put a board under the bucket to drill into, and go right through it into the floor. We left drill holes in hotel room floors all over Europe. Plus grease and tar over everything.*

"*You know the real miracle? It was that we didn't nail Rick when we were driving. There'd be two of us in the front, one driving, one talking to keep the other from nodding off. But what we talked about mostly was silly things like, 'Hey, I haven't dozed off for the last five minutes. How about you?' There's a point in sleep deprivation when you just keep on going, like a zombie. We hit that point and passed it. We just survived, that's all. We survived, and kept going.*"

For Mike Reid, who joined the tour in New Zealand, the relationship between Hansen and the crew was bizarre from the beginning. At twenty-three, fit and rested and eager for what he viewed as the great adventure, he was plunged into a situation in which everyone was operating on nerve, with an unrealistic perfectionist issuing orders that in some cases couldn't be carried out. As he began to fit in and take his share of the criticism, he developed a theory about the man in the chair.

"*He's tough, you know, sometimes to the point of being mean. And he's such a competitor that he's happiest when he's battling. The times when he got most prickly were the times when things were going well. It was like he'd see us doing well and want to challenge us to do better, or push us to make sure we wouldn't get slack. In a way, he was right. When we had everything going, when we knew what and where and when and how, that's when we'd get into trouble. We'd get careless. Little things would be forgotten, the same mistakes made twice. And it would drive him crazy.*

"You know when it was worst? During what I called the post-fishing syndrome. Every time he came back from a day off he'd spent fishing, he was just brutal. Nothing anyone could do was right. It was as though he'd been given a glimpse and a memory of what it was like in the normal world, and then he had to come back to our reality, which was wheeling and hurting and exhaustion.

"Quit? Sure I thought of quitting, lots of times. It was a rotten environment, and I knew that any time I felt like it I could just walk away. But every time, I'd ask myself: 'Is all this BS worth the end result?' And I could never quite bring myself to say 'No'. . ."

We flew out of Athens airport, bound for the island of Bahrain in the Persian Gulf and a whirlwind tour of the Middle East. As we left, I got a great lesson in airport psychology.

Two weeks earlier there'd been a major hijacking in the Athens airport. The security was drum tight. Everyone getting on board received a thorough search—except, of course, for the guy in the wheelchair. They gave me a cursory search, but never once checked my chair. I could have been carrying twenty pounds of explosives in the cushion. What if I was a terrorist, or an imposter? But no one thought of that.

In Bahrain we were catered to, pampered, quartered in a lovely hotel and given plenty of time between events on our one-day stay. We were, however, boycotted by the Arab press, because the feeling was that we were also going to Israel. We were, but we'd been briefed by our embassy not to admit it, no matter what.

"You mean, right up to *lying* about it?" I asked.

"Well, if it comes to that, no. But avoid the issue if you can."

So we dodged. The Bahrainian press kept asking us where we were going from there. We'd say, "From here to Jordan, and after we leave the Middle East we're going to New Zealand and Australia." I don't think we fooled anyone, but at least we didn't lie about it.

We wheeled 30 miles in Bahrain, a short stay but a warm one, then flew to Jordan, where we were greeted by a cousin of King Hussein, Prince Ra'ad Ben Zaid and his wife, Princess Majedeh. We then wheeled 24 miles from the airport to Amman, where there was a reception that night at the residence of the Canadian ambassador which had been made wheelchair-accessible. The security was tight because of the proximity of his residence to the headquarters of PLO leader Yassir Arafat. The next day, we headed for the Allenby Bridge to cross into Israel.

After all the buildup, the crossing was a bit of a letdown. I'd envisioned the bridge as a huge concrete structure bristling with guns and maybe a burned-out tank or two to one side. Instead, we came to this piddly little river spanned by a tiny wooden bridge. But there was nothing piddling about the security and the military emplacements on either side, and the contrast was incredible. On the Jordanian side, we were wheeling through dry, arid territory. On the Israeli side, everything was lush and green and irrigated.

You couldn't help but absorb a sense of history, biblical and otherwise. So many historical sites, so many cities that up till now we could only imagine: Bethlehem, Jerusalem . . . Okay, the tour was tough, but when it was over, the memories were going to be worth it. For us, one of the more moving was a visit to the new Israeli monument to the memory of Terry Fox, which his parents had dedicated only weeks before. It was special for me, because Terry had been with me in spirit all the way.

Things went relatively smoothly for us in the Middle East. There was good TV coverage, lots of interviews and plenty of wheeling company as we pushed from Jerusalem to Tel Aviv. When we said goodbye early the next morning and boarded the flight to New Zealand, it was with a sense of regret, and a feeling that this was a country we'd like to visit when we could just be tourists, taking our time and absorbing the culture.

Did I say we flew to New Zealand? Well, we did—but not directly. To save money on plane fares we were sent the long way around: Tel Aviv to Copenhagen, a day's rest, then Copenhagen to Los Angeles for a five-hour layover, then L.A. to Auckland. Layovers that weren't restful, time changes to knock the system for a loop—all because it was cheaper. Seemed like false economy. But then, why not go backwards? We were flying to the bottom of the world.

The temperature was in the nineties. Outside the hotel we could hear kids splashing in the pool, and a few miles down the road lay some of the world's finest sandy beach. All the ingredients were there for a great summer's day.

It was Christmas 1985.

We were finishing off a week's rest break in New Zealand before beginning a three-month wheeling session that would cover 850 miles there and 2,150 in Australia. Amanda had bought a plant to serve as our Christmas tree. She'd made little decorations and hung stockings for everyone. The two of us had made a shopping trip in downtown Auckland, where I told her to get lost for a few minutes, rushed into a store, and bought her a pair of diamond earrings.

It was a difficult Christmas, not only because it was summer and didn't feel right, but because we were in a strange land, far from home. The first Christmas on the road for the Man in Motion tour, and by now we knew or suspected there'd be one more before we were through. Deep down, everyone was asking whether it could be done, and how many of us would be left if and when it was.

Originally the plan was to finish the tour at the conclusion of Expo. But we weren't having a lot of success at the pace we were maintaining, because we were too tired and didn't have enough time to organize. So, should we turn it into a race and try to finish for Expo or at least before winter set in? Or should we remind ourselves of the purpose of the tour, which was to have an impact on people's awareness and to raise funds?

The only way to do that was to slow the project down to allow us the extra two to three hours per day to handle the public relations and get the minimum amount of quality sleep. Given those circumstances, the Canadian winter was upgraded from impossible to possible, and an extra six months on the road was now considered to be worth the result. Starting in Adelaide, we'd drop the wheeling day to 50 miles.

I knew it was the right decision. That didn't stop it from depressing me.

The New Zealand portion of the wheel began at Brown's Bay near Auckland on the North Island. We launched it the night before by getting robbed.

We were staying at the Poenama Motor Inn, a quadrangle built around the swimming pool and reception area. Because there was a Maori wedding in process and the place was packed, some of us decided to go elsewhere for dinner. While we were gone, someone reached through the window we'd left open a bit for ventilation, unlocked the door from the inside, and took about $3,000 worth of custom clothing and equipment, most of which was useful only to me.

Amanda's tape deck was gone, along with my diary tape of the time spent in Greece. What hurt most, though, was the loss of all my specially designed wheeling clothes. The stuff was designed to be functional, and tapered to fit my legs and body to prevent wrinkles that could create pressure sores. It had sponsors' logos all over it. The first thing any sensible robber would do was get rid of it. But then, sensible wasn't a word that came up much in the next few hours.

Amanda's brother, Mike, had just joined the tour. He's a big ex-junior hockey player, and from the moment the robbery was discovered he played policeman—which is more than I can say for the policemen sent out to investigate. He discovered that a hotel security man had actually passed the robber leaving the apartment. ("Hello." "Hi. Nice night.") Then the guy had gone back to the office and *phoned* the room to see if anything was wrong. When he didn't get an answer, he assumed everything must be all right.

Mike also found some of our things left on the inside of the fence around the motel. Obviously, the rest had been thrown over to an accomplice. He got a description of the car, which he gave to the police. They didn't even phone it in. They just stood there, making notes, just off their shift and obviously more concerned with getting home. Talk about "Car 54, Where Are You?" Those guys were lucky to find the motel, let alone the robbers.

It had a good side, though. The New Zealand *Herald* ran a big front page picture and made us the lead story. At least people now knew we were there, and why. Local people came by with donations of clothing and some money, and back home in Vancouver the ANZA (Australia–New Zealand) Club members were so embarrassed and apologetic they held a fund raiser to pay replacement costs for some of the gear.

But it was a lousy way to start the New Year. Everything seemed to be going wrong.

During the stopover in Los Angeles, Don had put the video camera down next to a bunch of our other baggage. I'd told him that under no circumstances was he to let it out of his sight. He maintained that he'd put it with stuff that other people on the crew were supposed to be watching. All I knew was that someone had walked off with it, and there went some irreplaceable tape of our journey through the Middle East.

We got to the Auckland airport to discover that two crates of equipment, including two wheelchairs, had been lost in transit. (Eventually they found one of them.)

The politics of organizational control back home were making it difficult for us to get on with the job. There were three people there who had different views on how the project should be run. My concern was that no matter who was in control, it was run in consultation with me. That's why I made a constant effort to to maintain communication—so that I was involved in all the major decisions. The dream of just wheeling and doing PR had evaporated, and as a result, the tour was going to be harder than it ever should have been.

The Lions Club members were out with a bucket brigade, running along by the motor home as we wheeled—but what good did that do when most of the people didn't know about us or why we were there?

Jim Taylor and his wife, Deb, who were down from Vancouver for a visit, even tried priming the pump. They circled the block in their rented car, pulled up next to Amanda, reached out and handed her some money.

"Great job you're doing! Wonderful cause!" he yelled.

Amanda almost fell off the bike. "What are you *doing?*" she asked.

"Seed money," he hissed. Then they drove ahead a block and did it again. I don't know how well it worked, but the tour was up $20—Taylor's money.

We were wheeling alone outside of Auckland—Rob Courtney, a local wheelchair athlete who held the world 100-metre record and was now in training for a meet in Houston, Texas, and me—when a police car pulled us over and the officer gave us a friendly piece of advice.

"You'll have to take another route," he said. "The road's washed out up ahead."

It had been raining for days, and from the look of the sky it would for days to come. One route was probably no better than another.

"How deep?" I asked.

He looked at the chair. "About axle high," he said.

I looked at Rob, who shrugged.

"Sounds about right," I told the officer. "Thank you very much."

We kept going until we got to the flood, paused for a minute, then plunged in. We got our butts soaked, but the wheeling wasn't bad, and on the other side, a surprise was waiting: two boys about thirteen and fifteen, each peeling in from one side of the road. They were in training for wheelchair sports competitions and wanted to wheel with Rob and me.

It was the greatest feeling, having them with us and seeing their enthusiasm. Until a day or so earlier they may never have heard of the tour, but they knew what I was there for and what I was trying to do, and they wanted to be a part of it.

They stuck at it for about an hour in bad weather on an uphill grade. One of the boys had a chair that wasn't the best for that sort of work, so whenever he started to fall behind, I'd reach back and "whip" him up level with us. In the motor home, Amanda winced at what I might be doing to my shoulders, but what the heck, this was special.

When we hit our break, they said good-bye and their parents picked them up. As they left, I looked back at the motor home. The moisture in my eyes wasn't all from the rain.

"Wasn't that great?" I called.

"Look up ahead," someone said.

I turned. About 30 feet ahead, two other kids in wheelchairs were coming out, one from each side of the road. They wheeled for an hour. When they left, two more took their place, and two more after them. Now we had children and adults, some on bikes, some running along beside us. Sure, it had to be organized. But nobody made them come. They just wanted to show that they were with me. Somehow, the rain didn't seem to matter much anymore.

There were other moments like that, other receptions where the media response was good, wheeling stretches where people cheered and seemed enthusiastic. Logistically, things had run smoothly, thanks in large measure to Nancy's organizational skills in her new position as tour manager. From that standpoint, New Zealand was a turning point for the project. But overall, New Zealand was built up as an exciting part of the tour, and that never materialized.

The mail I got from home didn't help. Remember the Spinal Cord Society of Canada, the cure-not-care people? Someone sent me a copy of a letter and response carried in the July 1985 edition of a newsletter published by the American parent body, the Spinal Cord Society. It read as follows (spelling untouched):

> *Dear Editor: Is SCS supporting the Rick Hansen wheeling around the world for cure project? (Signed) From Canada.*
> *Editor's reply:*
> *No. Rick Hanson of William's Lake, B.C. and an entourage including a motor home have embarked upon a tour around the globe to raise money for cure. They will be lucky if they raise enough to finance the tour much less "millions" for cure. Since spring he has appeared in Vancouver, California, Texas, Florida and Toronto, which must be some kind of wheeling record for even superman. According to the press, the APA [American Paraplegic Association] has been involved in this, but not SCS or SCS Canada. That authorization has not been given because it is believed this will turn out to be a stunt that will be essentially a world tour for those involved in it.*

Here we were, tearing ourselves apart mentally and physically to make this project work. We'd given up a year of our lives with at least another year to go—working for the same people this organization was trying to assist—and they're sitting back there, writing it off as some kind of jaunt around the world? Here was this radical organization, which represented only a small portion of spinal cord injured persons, spouting off without knowing—or asking—anything about what we were doing or how we were doing it. How do you fight a thing like that?

"Bring the writer or the editor out on the tour," I thought. "Show him what's going on. Run a towline from the motor home to his chair and see how he felt after a few days, even without having to push."

Taylor had an idea of his own.

"Finish the tour," he said. "Make it a triumph. Then write them a letter and tell them to stick their society up their ass."

I knew I could never do that. But I have to admit, it was tempting.

146

We had another ongoing problem: the situation with the crew was getting worse. We had Mike now, and Brian Rose, a big, dependable guy of thirty-five, a mountain climber and outdoorsman who ran a sporting goods store in Vancouver and was in for a stint as our advance man. We had the bodies, but the same mistakes were being made, over and over again.

Everyone was snappy, including me. From their perspective, I was probably acting like a jerk. From mine, I wasn't making demands on them any tougher than the ones I made on myself. But it did create a lot of tension for everyone, including Amanda. I found that out the hard way, when she threw her salad at me.

We were having dinner in our motel room just outside of Wellington. The main course was a disagreement about something or other, which wasn't unusual at the time. Suddenly, she just exploded, drew back her arm and fired her salad.

Oh, yeah? I picked up my salad and fired back.

"I'm leaving!" she yelled, and bolted out the door carrying nothing but her purse and her passport.

"Fine!" I yelled after her.

I sat there for a bit, just fuming. Then I started to think. I could see her out the window, crying and striding down the road. We were out in the country, fields and bushes on either side. Anything could happen out there.

I popped into the chair and took after her in the semidarkness. She turned and saw me coming. "You can send my stuff later!" she yelled, and began to run.

Amanda could run, but I was in the chair, desperate to catch her and gaining. When she saw me closing in she turned, jumped over a fence and headed toward the bush. Now I was scared. I felt helpless. She was young and beautiful and by herself, wandering through strange country with God knows what kind of danger—and I couldn't follow her any farther.

I wheeled back to the motel flat out, and got Mike. He took out after her. We could just see her face, off in the distance. He jumped the fence, caught up with her and had a long talk. She came back, and we talked it out.

By this time I realized that maybe she *should* go home. The stress that had begun to show in Rome had grown beyond her capacity to handle it.

It wasn't just the tour and its problems. She also had to deal with the strain of constantly being in the middle. To the crew she was my girl, and therefore lumped with me in any dispute. Yet she was a part of that crew on a daily basis. She was the buffer between me and the crew, between me and the office. And when I needed someone to unload on and talk things out late at night, she got that, too.

The load was too big. She just wasn't coping. As much as I wanted her to stay, it was better to lose her then and meet her again when it was over than to risk our relationship by having her stay. By the time we hit Wellington, it was obvious that something had to be done.

I sat her down and talked to her. I told her how much I valued her, how important our relationship was to me, how much I wanted it to be forever.

"So," I said, "I think it would be best if you went home."

It shook me as much as it did her. The line had been drawn. The words put it right out in the open. Now we started asking one another: "Can it be done? Can we both stick this out?"

Amanda believed that her survival on the tour meant the survival of our relationship, that we couldn't have one without the other. I believed that our relationship could survive even if Amanda had to leave. How many couples could survive being together twenty-four hours a day, seven days a week for two and one-half years under these conditions and still come out loving each other?

There were no promises. All we knew was that we were at a critical point in our relationship. There was nothing I could do to make it easier. Amanda had to dig a little deeper, fight her personal devils and go on. Because our relationship meant so much to her, she did.

No more food fights. We'd talk it out when we could, argue when we couldn't. But we'd started this thing together; we'd finish it together. And then we'd get on with our lives.

For a lot of reasons, the trip to Australia was like a tonic. Just getting off the plane in Sydney brought back memories of 1983, when I'd come there and won the Australian marathon. My brother, Brad, had taken his holidays to spend time with us on the road, and Amanda's parents would be flying in.

Before we began the wheel in Adelaide, we parked in front of a TV set and gave ourselves a fix of North Americana: the Chicago Bears winning the Super Bowl.

It was milestone time.

The second day out of Adelaide, we celebrated our arrival at the 12,000-mile mark with a unique little ceremony out in the middle of nowhere. Amanda carefully drew a line across the road with a spray can of whipping cream. Then, as I burst through the banner, the banner marked "12,000"—she carefully sprayed me right in the mush.

To tell the truth, I didn't like it much. The flies did, though. By now, I'd learned a lot about flies. Your basic Spanish type try to catch you, but if you outrun them at the start they get discouraged and quit. The Australian fly is smarter. He catches you, lands on your back to rest up, then goes straight for the nose, eyes, ears and throat. And if you happen to be wearing whipping cream at the time, wonderful.

The ceremony in Melbourne marking the halfway point— 12,450.775 miles—was somewhat more formal. The Lord Mayor was there in his ceremonial garb. I did an interview with "Good Morning, Australia," the country's biggest TV show, which gave me a great opportunity to explain again why we were here and what we were doing. The Melbourne ceremony was of tremendous significance to me. As a matter of routine I mentally split every wheeling challenge down the middle, because once I've done a half I can always tell myself I could do it again. I'd stuck to that all through the tour. Now we'd hit the biggest halfway of them all.

That night we all went out for Mexican food, and the boys gave me a mug inscribed "Half way 'round the world: A day to remember." I gave a world globe to everyone on the tour, including Tim, who was down visiting Nancy. He wasn't part of it then, but he'd been a vital part of it for a long time, and for that I'd always be grateful.

Along the way I'd posed with kangaroos and baby ostriches, and dodged $1 coins thrown to me by passing cars. It was a nice gesture, but when the car is doing 55 miles per hour, so is the thrown coin. I did an awful lot of ducking. Amanda, Don and I flew to Birdsville (pop. 200) so the Nike people could take the picture that became their official poster and, incidentally, the cover of this book. In Brisbane, we marked our first anniversary on the road. In Sydney we met TV actor Lorne Greene. ("Everybody wants to meet Rick," Brad said. "That's no big deal. But *Lorne Greene* . . . now there's a celebrity.") We finished the Australian portion of the tour in Brundenberg, then we went to Surfer's Paradise and vegged out for a week.

I knew I wasn't handling the situation with the boys as well as I should. Sometimes I expected too much or became unreasonable and too blunt in my demands. I was working on being more understanding, more of a diplomat. But it was a slow process, and at that point I was too beat to care.

We were halfway through the tour. It was a time for collecting memories, a time to take stock of how we'd lived and what we'd done. Back at the office, they'd even taken inventory. One year on the road equalled:

Postcards written: 1,086. Laundries done: 365. Flat tires: 63. Pairs of gloves worn out: 47. Rolls of tape used: 100. Times robbed: 4. Robberies solved: 0. Wheelchairs worn out: 1. Official receptions attended: 59. Wheelchair strokes: approximately 7,180,800.

Hopefully, we'd learned from the experience. "We'd better have," I thought. Because now we had it to do all over again.

10

"What would the emperor think?"

*T*he night before Rick Hansen began his world tour, in the midst of the pre-takeoff chaos, a friend looked at him and posed a question that had been bugging him for days.

"What do you want out of this tour?" he asked. "Never mind the tour objectives. I know about those, and they're fine. But what do you want to come out of it with? You—personally?"

Hansen thought a moment.

"When I come back and it's all over," he said, "I want to be able to wake up in the morning, look at the bedroom wall, and see a picture of me in the wheelchair, sitting on the Great Wall of China."

"That's it?" his friend asked.

"That's it. I want to be able to lie there for a minute, and stare at it, and remember what it took to get there, and remind myself that there are no walls too big to climb."

The wall and Chinese culture had always intrigued him. When he began toying with the notion that a man might be able to push a wheelchair around the world, China was one of the first countries that came to mind. China, and the wall.

And now he was a few days away from trying it.

He knew a fair bit about the wall. Twenty-two centuries old, some of it, built to repel the invaders from the north, and gradually extended to a length of 1,500 miles, making it the only man-made structure visible from outer space. Twenty to thirty feet high, twenty-five feet wide at the base, tapering to fifteen at the top. There'd be stairs, of course. He'd need to be lifted up those. The slope on the parts he could wheel would be worse than any mountains he'd faced to date—forty-five to sixty degrees. He had no illusions about how tough it would be. Too tough, maybe.

The Chinese people. How would they accept the Man in Motion tour?

He was heading into a totally different culture. The focus would be on the most important part of the tour: the message and awareness theme. There'd be no fund raising as he wheeled 750 miles of the distance between Beijing and Shanghai. He was confident that he could breach the political, cultural and linguistic barriers to get that message through. The quality of response had been high everywhere providing that the organization and support had been there to get the word out in advance as to what the tour was about and give people the opportunity to respond. But would it be there in China? He didn't know. It was almost like the first day, sitting on the stage at Oakridge, knowing what he had to do, what he'd promised to do, but not knowing what he might face in trying to do it.

The rest of it—the injuries, the tour pressures, the problems with the office, the million-and-one details that seemed to fall on him like a cloudburst every day—he'd simply have to put behind him for a while. This was it: China and the Great Wall, the picture on the bedroom wall, live and in colour.

Well, he was as ready as he could be. The crew problems had been resolved, at least to the point where they were still all together. And one thing he knew for certain: in this version of the Long March across China, the bitter, driving winds would be at his back. They'd had an advance man over here months ago, laying out the route with that in mind.

"No head winds," he'd told the office. "If you make sure of nothing else, make sure of that. It's vital. In the condition I'm in, head winds would finish me."

Thank goodness, he didn't have to worry about that.

I was leaning back in the plush comfort of a limousine on the way out of the Beijing airport when the official who'd picked me up leaned forward and popped a cassette into the tape deck.

"Welcome to China, Mr. Hansen," he beamed. "This is for you." Traditional Chinese music? No—"St. Elmo's Fire," as performed by David Foster and John Parr. I was flabbergasted. Even in China! The song had followed us around the world.

David Holtzman, who'd done the advance reccy, had told us the Chinese people were really going to lay it on. They weren't just providing vehicles, they were supplying drivers. I scrunched down into the upholstery and gazed out the window for my first glimpse of China as we headed for the Great Wall Sheraton on the edge of the city of Beijing.

As we were to discover, our hosts had done everything possible to ease the rigours of the tour. We knew well in advance the time and place we were supposed to be, how long we could stay and where we could and couldn't go. There was a reason for the all-out effort, and for the relative ease with which we got the necessary travel clearances. His name was Deng Pufang.

Deng was chairman of the Chinese Welfare Fund for the Disabled —and the son of Deng Xiaoping, chairman of the Central Advisory Committee of the Communist party and president of the Central Military Commission. Deng Pufang was paraplegic, the result, it was said, of being thrown from a third-storey balcony during the Cultural Revolution. His father cared for him and eventually sent him to Canada for surgery. He joked that he had quite a few pints of Canadian blood in him. Thus we had an influential supporter through his work for the disabled and through his feeling for Canada. From the instant the plane landed, the red carpet was out.

Well, great. We could use a little of that. We'd had a long trip from Australia—Sydney to Singapore, then to Hong Kong for a day, then on to Beijing. There had been time for a bit of shopping in Hong Kong to go with a 10-mile wheel. We didn't draw many people, but the TV and newspaper coverage was good. We were tired, and now that we were there in China at what I'd always considered one of the true high points of the tour, the easier they made it, the better. No matter how tough it got, this was going to be one of the fun parts. With the wind at my back from there to Shanghai, how could I lose?

Cuisine was a problem—not the kind of food, but the amount and the ceremony involved in serving it. Our hosts were so good to us there were sometimes two official meals in a day, and as much as I wanted to stay—I love Chinese food and you couldn't have a more authentic source—my wheeling and rest schedule just didn't permit it. The food was so loaded with the traditional flavour enhancer, monosodium glutamate, that we all began to get what we called an MSG "buzz"—wild dreams, even nightmares.

And then there was the dreaded Curse of Ganbei.

Every country has its own version of "Ganbei!": "Bottoms up!" "Skoal!" A dozen more. In every language it means essentially the same thing: "Pick it up and knock it back." In China, "Ganbei!" was white lightning in a shot glass. Rocket fuel, the boys called it, and they were soon in a position to know. After one try, in which I made a toast to our hosts for the evening, threw back the drink and was reduced to a teary, beet-red, coughing mess, I pleaded weariness and the need to prepare for the next day's wheeling. The crew became my designated shooters.

It wasn't an easy job.

The protocol seldom changed. The crew and everyone with us, which usually included the North American journalists, were spread

152

around the hall, one or two at each table with local dignitaries and special guests. At each setting was a beer glass, a wine glass and a shot glass. The food just kept coming—if we entered a province and the chef there wasn't considered first-rate, a chef from a nearby province was brought in for the occasion—and the "Ganbeis" grew in number and intensity as the evening progressed. In the initial stages someone would stand up, offer a toast to one of us, or to the tour, or whatever, say "Ganbei!" and take a sip of the red wine. But at some point in the evening the wine was put aside, the "Ganbeis" came fast and furious—and this time they were done with the rocket fuel.

One of the local people at the table—usually an old man with a suspicious twinkle in his eye—would propose a toast, shout "Ganbei!" and toss off the shot, then point his empty glass at us to show he'd downed it all. Naturally, the guests had to reciprocate. Naturally, so did the old man.

In the city of Tianjin, the evening was near the end when Miss Wong, the translator for the media, heard one of us say "Cheers."

"Ah," she asked. " 'Cheers' is Canadian for 'Ganbei'?"

"Oh, no," said Joe King, a cameraman in to film the *Heart of the Dragon* video on the tour, being produced by a Vancouver lady named Anna French. " 'Cheers' is British for 'Ganbei.' In Canada we have our own toast."

He leaned over and told her what it was.

Well, Miss Wong practised for a few rounds. Then, on the final "Ganbei" of the evening, with everyone standing with glasses raised, she spotted CBC cameraman Fred Cawsey of Vancouver at the other end of the room.

"Fr-e-d!" she shouted gaily, *"Up yours!"*

Don't you just love cultural exchange?

The last census listed Beijing as a city of 7,570,000 people. To me, it seemed to have at least that many bicycles and hand-drawn carts. The sheer volume was incredible. And the contrast: people, bikes, horses, some oxen, plus Mercedes, limousines and rickshaws. And, darting in and out of the confusion, guys running with hundred-pound packs on their backs, held in place by a strap across the forehead.

We'd roll slowly along on our exhibition wheel, trying to absorb all that, and suddenly our hosts would guide us in a different direction and into another age. We were taken into the Forbidden City, and also to the Ming Tombs. To get to them we went along Animal Alley, with its carvings of animals alternately posed standing and sitting, the sitters resting so they wouldn't fall asleep while guarding the tomb during the night watch.

There was so much to see, and so little time. But on the second day there we were in front of the Great Wall, preparing for the climb.

It didn't start well. For ninety minutes, it didn't start at all. Don had forgotten to fix the chair with the biggest push rims and the smallest wheels. He had to go rushing back through all that traffic, bring them back and put them on. But eventually I took a deep breath and pushed to the wall.

It was a perfect day for the climb, hazy and a bit overcast, but with good lighting. We'd hired a commercial photographer. Both the CBC and CTV networks had cameras there. The wire services were well represented. My attack plan was simple: in places where there were stairs, the crew would have to lift me. Otherwise, no matter what the grade, all they were to do was stay behind me to grab the chair if necessary. I wanted to climb this thing, not be carried.

It was unbelievably difficult. The books hadn't lied about the grade—forty-five to sixty degrees. After every stroke forward someone had to be there to keep the chair from rolling backward because at the end of my stroke I couldn't get my hands back up to the top of the push rims in time to brake it myself. When we came to the stairs —which was about every 100 yards—they'd carry me. The total, I'm told, was 103 steps. Otherwise, it was me and the wall, just as I'd always pictured it.

I pushed too hard. I think I injured my hand. But when I was finally too beat to go an inch farther, we stopped and did the photos. Funny, I'd always pictured this moment as one of solitude, a sense of isolation. As I gazed out over Mongolia I found myself wondering what that first emperor would have thought, if he'd known that some day the wall he started to build to keep outsiders from his kingdom would be climbed by a man in a wheelchair, with mobs of tourists from a dozen countries swarming out of busses to gather round. Not much, probably. Not much at all.

We spent forty-five minutes on the wall, then rolled back down about 800 metres, brakes on all the way. One slip and I was in Mongolia. Then we drove to the hospital for a private visit with Deng Pufang and later with Wan Li, one of five vice-premiers of China's State Council. I felt a great bond with Deng because of the work he was doing for the disabled, and a sense that we'd meet again. Given the work yet to be done, perhaps we will.

We took a three-day rest break in preparation for the first wheel. Either we didn't get out much or I wasn't paying attention, because until we attended the big outdoor farewell ceremony, I still hadn't twigged in.

The wind. It was blowing into my face. All the planning, all the reminders, all the reccy work, and I was wheeling into the teeth of a 30-mile-an-hour wind.

There was no mystery as to what had happened. The cutback to 50-mile wheeling days in Australia had put us six weeks behind schedule. The reccy had been done based on our arrival in early March. Had we started out then, the winds might have blown us all the way to Shanghai. Now it was April, the warm air had blown up from the south, and the wind was in our teeth.

Now I really was climbing the wall. We'd known in January we'd be late arriving in China, and nobody had checked to see if that meant a change in the weather? If we'd known, we could have done the wheel backwards, Shanghai to Beijing, had the wind with us all the way, and finished on a high at the Great Wall. But no—we forget to check. This wasn't just another logistical foul-up. This time I was in jeopardy.

I should have known something was wrong at the farewell ceremony. They gave me a pigeon to throw into the sky as a symbol of freedom. As it left it dumped all over me. It was a symbol, all right, but not of what they thought.

The wind made the wheeling pure agony, but the reception across China was heaven. We had a virtual wagon train—five vehicles including our little van, each with its own Chinese driver, plus our crew, Fred Cawsey and a few other media. The *Heart of the Dragon* group was still with us, and that meant a lot to me. Anna French of Vancouver was in the midst of a long battle with cancer and already had lost a leg. When she heard about the tour she wanted to help, so she and her husband, Michael, and two cameramen packed up and came to China. The video would be her gift, her way of helping us spread the message.

It became quite a friendly mob. Each night there'd be the best of food, plus beer, fruit and bottled water. Dining did, however, provide its interesting moments. The boys ate dog once without knowing it until the meal was over. I had turtle soup, which turned out to be a big tureen full of boiling water, with a turtle in the bottom. We just kept matching them smile for smile, bow for bow, ganbei for ganbei.

The Chinese drivers were fascinated by Mike's size. They always wanted to check how strong he was by wrestling. At 6'2" and 205 pounds, he'd pick up a couple and bounce them off one of the vehicles, and they'd bounce up grinning, looking for more.

It wasn't all wonderful. Lee just about went crazy when he saw the vehicle in which he was expected to cook when we were on the road. It looked like one of those trucks at home where the driver props up the sides to display sandwiches for sale. The cracks in the roof were so wide it was a see-through truck. There was a tiny icebox under a tiny gas stove, plastic dishes and utensils, and dust everywhere. Besides, Lee never knew when he could cook, because the driver kept taking it up ahead or scooting back down the road. Occasionally, I'd come in for my break and there'd be no food ready. Lee would be there, but the truck wouldn't.

We didn't know what to expect in the way of response from the Chinese people. There weren't many in evidence on the first leg between Beijing and Tianjin, but as we approached the outskirts of the city itself, the crowds grew from a trickle to a mob. All at once we had a motorcycle police escort and were surrounded by thousands upon thousands of people, all waving and yelling and throwing flowers. For a minute, I almost panicked.

The police would zoom their motorcyles at the crowd, which would fade to make an opening, then flow back. The support strap for my feet broke off, leaving them dangling, but I couldn't stop for fear of being engulfed. Even then, I had this grin plastered all over my face. I just couldn't stop. Later I was told the people were comparing me to Dr. Norman Bethune, the Canadian surgeon who came to China in 1938 and set up a clinic to treat the Chinese during the Japanese invasion. Drums were beating, people were squeezing out to touch me. The atmosphere was electric. Something magical was happening.

I wasn't sure the grin would ever come off.

We kept heading south, into a wind that blew gritty, sandpaper dust into my eyes and nose and ground the skin of my face until I felt as though I'd shaved all over with a dull blade. On the highways the drivers were aggressive, one hand on the wheel and one on the horn, but 30 feet away there'd be endless rice paddies, the people tending the crops as they'd been tended for generations, with hands and feet and primitive hoe and plow.

The fields were dotted with what looked like clay funnels that turned out to be graves. The people were buried where they'd laboured, with a hole at the top of the cone to let the spirit out. The others just plowed around the graves, as some day someone would plow around theirs.

We must have been the first foreigners some of them had ever seen. They'd drop everything and run to stare in amazement at this guy in the wheelchair surrounded by motor vehicles and police cycles with flashing lights. There was an innocence about them, an unaffected curiosity. They'd come right up to me, nose to nose, and stare for the longest time.

"If I'm the first foreigner they've ever seen, we're in trouble," I told

Amanda. "They'll go home thinking we all travel this way and can't use our legs."

That curiosity was to be evident everywhere we went. Once when the rest of the crew was away on a lunch break, Amanda and I felt the motor home shaking. She opened the curtains, and all she could see was eyeballs and noses pressed against the glass. There were so many people trying for a glimpse inside that they were actually rocking the van. It got a little claustrophobic—to the point where Amanda started waving her arms at the glass. "Shoo!" she yelled. "Shoo!" And they did, leaving us wondering what "Shoo" might mean in Chinese.

The contrast between today and yesterday was inescapable. We'd see the expensive cars, hear the jet planes, visit the huge cities—then come to a little town like the one in which a major archaeological dig had been suspended until modern science could devise a method of preserving what they'd begun to uncover. They'd discovered another nest of the little clay soldiers, these brightly coloured. But exposure to air oxidized the colors and turned the soldiers grey, so there'd be no more digging until they found a way to protect them. What was another ten years, or twenty, or one hundred, when they'd been there for thousands?

It was a difficult challenge to convey how we wanted things done, based on our experiences on the road, because of the language barrier and their ability to transform our requests into action. China was a different culture, and compromise became the rule of thumb.

Our co-ordinator, Mr. Soo, thought the important thing was how many events could be crammed into the schedule. It hadn't been made clear to him that our priority list was based on putting in the miles, staying healthy and rested, then getting in as many events as possible. The conflict made for some interesting wheeling. At one point I was challenged by some of my disabled escort wheelers, who were using three-wheel carts with cranks and gears. I dusted them, and spent the next day teaching them about chairs. Meanwhile Mr. Soo's group, somehow convinced that I couldn't wheel over steep hills, had made plans to drive through the tough areas. I won that argument, then hit a construction site where the rain had turned a short patch of the road to gravel soup. I got three flat tires—the boys slopping through the muck to change them each time—before I gave up and we drove through it.

China was marvellous. We'd learned and seen so much, and the tour had won such great acceptance. But an unfortunate incident occurred at our finish in Shanghai.

China has five wheelchair basketball teams. I'd conducted two clinics for them. The local team staged an exhibition game as part of the farewell ceremonies, after which four of the twelve players rolled out of the gym with me to complete the final wheeling segment in China.

Apparently someone from the embassy didn't understand that disabled athletes who play wheelchair sport are not necessarily wheelchair-bound. Some are amputees and can stand on artificial legs or crutches. Others have disabilities that allow them to stand for brief periods, or even to walk. When we'd left and he saw some of the others rise, fold their competition wheelchairs and store them away, he jumped to a hasty and totally erroneous conclusion.

He told a correspondent for the Toronto *Globe and Mail* that the Chinese athletes were not truly handicapped, and described them as "fake." Naturally, the wire services picked it up. Deng Pufang and the Chinese Welfare Fund for the Disabled were embarrassed. We were embarrassed. Eventually, apologies flew.

Of all the countries we'd visited, China was the most significant, the first in which we reached all levels of society, from government to school children to farmers in the fields. We were treated with respect and dignity. The people did everything they could to make our stay as comfortable as possible. We will remember China with warmth and affection, both for its response to the tour and for the treatment we received.

When I conducted the basketball clinics I thought how nice it would be to come back someday to teach and coach. Now I was sure that someday, somehow, it would happen.

I was in South Korea, somewhere between Pusan and Seoul, talking to a bunch of people and crying. I couldn't figure out why. I looked around, and everyone else had tears in their eyes, too. It seems that an hour earlier, on this very spot, police had used tear gas to break up a student demonstration. Welcome to the land of the 1988 Summer Olympic Games.

Our co-hosts were the Korean Broadcasting System, reportedly one of the wealthiest TV networks in the world, and the Ching Nip Polio Centre, headed by Dr. Wong. Stricken by polio as a child, she'd persevered until she was allowed into a normal school. Later, after great effort, she went on to become the first disabled person in Korea to become a doctor and was a driving force in the cause of disabled persons in her country.

We stayed four days and wheeled 160 miles. The response of the people was good, particularly at gatherings like the Children's Day Festival in Seoul, where 30,000 young people waved and cheered and seemed to have a good feeling for what we were doing. But in the early stages of the visit we ran into the same problem we'd hit in southern China: the theory that events were everything, wheeling incidental.

The KBS obviously viewed the whole thing as a potential documentary to be used as publicity for the Paralympics, the games for the disabled to be held in Seoul following the 1988 Summer Olympic Games. So we'd get, "Okay, you stop now!" then "Okay, you go now. Wheel!" Nothing seemed to matter but keeping their schedule. Once, with me sick in the back and Mike driving and waving, we boomed right on through one village with the mayor standing at a podium ready to make a speech. It seems there was a bigger village and a more important mayor up ahead, and we were late. That really upset me.

We finished up one of the wheeling days at a city hall. I had the flu again, it had been a tough wheel, and I was beat—but here was this tour co-ordinator who'd been more or less ignoring our wishes and pushing his own schedule, insisting that there was one more event we didn't know about, a trip to a children's rehab home or hospital.

I was on the bed. I sent a message out: "No way. I can't." The motor home starts up to take us to the hotel. Suddenly, it occurs to me we're not making much progress. I look out the front window and there are the twelve athletes who'd been wheeling with me all day. They're still wheeling, the cameras are still rolling, and we're going to the hospital.

Now I'm really mad, and this guy is sweating. He's actually down on his knees: "Please, Mr. Hansen! For the children!" And now there are kids outside the motor home. What can I say? I come out and visit, we discuss the whole thing later, and after that, everything in Korea goes like clockwork.

Okay, I admit it, I'm a competitor. On the tour I mostly tucked that side of my nature away, but here was one of my escort wheelers, giving me the business for two days. He'd keep his chair in front of mine all the time, and turn and make hurry-up motions with his hand.

Finally, as we got close to Seoul on the third day, I thought "Now!" I had Don put on the twelve-inch rims and the largest wheels.

We started out, and the guy tried to take his usual spot. But the harder he pushed, the harder I pushed. Pretty soon it was a sprint—a race over the last 4 miles of the first 13-mile segment.

There was a hill up ahead, with a turn scheduled at the top. I figured I'd gas him there, then wait for him around the corner. I left him gasping, made the turn figuring to slow down—and there was another hill, and another turn. And after that, another. By the time I got

159

to the top of the last one I was worn to a nub myself. I had a nice rest then, though, waiting for this guy. He was a long time coming, and he didn't look good when he arrived.

As he turned the last corner, I grinned, started out again—then looked back, and made a little hurry-up gesture.

We saw the Olympic Games sites and met with the Paralympics organizing committee, where we discussed the progress toward and the pressing need to have wheelchair sports representation in the Olympics—not as exhibition or demonstration sports but as regular Olympic events in which we were athletes competing among our peers. It's going to come—perhaps one representative event in the summer games and one in the winter—but it's been a long, hard struggle, and it wasn't over yet. Then we flew to Tokyo, the last country on the Asian tour, to put in a final 1,000 miles before flying back to Miami.

The prospects of wheeling in Japan had not looked good because of the tremendous amount of red tape and their concern over the congestion and traffic conditions. Thank goodness that Prince Tomohito of Mikasa became interested at the eleventh hour and agreed to be our honorary chairman. When he snapped his fingers, things happened. He got corporations like IBM and Toyota involved. We were received with open arms, and although the weather wasn't the best for wheeling and we had our usual getting-lost escapades, we found the people just as warm as they'd been during my visits to Oita for the marathons.

Mind you, there were a few mad moments that were strictly off the wall. Like the washroom in one of the smaller towns. How does a guy in a wheelchair squat over a slit trench? Or the short, deep bathtubs. Getting in was easy. Getting out was something else. Or how about the eye doctor, who treated my eye infection in his cloakroom by flashlight because tradition said you take off your shoes before you enter a room and he didn't think cleaning the wheels of the chair counted? Fixed the infection, though.

And then there was the night in Tokyo when we sent Mike and Nancy on a hamburger run to a McDonald's two blocks down the street, and they were gone for seven hours.

The way they told it, it sounds almost logical. To be certain they'd get to the restaurant and not get confused in the Tokyo streets, they took a cab. The cabbie drove for about an hour. Now they were really lost. They took another cab and tried to get back—but they couldn't remember the name of our hotel.

A few hours of this and they had an inspiration: Muriel Honey, our

Man in Motion

Home in Canada at last, Hansen is greeted in Cape Speare, Newfoundland, by old friend and competitor Mel Fitzgerald (front, bearded)—and swamped by autograph hounds.

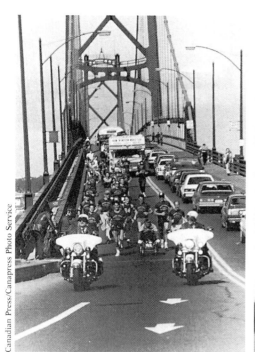

Canadian Press/Canapress Photo Service

Man in Motion

Left: Runners by the dozen hit the bridge to escort the Man in Motion tour into Halifax. "You could feel the momentum growing," Hansen said.

Right: In Prince Edward Island, the message around the outside of the "medal" said it all: "Be strong and of good courage, and *do* it!"

Man in Motion

Top: "Welcome to Quebec, my friend!" Wheelchair athlete André Viger, a star in his own right, greets Hansen.

Bottom: On a hill in Montreal, the sign on the Man in Motion motor home tells the story: 19,671 miles behind them, heading west and home.

Norm Betts/Canada Wide

The million-dollar drop in the bucket. On Parliament Hill, Prime Minister Brian Mulroney presents Canada's gift to Man in Motion.

Facing page: When a single wrinkle could cause discomfort or create a pressure sore, a clothing check is all important. Amanda Reid checks Rick's outfit for the day.

Wintertime, and the livin' ain't easy. Wheeling through the snow in northern Ontario—and just think: pretty soon, we hit the prairies.

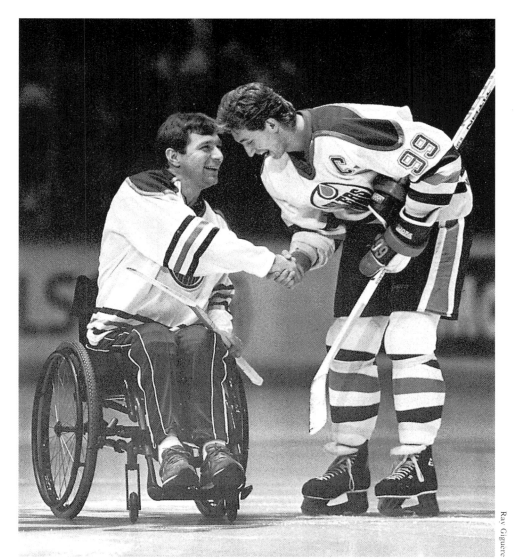

Ray Giguere

Jim Cochrane/Edmonton Journal

Top: When champions meet: Hansen and Wayne Gretzky at centre ice in Edmonton. The two shared Canada's athlete-of-the-year award in 1983.

Bottom: "Sorry son, gotta run." In Alberta, a woman races to get her child close enough to shake hands with a hero. She made it—but just barely.

Christine and Marv Hansen dry off the thousands of coins dropped in fountains at Expo 86 and donated to Man in Motion.

PR lady, would have the hotel name and number. They'd phone Muriel. Muriel was in Vancouver, but so what?

There was only one problem. It was the middle of the night in Vancouver—and they didn't have Muriel's home number.

"I've got it," Mike said. "I'll phone home and get Muriel's number from Mom and Dad. Then we'll phone Muriel, she'll give us the name and number, and we'll have it made."

By this time they don't know whether to laugh or cry. It's raining, they're cold and wet and most of all hungry, and Mike's on the phone talking to Patrick:

"Dad," he said. "Remember when you told me that if I ever needed anything, to call you? Well, I need something. Have you got Muriel Honey's phone number . . . ?"

Two blocks. Two trans-Pacific telephone calls and seven hours later, they're back in the hotel. And they hadn't brought the hamburgers.

Speaking of food, Lee rushed out to see the cooking facilities he'd be using on the road. It was smaller than the see-through sandwich van he'd struggled with in China, about the size of a bread truck. It had no fridge, no water and a bunsen burner stove about ten inches square. Every time he climbed in, he bumped his head. If there's ever an Olympic event for cooking while standing up in a moving vehicle while balancing three things at once, Lee wins.

One of the unfortunate aspects of the tour was that there was never much of an opportunity for me to see the night life. I was being iced down or worked over or trying to catch up on my sleep. But I was lucky: I had my girl with me. Don and Lee and Mike were out there, young and single. Understandably, there were times when they felt the urge to sample the local downtown culture.

One night in Tokyo they found themselves at the famous Singing Bar, where they have a huge supply of cassette tapes featuring the the melodies of popular songs, with lyrics to match. If you feel the urge to sing, you find your song in the book, they plug in the cassette, you jump up on stage in front of the microphone while the lyrics run across a little TV monitor in front of you.

Well, Don is a professional musician. He also is the kind of guy who's either terribly quiet and withdrawn, or totally into it. On this night, he decided to sing Elvis Presley's "Love Me Tender."

They plug it in, he gets up in front of the mike and starts singing. He is an instant smash. People are rolling off their chairs. "But why are they laughing?" he wonders. "This is a ballad, man!" He can't

161

understand it. Finally, he notices that they seem to be looking behind him. He turns to see what's back there. Playing on a gigantic screen behind him is a pornographic video. While Don was loving them tenderly, two people on the screen were loving each other, uh, differently.

We were leaving Asia, and leaving a part of us there forever. For all the problems, the tour had been a major success, in Asia more than anywhere it had come alive. The people had responded. We left knowing that the message had, indeed, gotten through.

Partially it was because people like Deng Pufang and Prince Tomohito cared enough to become deeply involved. We even met the prince's cousins, Crown Prince Akihito and Princess Michiko, who expressed great interest in the project. But mainly I think because the people could see us giving it everything and asking them for nothing but a willingness to listen and become aware of the problems, daily battles and potential of people who, in so many parts of the world, had been ignored or pushed aside.

Amanda, Nancy and Mike had left Japan a week early and gone back to Vancouver to see Expo. Clyde Smith, a good friend from Vancouver, was in as a replacement physio. He must have gotten awfully tired of me mooning around saying how much I missed Amanda.

Ah, well, we were off for Miami. Amanda would rejoin us there. And from there, we'd make the last run for home.

11

"Doin' it for the b'y."

*S*eventeen months, three days and thirty-three countries from the day it banged its way out of the Oakridge shopping centre in Vancouver, the Man in Motion tour was back in Canada—leaner now, and tougher. Beneath the smiles and waves was a commando unit, fit and ready for the final push.

There had been casualties. Tim Frick was gone, and now Lee Gibson, who left in New York for personal reasons. The survivors simply pulled the walls in tighter. "We worked the bugs out coming up the coast from Miami," Mike Reid says. "We knew in Canada we'd have to be pro, and by the time we got there, we were."

There were new troops: Simon Cumming, Mike and Amanda Reid's cousin and a veteran of the Up With People tour of the U.S. and Europe, started by doing the advance work for the wheel up the east coast. Rico Bondi, who had been working on the cross-Canada reccy since July of 1985 as well as in the Vancouver office, joined the road crew full time as it reached Newfoundland. Mike "The Mechanic" Pomponi would come aboard in his native Hamilton to maintain the vehicles through the winter months. Derrick Hill—the Maytag Man, they called him—was a Kinsman with the loneliest job on the tour, crossing Canada a day or so in advance, co-ordinating the sale of Man in Motion merchandise with local Kinsmen and selling it himself out of a crammed motor home. Derrick had worked out of a basement as co-ordinator of Terry Fox's run, but had never had a chance to run with him. For him, seeing this tour through to the end was a special, personal commitment.

In the beginning, the four were of the team but not part of the team. Again, the war analogy. Until they'd been blooded, new troops were always viewed with suspicion.

"Everybody was nice," Rico Bondi recalls. "But when it came to doing something to help, it was like I wasn't there. They'd been out so long, had the routine so firmly locked into place, that asking to help was like an intrusion. Then, gradually, I was absorbed into the unit. And you know something? Later on, when The Mechanic joined us, I treated him exactly the same way. Because now I was part of the team, and he was an outsider."

For weeks now, they'd been hearing that Canada was going to be big, that the whole country had turned Man in Motion crazy. "Great," they said. But they didn't count on it. If they'd learned one thing on the road, it was to hope for the best and prepare for the worst. Far too often, it had saved their necks.

The No. 1 priority had always been awareness. Even in the half-dozen or so countries where fund raising was a main part of the focus, they had met with dismal results. After a slow start, the awareness program had built to become an enormous success. But they knew that wouldn't cut any ice with the critics, some of whom were already coming out of the woodwork to write the tour off as "a media circus." Awareness was difficult to define or measure in terms of success. Money was an easy way of keeping score. The knockers would take two unrelated figures and hang them out side by side:

Coming into Canada, the tour that was budgeted at $1.5 million and set a fund-raising target of $10 million had raised $174,000. If Canada didn't come through, the tour would be perceived in many places as a failure. And for all their brave talk, for all the excitement of coming home, the crew had mental fingers crossed.

"I was beginning to wonder whether the response at home would be like the brass bands in the U.S.," Mike Reid says. "You know—always going to happen in the next town, but never ever there."

They were too far away to hear the sound of the fiddles. Up ahead in Newfoundland, the easternmost Canadians were tuning up . . .

Her name was Debbie Prim, and after about thirty seconds with her, you didn't notice that she was in a wheelchair. She'd sweep up, stick out her hand and say, "Hi. Debbie Prim. Polio, '62. How are you?" And that was out of the way.

At age twenty-seven, Debbie was chairperson of the tour's Newfoundland organizing committee, one of many such groups for the disabled for whom she laboured. She'd also been a medal winner at the National Wheelchair Games in Vancouver in 1973, attended other NWG events in 1976, 1977 and 1978, and the Pan-American Games for the Disabled in Halifax in 1982. She'd been chairman of the Newfoundland organizing committee for the Year of the Disabled, winner of the Newfoundland Disabled Person of the Year award for 1980. All these things were spare-time activities away from her job with the Royal Newfoundland Constabulary as a PBX operator.

She was, in short, a person who accepted her disability as a factor in her life, not a deterrent. "I had a bout with polio when I was two," she quipped. "That's what they call it, a bout with polio. Well, I'm still having a bout with polio." She hadn't beaten it, but she'd wrestled it to a draw, and as I looked around the podium at Cape Speare, Newfoundland, at the reception she'd done so much to organize, I couldn't help but think how much she stood for what our tour was all about.

It was beautiful out there. The easternmost point in Canada, and in many ways it could have been a century ago. The Atlantic waves pounded on the rocks behind us. Off to one side stood a lighthouse that's been in use since 1841. The job of lighthouse keeper has been handed down, father to son, for 141 years.

Up on the podium, three generations of fiddlers offered entertainment for civic, provincial and federal dignitaries, committee members, representatives of our corporate sponsors and a surprise visitor, mayor Ethel Winger from Williams Lake. Musicians Kelly Russell, who looked to be in his thirties, eleven-year-old Paddy Moran and a Newfoundland legend named Rufus Guinchard, age eighty-seven, played the "Traveller's Reel," a number Rufus had written in 1930.

It made a wonderful picture: Rufus, holding the bow up in the middle in the old-fashioned way, sitting there keeping time with both feet going like a clog-dancer's; out front, the flags and Man in Motion pennants whipping in the wind; the 325-foot-long telegram from Vancouver containing 41,080 signatures—and down in the crowd, my old friend and competitor Mel Fitzgerald, one of the finest athletes I've ever known.

We'd be starting out the next day, and we knew the toughest part of the tour lay ahead. But we were back in Canada, sitting in a nice, friendly time capsule with some of the nicest people you'd ever want to meet. Work was for tomorrow—and hey, tomorrow I'd be twenty-nine years old!

The trip up the coast from Miami had been eventful if not lucrative and, in a sense, ironic. Finally, on the delayed last leg of our trip through their country, the Americans were becoming aware that we were there.

We'd done the "Today" show, met New York mayor Ed Koch and Burnaby actor Michael J. Fox, just about the hottest thing on TV through his work on the "Family Ties" series, and been guests at a luncheon hosted by Ken Taylor, the Canadian ambassador to Iran who'd become a hero in America through his protection of U.S. citizens there during the hostage crisis. We'd had a private tour of the United Nations building, and held a press conference with the U.N.

media. In Boston I'd had lunch with my hero, Bobby Orr, who presented me with one of his No. 4 hockey jerseys (which I proudly wore later as we wheeled into his home town of Parry Sound, Ontario). In Bar Harbor, Maine, we'd completed our three-hundredth wheeling day—our last day in the U.S.

But now we were in the final country—our country—about to find out if what people had been telling me since Day One of the tour was true. "You'll get moral support everywhere else," they kept saying. "But if the money side of it is going to happen, it won't happen until you get back into Canada."

I believed that. What other choice did I have? But in the back of my mind I thought a little miracle would be nice. And we got one.

As we'd pulled out of Cape Speare after the welcoming ceremony the day before, a girl named Leslie Tomblin had ridden up on her bike. She was from Vancouver, now two years a Newfie, and she had a suggestion.

"You're missing donations," she said. "The motor home pulls away before people realize. Would you mind if I came out and rode behind you tomorrow? I could put a donation bucket on the back of the bike and pick up the money."

"Sure," we said. "Go ahead."

She was there early the next morning, two of those round cardboard ice cream containers strapped behind the seat of her bike under a DONATIONS sign, a packsack on her back. And off we went, first to St. John's for receptions, then out onto the highway.

In mid-afternoon, Leslie pulled the bike up beside the lead escort car, where tour people were also taking donations pressed through the window.

"Can I put my pack in your van?" she asked.

"What's in it?"

"Money," she said faintly. "The cartons kept filling and I didn't want to stop. So I kept reaching back and emptying them into the pack. Now it's full, and . . ."

The pack was transferred to the car. They weren't quite sure what to do with it. Up till then there'd been no problem because the volume of donations had never been that high. Now we had the money Leslie had gathered, plus what had been picked up by the escort car and poked through the window of the motor home. Obviously, the white wooden box with the slot in the top was no longer big enough. So we dumped it in a big green garbage bag.

We handed the bag to Muriel Honey, our PR person out from Vancouver, and to Jim Taylor, who had joined us to work on the book. They drove back to the Newfoundlander hotel in St. John's, took it into Muriel's room, and dumped it on the bed.

166

There was so much it spilled out onto the floor. Giggling madly, they set about counting it. It took an hour, and the total left lumps in their throats. Dollar bills: 351. Two-dollar bills: 162. Five-dollar bills: 154. Ten-dollar bills: 51. Twenty-dollar bills: 31. Fifty-dollar bills: four. Plus $1,890 in cheques, $22.90 in change, $13 in U.S. funds, three Newfoundland buttons, a religious charm on a chain, and a motel key.

Total from one green garbage bag containing the love and respect and hard-earned dollars of a small part of a province in which so many people live near the poverty level: $4,700.90.

But dollar figures could never tell the story of what had happened that day along the hilly roads from St. John's through Topsail, Foxtrap, Kelligrewe, Upper Gullies and Seal Cove to Holyrood. What happened was that people living in a province with a twenty-five per cent unemployment rate came out with crumpled bills, an Atlantic salmon, blueberry muffins and seven home-made birthday cakes. Kids on crutches waited on the roadside to wave or hobble over with a birthday card or a quarter.

We knew by now that incredible things were starting to happen at the political and corporate level. At a mid-day birthday party in St. John's, there'd been a $10,000 cheque from Premier Brian Peckford. Company employees were collecting in the office—trucking companies, banks, oil companies, Revenue Canada.

And Ronald McDonald.

McDonald's restaurants had been supportive of the tour from the beginning through western vice-president Ron Marcoux of Vancouver. Then George Cohon, president of McDonald's Canada, saw me on the "Today" show and was so impressed by the interview that he called Marcoux from Toronto. "What are we doing for this kid?" he asked. "I think we should really get involved."

That call triggered a commitment from McDonald's to raise a minimum $250,000 in Canada, the first installment being a cheque for $4,500 presented by Mr. Cohon in St. John's, representing $1 for every Big Mac sold in the area during a special drive. But it wasn't just the money. Ron and George made a personal commitment to support the tour in any way they could. Ronald was at so many functions somebody called me the McMan in McMotion.

In under two days the people of Newfoundland raised and donated $97,387.93. Still, what touched me most were gifts of another kind—lasting gifts like ramped corner sidewalks and wheelchair ramps like the one up to the entrance of city hall in South Conception Bay, still unpainted, so new that the pitch was oozing out of the wood. It had been planned for a long time, but there was no money.

167

When they heard I'd be stopping, they built it through volunteer labour.

We didn't know it then, but it was to be like that all through the province and the Maritimes: people without much giving what they could, lining the roads to give it. And where there could be no money, a wheelchair ramp to a store or civic building previously inaccessible.

During the stop at South Conception Bay, one of the policemen in our escort was asked how it could happen this way.

"Well," he said thoughtfully, "when Terry Fox came he was just startin', and Newfoundland didn't do him well. We did a little better with Steve Fonyo, but he was just startin', too.

"But the b'y, Rick, has come three-quarters of the way around the world. How could anyone let him go home without showin' him we care? That's what this is all about: We're doin' it for the b'y."

On September 30 I arrived in Petitcodiac, New Brunswick, around supper time after a 50-mile wheel, flopped on my bed in the motel, flipped on the TV set, and found out that Amanda and I were engaged.

Well, we knew that, but nobody else was supposed to know. We hadn't even told our parents. But there was this lady on TV, saying that a tour spokesperson had announced that we were engaged! I lunged for the telephone and called the office in Vancouver. Not unexpectedly, the people there were trying to phone me. The conversation got a little bit hectic.

"Rick! There's a story on the wire that says . . ."

"There's a lady on TV here who says we're . . ."

"That you and Amanda are engaged and . . ."

"Who's this 'tour spokesperson'? Who would make an announcement like that without . . ."

"And it's on the wire and all these reporters are phoning and we don't know anything, and . . ."

"Wait a minute! You mean you didn't make any . . . ?"

"You mean you didn't tell anyone that . . . ?"

"*No!*"

"*No!*"

"Well then, how . . ."

I slumped back onto the bed. Sure, we were engaged. We almost always knew we would be, eventually. I'd even bought the ring back in Raleigh, North Carolina. It had taken some juggling.

I hadn't carried any money—none—since the day we left Vancouver. There was no need. Every minute of the day when I wasn't wheeling I had someone with me, usually Amanda, who'd look after and record the day-to-day expenses. Obviously, I couldn't ask

Amanda for the kind of money necessary to buy a ring. I borrowed it from the tour "float" fund and paid it back later with money from my account at home. Then I deliberately started a fight with Amanda so I could storm out of the room and get away from her, and asked Mike to come with me while I shopped for a new scope sight for my rifle because they were cheaper in the U.S. Instead, we hit a jewellery store and bought the ring—a gold band with a single diamond set among four square-cut diamonds. I'd kept it secret from everyone but Mike, and left the ring in his care until the right moment.

There was no rush to give the ring to Amanda. Originally we'd planned to wait until the tour was over. We knew what we had, and it wouldn't change just because we weren't engaged. But on September 29, in Shediac, New Brunswick, in a suite in the Neptune Motel obviously designed for romance, over a fine dinner with the perfect white wine and the stereo playing softly in the background, I popped the question and gave her the ring.

And now, less than twenty-four hours later, it was on TV and the wire service? How in blazes . . . ?

I grabbed the phone again. Maybe it wasn't too late.

"Hello, Dad? Amanda and I are engaged."

"I know. One of the guys at work told me. He heard it on the radio."

"Oh. Well, I better phone Brad. He'll . . ."

"He knows. He phoned to tell me."

"Oh."

Amanda made the same kind of calls to her folks, and got the same answers. So much for the quiet engagement.

In checking out of the Neptune Motel, we'd quietly thanked the manager for the great service and mentioned to him that we'd never forget the place because it was where we got engaged. As we heard it later, a member of the Maritimes organizing committee overheard us. He worked for a radio station. Bingo.

I guess we were kind of naive. We hadn't planned to make it a big secret. We figured if anyone noticed the ring on her finger, we'd say yes, we were engaged. For us it was a big deal. But with so many great things happening with the tour, with the response through the Maritimes so magnificent, of what interest could it possibly be to anyone else?

Wrong again. I guess everyone loves a love story. Like it or not—and we didn't, particularly—The Rick and Amanda Romance had become a big deal across the land.

We'd already grown tired of answering The Big Question, thrown from all angles: "Uh, Amanda, we were just wondering, you know, with Rick being paraplegic and everything . . . well, uh, can he . . . ? Do you . . . ? I mean . . . ?"

It was something they wouldn't let go. The simple, truthful answers—"Yes, we do want children. No, there's no reason why we shouldn't be able to have any. Disabled people are like anyone else: some can, and some can't—and, incidentally, do you ask able-bodied people questions like that?"—apparently weren't good enough.

We didn't have much private life. What we had, we fought to protect. When it got to that point, our stock answer was, "That's personal. Let's talk about the tour."

And the tour was exploding.

Remember the wave I'd visualized, way back when we were struggling through Washington? Vancouver had begun the wave. Newfoundland was the second section, the spark that ignited the stadium. Nova Scotia picked it up, Prince Edward Island jumped in, Quebec got involved, and by the time we hit Ontario, eastern Canada was one big stadium, rocking to the beat of "St. Elmo's Fire" and the message of Man in Motion.

I couldn't begin to list the things that happened, the different responses we on the streets, at the receptions and in the dozens of schools, rehab centres and hospitals we visited along the way. They came so quickly there was barely time to react before we got hit by another one.

Simon turned up in Sydney, Nova Scotia, to do the advance work—and found himself holding $26,000 in money and cheques, already collected. He was so worried about having it in his possession overnight that he dropped everything in a green garbage bag, put it in the bathroom of his motel room, then stayed up half the night fretting over it. The next morning he was a half-hour down the road in the van before he realized he'd left the bag at the motel.

"Garbage bag," he groaned as he turned the van and floored it. "Maids throw out garbage bags. They throw them down the shoot into the incinera . . . Omigod!"

He got there in time. If he hadn't, he'd likely just have kept on driving till he hit the ocean.

In Truro, Nova Scotia, Mike kept telling the policeman in charge of the escort that he didn't have enough men. The guy insisted he did. What the heck, the town population wasn't more than 12,000. "You let us handle it, son," he said.

"Right," Mike said resignedly. That afternoon 10,000 people jammed the parking lot leading to the band shell where I was to speak. The police did their best, but crowd control was impossible.

"I guess you were right," the policeman said.

"Right," said Mike.

You couldn't blame the policeman. Mike had been in China. He'd seen crowds of thousands. The local police had no reason to expect anything that huge. And this young guy who wasn't even a policeman was telling them how they should be doing things? No way.

It was a lesson well learned, and passed along. Traffic and crowd control, security and police escorts don't just happen. They're the result of hours and days of careful planning and co-operation. We had the best, and the police seemed to like us—partly, I think, because of the hats.

Every provincial or district police branch has a hat featuring its own logo on the front. I made it a point to get the proper one as soon as we were turned over to another branch, and wear it as long as we were with them. It became a tour tradition, and something that seemed to make us honorary members of the police family wherever we went.

Mike was our security chief. He was the one with the walkie-talkie, riding beside me or going on ahead, keeping in touch with the police and our various vehicles. But in the newspapers and on TV he was always referred to as "Rick Hansen's bodyguard," probably because of his size, his thick black moustache, and his junior hockey upbringing, which had taught him that when pushed, you push back. Like all of us, though, he had to pick up a little diplomacy and public relations polish. He showed us in Montreal how well the lessons were sinking in.

The photographers were jamming around me, fighting for angles. One guy was being particularly obnoxious. Twice, Mike asked him to stay back. The second time, he gave Mike a shove as he went by. Hockey instinct took over. Mike gave him a half shove, half punch that got him out of the way. Ah, but then the PR instincts took over.

Mike knew that the guy would turn his camera on him, trying for a shot of the big bully security man. By the time he had the camera up, Mike had already picked out a little kid in the crowd and was leaning over him, smiling and laughing and asking him what he thought of the tour. Fortunately, the guy gave up. Mike would have stayed there till he ran out of film.

We're a bilingual country, and I'd tried hard to prepare for the tour's time in Quebec, dusting off my grade eleven and grade twelve French, and working with Amanda to pull it up to the point where it was at least passable. André Viger, Quebec's own hero and wheelchair marathon champion, was our ambassador there, meeting me at the border and wheeling with me. But the language differences definitely affected our situation in Quebec. All our written information had been

171

sent out in French, but there'd been very little in the way of advance PR. We had to build momentum from scratch. It happened, but by the time it did, it was almost time for us to leave.

I suppose almost everyone in Canada knows that Prime Minister Brian Mulroney presented me with a cheque for $1 million outside the Parliament Buildings in Ottawa. Most of the newspapers ran the picture, me holding a Kinsmen donations bucket, the prime minister dropping it in. "The $1 Million Drop in the Bucket," they called it.

They were right, but they didn't know the half of it.

I'd said good-bye to André in Hull, Quebec, and wheeled across the bridge into Ottawa on Friday, October 23, smack into one of the busiest and most satisfying three days on the tour.

Saturday began with a trip to a community centre to speak in a gym packed with Brownies, Scouts and Cubs, then to a rink where the kids were playing sledge hockey, a great winter sport for disabled youngsters. The kids ride sleds that look like cut-down versions of the old Flexible Flyers, and carry sticks with points or picks at one end to jab into the ice and push off for propulsion. When they get to the puck, they reverse the stick and hit it with the other end. For kids who can't manage that part of it, there are two-seater sleds, allowing a friend or relative to do the pushing while the youngster plays the game. They really go at it, and it takes a lot of skill to manoeuvre the sleds because they have no brakes. To stop, you fall off—something that wasn't explained to the media types who took part in a race of their own and kept running into the boards.

Then it was back to the hotel for a march to the Parliament Buildings, complete with thousands of people, reporters, TV cameras—and yes, a marching band. That's where the fun started.

The prime minister had phoned me when we were in Newfoundland to tell me that the government would donate $1 million whenever and wherever we wanted it. He'd fly out and present it the next day on the road if I thought it best. I gulped and thanked him for both the donation and his consideration. Later we decided that Ottawa would be the ideal place for it to happen.

The ceremony took place outside the buildings. Right away I knew I was in trouble: my chair was on a hill. Either I held a wheel with one hand, or took off. The second thing I noticed was that Kinsmen flags and buckets were everywhere. Well, they were doing the fund raising, but I thought it looked a shade too commercial for a ceremony like this. So, I put my other hand around the bucket in my lap to cover the Kinsmen sign.

I was doing fine through the speeches. Then the prime minister tried to hand me the cheque.

Well, I'd run out of hands. So he held the cheque up to the crowd, then dropped it into the bucket. It was great theatre, great politics, a great camera shot. For us, it couldn't have been better. We shook hands, the crowd dispersed, and we headed back to the hotel.

What we didn't know was that, as we were leaving, one of the prime minister's aides rightly thought that a donation bucket was no place to leave a $1 million cheque. So he reached in and took it out. The only thing he didn't do was tell anybody.

A few minutes later, Muriel Honey and Jim Taylor are wandering back to the hotel when the aide rushes up, holds out the cheque and says, "Muriel, what should I do with this?"

They look at it for a moment: one million bucks. Briefly, they discuss Acapulco. Then Muriel takes charge of it and they walk into the hotel lobby—where Kinsmen are frantically pawing through buckets and muttering:

"It's got to be here somewhere! You don't just lose a $1 million cheque!"

Muriel walks over, waving the cheque.

"Looking for this, boys?" she asks.

The cheque meant more than money. It meant that the prime minister and the government were committed to the Man in Motion project and what it stood for. There was further evidence that night, when we were guests of honour at a fund-raising "roast" of transport minister John Crosbie.

During intermission I was able to have a quiet meeting with Mr. Mulroney in his room. He took off his jacket, relaxed, and we had an interesting, casual conversation.

Then I brought out my little piece of paper. "I hope I'm not being presumptuous, sir," I said, "but there are some issues about disabled persons in this country that I'd like to discuss."

His eyebrows shot up for a second. "Of course," he said, and we got down to it until it was time to return to the dinner.

Look, the tour was opening doors. It was my job to get through them and have the issues heard. There might never be another opportunity like it.

During our stay in Ontario I also met with federal sports minister Otto Jelinek, Secretary of State David Crombie, Ontario premier David Peterson and other government officials—often with representatives of organizations for disabled persons—and obtained commitments that the problems of the disabled would be pursued with new vigour—not just during the tour, but on an ongoing basis.

Mr. Jelinek, for instance, promised to ensure that disabled athletes in Canada were recognized as athletes and allowed to take their rightful place in the athletic world. He also promised to pursue the International Olympic Committee regarding our dream of getting at least two wheelchair events into the Olympiad—one in the summer games, one in the winter—not as demonstration or exhibition sports, but on equal footing with the rest.

Mr. Peterson expressed great interest in a program we'd developed, along with the Canadian Dairy Bureau, in which able-bodied children would be educated as to the potential of the disabled, and made aware of the barriers in society. Ideally it would be built into the elementary school curriculum across the country, giving able-bodied and disabled kids a better chance to interact. If there is to be progress, then the training must start at that level, where attitudes are formed among those who'll someday shape the country.

It wasn't a part of the tour that got a lot of publicity. ("You've blown it, Rick," wrote a lady from Nova Scotia who was herself in a wheelchair. "You're not doing anything but trying to raise money.")

That just wasn't true. Unfortunately, when it came to the tour, the media were more interested in the sizzle than the steak.

Promoting awareness is always a hard sell. There are too many terms, too many definitions. Sometimes I have trouble keeping track of them myself. Am I "physically challenged?" Am I "special?" "Handicapped?" "Disabled?" Am I an "invalid?" A "cripple?" A "gimp?"

People get caught up in the terminology. It's easier to give money. You make the donation, watch the papers and TV, see the fund raising go up, feel good about what you've done.

Yet, giving money can't create awareness. I've known people who've worked for and donated to worthy causes for years, and their awareness level hasn't changed one bit. But an awareness and a greater understanding can and will provide the knowledge of the need for funds, and how those funds can make a difference.

Okay, you say, define awareness.

For the Man in Motion tour, awareness meant being a catalyst for good things to happen in a community, to help remove barriers— physical or those erected by social attitudes.

We were trying to be a messenger, to let people know that no matter what the form of physical disability—loss of limb, blindness, cerebral palsy, paralysis—everyone has hopes and dreams. And that my dream of wheeling around the world was no more significant than the dream of someone trying to make the long journey from a hospital bed to an electric wheelchair and thus lead a more independent life.

I wasn't trying to be a physical role model for disabled persons. It would be wrong for me to be one. We were trying to provide an illustration that all disabled persons must struggle every day in pursuit of a normal life and that, as with the tour, amazing things can happen once those obstacles are removed.

Awareness isn't just about helping people with spinal cord injuries. If a town has no one in a wheelchair, but ten blind persons, you don't launch a program to ramp sidewalks, you do something to ease the burdens of blindness.

And that brings us back to definitions, and two that might help ease the confusion:

My disability is that I cannot use my legs. My handicap is your negative perception of that disability, and thus of me.

The tour rolled on. In villages, towns and cities we drew crowds beyond our wildest expectations. In Belleville, Ontario, we passed the 20,000-mile mark, the last major milestone. From now on the measuring stick would be provincial borders—and there were only four of them left! In Napanee, thousands waited for hours in the rain just to cheer us in. We were like a snowball rolling downhill now, picking up people and media with every roll.

There must have been 100,000 people lining the streets of Toronto, and another 10,000 at the reception in Nathan Phillips Square. Gazing over the upturned faces, I couldn't help but think of Terry, and how he'd felt, standing where I now sat. Before the visit was over we'd joined rock star Bryan Adams on the nationally televised Juno Awards (presenting the group-of-the-year award to Honeymoon Suite) and attended two major fund raisers: an invitation-only $5,000-per-couple dinner co-hosted by Ontario premier David Peterson, the Honourable John B. Aird and George Cohon in the McDonald Building, and a $200-a-plate, black-tie Man in Motion tribute dinner that drew a sellout crowd of fifteen hundred. David Foster and John Parr—whom I finally got to meet—came in for that one, bringing with them the background tracks that allowed them full-orchestra sound as they brought down the house with "St. Elmo's Fire."

It couldn't have been better. But my scheduled nine-day rest in Toronto had evaporated under the heat of events to a single day. I was dead tired, and in the back of my mind I knew that the toughest challenge still lay ahead: northern Ontario and the prairies, in the dead of winter. In spite of myself, I shivered at the thought.

175

We'd tried to think of every eventuality as we planned for the assault on Canada's winter.

We put Brian Rose in charge of the winter project, gave him a near-impossible deadline, and he met it. We had specially designed clothing, some it made of an experimental material the Japanese hadn't yet put on the market. Friends of mine like Chris Sammis and Lennie Marriott—wearing "I was a Guinea Pig For Rick Hansen" T-shirts underneath—had tested it in the cold room at Simon Fraser University's department of kinesiology.

Lennie also road tested a special winter chair co-designed by Pete Turno and another friend named Gerry Smith in Florida. The Ford motor company provided us with additional vehicles. Honda provided an all-terrain vehicle so someone could ride along beside me, or get out for help should we ever be trapped on a wilderness road. We even had a piece of electronic equipment hooked into sensors that would run to areas on my legs and flash warnings if the temperature fell near the danger point. Otherwise, with no feeling in my legs, they could easily freeze without my knowing it, and I'd be bucking for amputation.

We had all these scientific wonders—but we didn't have a cure for the flu.

It began with a sore throat around Oakville as we continued a long, meandering route through Ontario in order to pick up those "lost" miles we'd so carefully listed in Europe and Asia. The next day I was hacking and wheezing and on antibiotics. By the time we hit London, the flu had settled into my chest and my right shoulder was acting up. We'd learned a hard lesson in Europe about pushing on regardless in that situation. We took three days off in Sudbury—three days in which the weather was perfect. The day we resumed wheeling, we went right into the teeth of a blizzard.

The winds were in my face, the snow falling so thickly it was almost a whiteout. It took better than twelve hours to do our 50 miles. At one point the Ontario police diverted us from the main road as a safety precaution, which made things even tougher. With more clinging snow, the push rims iced up, it was difficult to get a grip, and my hands were so cold they began to spasm.

But in a way, I was glad. Mother Nature had thrown her best shot, and we'd survived. The next day she let up on the cold, gave us tail winds, and we had our scheduled 40 miles in the bank by just after lunch. Maybe she's a nice old lady after all.

In Sudbury we met the Mayors in Motion—six mayors from the city and nearby municipalities who'd vowed to spend one full working

Top: Crossing the last border, Hansen wheels out of Alberta and into B.C. and home. "Just think," Amanda cried. "We're in the 604 area code!"

Bottom: Among those waiting to welcome Rick at the border was his mother, Joan.

Top: The Man in Motion crew follows the leader over the Alberta-B.C. border. Left to right: Simon Cumming, Lee Gibson, Don Alder, Nancy Thompson, Amanda Reid, Mike Reid, Mike Pomponi, Tim Frick, Rico Bondi.

Bottom: Amanda and Rick look ahead to the finish of the tour.

Tim Pelling

Tim Pelling

Top: All but lost in a forest of microphones, Hansen fields the No. 1 question from media across the country. "Yes, it does feel great to be home."

Bottom: His wheelchair athlete honour guard rolling proudly alongside, Rick Hansen covers the final miles to the cheers of thousands in downtown Vancouver.

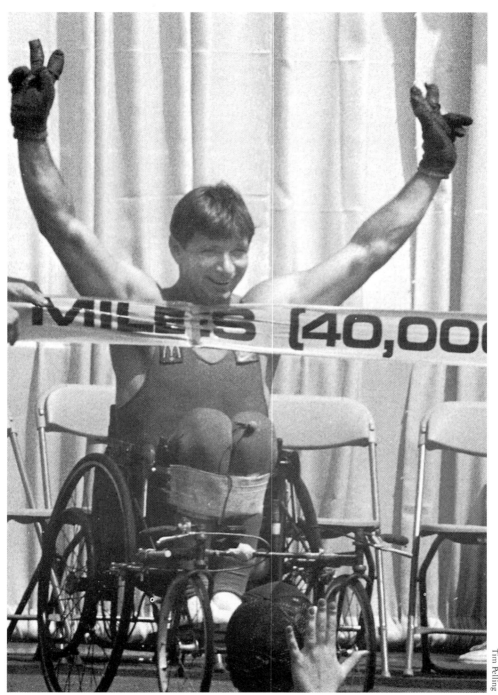

Twenty-six months plus one day and 24,901.55 miles later, Rick Hansen breaks the final, symbolic tape. At last, the journey is ended.

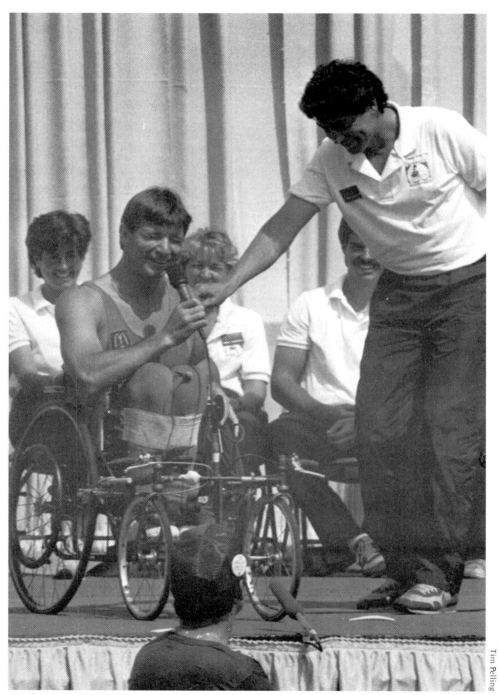

Don Alder, the lifelong friend who was with him in the accident that changed his life, obliges Hansen with a just-in-case pinch.

FLASHCARDS

YAMAHA

A crew for all seasons. Front, left to right: Nancy Thompson, Rick, Amanda. Back, left to right: Rico Bondi, Derrick Hill, Mike Reid, Simon Cumming, Don Alder.

Previous page: Led by David Foster and John Parr (inset), whose "little piece of music" became the theme for Man in Motion, B.C. throws a party for a hero come home.

day in a wheelchair to gain a better understanding of the problem. They learned a lot, particularly about access.

Naturally, there were reporters and cameramen all around when one of the mayors decided he had to go to the bathroom. He crashed his chair through the door to the public washroom. There was no wheelchair-size cubicle. He could get the chair in—but he couldn't turn it, or even close the door. There was a lot of crashing and smashing and eventually he got out. But he still hadn't gone to the bathroom.

We spent our second Christmas on the road in a log cabin unit of a motel in Wa Wa, Ontario, complete with kitchen, fireplace and a gorgeous view of a winter wonderland which I could stare at while nursing my bladder infection. "I can see the headline now," Taylor chortled over the phone from Vancouver. "Rick Can't Go Wee-wee in Wa Wa."

On the morning of December 23, the stomach cramps and headaches had been so bad a doctor was brought out to check me on the roadway. He sent me straight to hospital in Wa Wa. All the old anxieties and doubts about injuries and what they could do to the tour came zooming up from the back of my mind for reruns. I'd been thinking a lot about Terry Fox as we drew closer to the place where he'd had to end his Marathon of Hope. Naturally it spooked me when I developed this problem so close to that spot. Had I pushed too far? Should I have taken the full nine days of rest in Toronto? What was it —and could it come back? Would it stop me?

The media circled like sharks, and we took extra care not to make any comment or allow any pictures or interviews until we knew for certain what the problem was.

The hospital verdict: bladder infection. Treatment: antibiotics and rest. Merry Christmas.

We had a real Christmas tree, all kinds of presents from people we knew and people we didn't, tons of mail, and a fabulous dinner cooked by Nancy and Amanda, served in the biggest cabin with chairs brought in from the others. Then everyone hit the phones and called home. But in spite of the wonderful setting, I couldn't enjoy it because of the punishment from the infection. New Year's Eve was quiet, too—the crew off to the curling club dance in Terrace Bay, Amanda and I staying in the hotel to see the New Year in on TV and count our blessings and our memories.

Oh, we'd had our troubles. There'd been times when we didn't know how long we could go on—or if. We were in hill country and I was wheeling in 20-below-zero weather. But we were sitting there knowing the Legacy Fund now stood at $5 million, knowing that the awareness message was getting through—and knowing that next Christmas and New Year's Eve we'd be in our own home, surrounded by our own things, and starting a new life together.

Show me a better New Year's Eve than that.

There was one more highlight in Ontario, a special one for me that I'd hoped to keep private and media-free: a stop at the monument outside Thunder Bay, at the spot where Terry had to end his Marathon of Hope.

I'd made one of my naive little requests that the stop be kept secret, that I'd like a few moments alone with my friend. What happened? Someone on our staff told the media that I'd be there, but wanted privacy. They carried the story and people turned out by the hundreds, pressing in against the restraining rope, cameras popping.

I found it difficult to control myself. I wanted to concentrate on just being there. Instead, I had to try to do that while not losing my grip on my emotions in front of all those people and the TV cameras. I stayed only long enough to look at the statue, read the inscription, and send a silent message. Wherever he was up there, he'd know.

12

"... All I need is a pair of wheels."

By now the wave had reached tidal proportions, and despite the prairies and the mountains ahead, Rick Hansen seemed certain to ride it clear to Vancouver. The Man in Motion tour had the country in the palm of its hand.

The Legacy Fund had topped $5 million as he left Ontario. The dream of reaching $10 million — a figure more or less pulled out of the hat in the pre-takeoff days of 1985 — didn't seem merely attainable now; there was a growing suspicion that Hansen, who'd based his life on setting seemingly unreachable goals, may have underestimated.

Still, there were critics. The words "slick" and "circus" began to appear in newspaper articles — which made the crew laugh, considering the frantic, day-to-day, seat-of-the-pants manner by which the tour progressed and survived. "Slick?" Don Alder scoffed. "What tour are they following?"

The CBC's "Fifth Estate" ran a national TV show in which some disabled persons questioned the long-range value of the project. One of those interviewed was a Sydney, Nova Scotia, journalist named Peter Kavanagh, who suffered with a twisted hip and had already published one article in the Globe and Mail *bemoaning such "stunts" and suggesting that "neither the able-bodied nor the disabled really benefit from Mr. Hansen's campaign."*

"I want Rick Hansen to stop what he's doing," Kavanagh told "Fifth Estate." "If he's doing it for me, if he's doing it for other disabled people, if he's doing it for spinal cord victims, stop it! Who wants him to do this? We didn't ask him to do this!"

Hansen could only shake his head. "Fifth Estate" had interviewed him. He'd answered all the questions raised by the show. His answers wound up on the cutting room floor. The program was in no sense a balanced discussion. No one was interviewed from the Canadian Para-

plegic Association, the umbrella group for perhaps 90 per cent of the country's disabled; only those from small, anti-tour groups. Among all the spinal cord injured persons interviewed, only one seemed to have any real sense of what was happening: a teen-age girl in a wheelchair, interviewed as the tour passed by. "He makes me feel good about myself," she said.

"Hatchet job," snapped Cam Tait, a cerebral palsy victim wheelchairbound for life. As a reporter for the Edmonton Journal he'd followed the tour closely since its inception, and travelled with it several times.

"Listen, I've had parents come and snatch their children from in front of me because my voice is strange and my arms wave around a lot. I've had other children laugh at me. That's not an easy thing to accept. Rick has changed that. In Newfoundland, I saw parents running down the highway with their children, trying to get a handshake or an autograph. And the kids? They love him. You think that isn't going to make a difference?"

There was a sad sort of irony to the "Fifth Estate" telecast. Hansen wanted the tour to foster national discussion. Because of the tour, "Fifth Estate" had done the show. Because the show was controversial, it triggered response around the country on radio, TV and in newspapers. Had there been no tour, would the very groups who were knocking it ever had that kind of forum for their viewpoints? History said no.

The "circus" and "show biz" tags bothered Hansen, but they were out of his hands. The people had fallen in love with the tour. Despite continued efforts to downplay it, the Amanda-and-Rick romance had captured their imaginations. And Rick Hansen was a hero.

He'd tried to change the focus at the Man in Motion fund raiser in Toronto. He was frazzled from tour appearances pressed upon him during what was to have been a nine-day break, weak from the oncoming flu. Some of those close to the tour were wondering if he could get through the evening, let alone make a speech. But he did, and as the applause washed over him, he added a final plea:

"I view this tour like trying to push a boulder up a steep hill," he said. "Lately, a lot of people have tried to take me from behind that boulder and set me on top of it, make something special out of me. I ask you: please *put me back behind the boulder, and let me try to push it a little bit further."*

His chin was almost on his chest as he wheeled wearily out of the ballroom. Behind him, the people were on their feet, applauding more loudly than ever. They knew and accepted what he'd said, but one part of the argument he was never going to win.

Like it or not, he was a hero. And the hero was coming home.

Of the dozens and dozens of calls we received during a seven-day layover in Winnipeg (three scheduled, four more to win a bout with flu), I most remember two.

The first came from a doctor at one of the hospitals we were scheduled to visit. He was worried about a patient, a boy named Kevin, maybe fourteen years old, who had a disease called Guillian Barre Syndrome, which attacks the spinal cord, can cause paralysis and makes regular breathing difficult. Kevin was in intensive care, on a respirator. Fortunately, the recovery rate is about 90 per cent—but mental attitude is one of the key factors in that recovery, and Kevin's wasn't good. Could I talk with him?

During the hospital visit I spent a few minutes with Kevin and laid it on the line: how a positive attitude was so necessary to keep me going on the tour, how much easier it made things when the going was at its worst, and how it was up to him to show the kind of fighter he was in getting rid of that respirator and going home as quickly as he could.

The second call came from the same doctor, just before we left Winnipeg. He said Kevin had undergone a complete turnaround, that he was out of the respirator, out of intensive care, and talking about going home.

Did the pep talk make a difference? I don't know. But *trying* to make that difference is what this tour is all about, and we had hundreds of letters—from both disabled and able-bodied persons—offering evidence that it was working. That's why, despite the cold, we came across the prairies chilled a bit on the surface but warm as toast inside.

It wasn't just a case of feeling the awareness and excitement growing. The farther west we came, the more we could *see* it. There were more curbs lowered for wheelchair accessibility, more pledges from companies to construct ramps in the workplace, more media interviews—in Winnipeg we set a Man in Motion record with eighteen interviews in one day—and, just as important, more signs that the media weren't going to turn away from the problems of the disabled once we'd passed through.

In Regina, for example, a reporter wrote a lengthy article in the *Leader-Post* after checking places like the post office, universities, hotels, the stadium, the hockey rink, downtown office buildings and the legislature, and grading them on accessibility. Included in that survey was the office of the *Leader-Post* itself. ("Too many heavy doors. Stairs at the front door. The washrooms don't provide for wheelchairs.") "If he wasn't the Man in Motion," the article stated, "if he was just a regular guy in a wheelchair, he'd spend a lot of time sneaking in the back doors of buildings like a common thief."

The reporter must have been reading my mind. Not about Regina in particular, but about developing a system to make certain that awareness and accessibility would be an ongoing concern in every community, all over the country. My idea was the establishment of an annual National Access Awareness Week, during which communities would study the local situation and give themselves a "report card" recognizing the improvements and initiatives of the previous year along with the people responsible, and identifying projects for the coming year. Slowly but surely, we could remove the barriers that society has erected.

Regina, for instance, could look back on 1987 with justifiable pride. Plans were announced for a city playground—to be named in my honour—that would be totally accessible to disabled children, including the blind. By touching a "guidance wall," they'd be able to read braille instructions as to what was in that area, and what was ahead as they followed the wall. And the nice part was, it wasn't a park for disabled children, it was a park designed so disabled and able-bodied kids could play together.

I'd spoken to the prime minister about such a week, and broached the subject to every provincial premier as we headed west. It was a matter of another kind of accessibility. I was in the right place at the right time. The suggestion was greeted warmly. Maybe we could pull it off, at that.

Near Kenora, Ontario, we'd had to use the sensors on my legs for the first and only time. Like the new winter clothing, they worked like a charm. And speaking of charms, somebody up there was looking after the weather for us. There were bad days, freezing, bitterly cold and snowy days, but over the prairie haul we got better weather than we'd been gearing ourselves to expect. "Maybe," I thought, "it's even-up time. Maybe this is for all the bad days and the rain and cold and wind in Europe."

Whatever it was, our timing was tremendous. We came into Regina in good weather. The afternoon of the day we left, the city was hit by a snowstorm so severe planes were grounded while we wheeled merrily on to Moose Jaw—stopping for a while to visit the Town in Motion, Saskatoon. When the people there heard we weren't going to visit, about two hundred of them packed and came down the highway to meet us, building a mock-up of the town in a field on the roadside. I wheeled into Swift Current in my shirtsleeves, it stormed all through our rest day, and the next morning we took off in warm weather. Somebody said it was like Moses parting the Red Sea.

We rode tail winds all the way across Saskatchewan to the next border, where Alberta premier Don Getty renewed a promise: his government would match, dollar for dollar, the total donations made in Alberta, with the government match staying in the province to support projects similar to those the Legacy Fund would be supporting elsewhere. The match turned out to be $2.45 million.

The route across the province had been "sold" for $100 per kilometre, the buyers putting up signs with their names on them. They made great reading. At K4, I saw the name Reg McClelland. I'd competed with and against him many times in wheelchair basketball, and No. 4 was his jersey number. And speaking of jersey numbers, we got to K99 and there it was: Wayne Gretzky.

Gretzky was also there to help me at an Edmonton Oilers' National Hockey League game (as Doug Risebrough did at a Flames game in Calgary) for puck-shooting competitions involving the mayors of the two cities. We shot from centre ice—one $10,000 shot for me, twenty shots for the mayor, all on the empty net. Every puck the mayor put in the net was worth $5,000 for Man in Motion, every miss $2,500.

I'd never shot a puck from a wheelchair before, but at that price I'd shoot all day. Besides, I was really pumped up. The day before, I'd seen the Rockies. And on the other side of them was Vancouver and home.

On the road between Calgary and Edmonton we found more gratifying evidence that the tour had crossed all cultural lines.

Mike Reno and Matt Frenette of the Vancouver-based rock group, Loverboy, flew in to present a cheque for $25,000. They'd been behind the tour from the start, and were always giving their support to worthwhile causes. Ron Minor, my friend and racing rival, was there to wheel with me. I had the opportunity to see Reg McClelland again, and Gary McPherson, Alberta's answer to Stan Stronge. The two of them had been instrumental in organizing the Alberta portion of the tour.

We stopped in at the Bowden Correctional Centre, where the inmates were excited about the tour. (Amanda appreciated the ball and chain they gave me. Always thinking ahead, that girl.) The institute had just been made wheelchair accessible, and we spoke with a disabled inmate, an accountant serving time for fraud.

At the Hobbema Indian Reserve, representatives of four Indian nations packed the gymnasium and showed that they, too, were caught up in the spirit of the tour. A tribal elder, tears running down his face, offered a prayer for us. They performed traditional dances in our honour, presented us with blankets, moccasins, gloves and $23,000 in donations, and made me an honorary member of the band.

As we left, they gave me an eagle feather. "For strength," they said, "and for power to make it through the mountains and home."

Two years less a day since we left Oakridge shopping centre full of hopes and dreams, and yes, a little bit scared, I was wheeling the final mile to the B.C. border. The temptation to break into a sprint was overwhelming.

We'd come a long way for this moment. There'd be hundreds of people up there, including my mother and father, whom I hadn't seen for two years, Brad, Christine, Cindy, uncles, aunts, cousins, friends and the newest addition to the family—my new baby niece, Brad and Shelly's daughter, Jenna.

The crew had been bouncing for the last couple of days. So there'd still be 2,000 miles to go. So it was some of the toughest terrain we'd face, with two more twists in and out of the Rockies, and long and killing hills. B.C. meant home, and we were almost there. Back in the motor home, Amanda put it all into perspective:

"Omigosh!" she said, her eyes moistening. "We're going to be in the 604 *area code!*"

My mother had a yellow band tied around her arm, a yellow ribbon on her lapel. Everywhere I looked there were yellow ribbons, yellow balloons, yellow armbands—all bearing the same message: WELCOME HOME, RICK. The sounds of "Tie a Yellow Ribbon 'Round the Old Oak Tree" blared out of the public address system. With the snow falling softly, there was an exciting, magical sort of quality to it.

In our situation, "coming home" had several definitions: home to B.C., home to Williams Lake, home to Vancouver where the journey had begun. But I know the instant it happened. "Hello, son," my mother said, giving me a big hug. "Welcome home." Nobody would say it better than that.

The stop at the border was actually quite brief. We'd come down the Yellowhead Highway (there's that colour again), rolled under the big banner marking the border, mounted a stage erected on the road-side and listened as the Alberta Man in Motion committee turned us over to their B.C. counterparts. Now it was time for the official welcome by Premier Bill Vander Zalm. I cocked both ears for that one. There was a lot riding on what he had to say.

We knew the provincial government would be adding a substantial donation to the Legacy Fund. We knew that donations by the people of B.C. might be a staggering total indeed. The question was, would the premier announce a flat donation, a matching grant arrangement such as that in Alberta, with the government's half supporting other projects similar to ours within the province—or would he shoot the works, match the B.C. contributions and give it all to the Legacy Fund?

It was a more-than-million-dollar question, and he came through with the answer we wanted. B.C.'s government would match B.C.'s people dollar for dollar from that moment until the tour ended, and he hoped it would cost him millions. As it turned out, it cost him $5.45 million.

And now we were wheeling down familiar roads. I knew what lay around every corner not because I had reccy and advance people and a map. I'd driven these roads a hundred times. Friends honked horns or stopped to say hello. I was in *my territory*. You have no idea how much difference that made.

The media were interested in one particular stretch of road in the Williams Lake area, the place where I'd had the accident. Did I go over it? No, it was 35 miles to the west. Did I think about it as we wheeled through the area? No. Did I ever think about what might have been, had the accident not happened? Yes, but not in the way they assumed.

I've travelled that stretch of road on fishing or hunting trips, or coming home for a holiday. I might look at it, but I don't dwell on it. This may be hard to understand, but it's the truth.

The accident shattered me at the time. I was fifteen years old, and I was going to spend the rest of my life in a wheelchair. There's been a continual struggle since then, a lot of physical and emotional adjustments, a great deal of pain. But if I had a choice right now to erase all of it, to start over again hitchhiking home from a fishing trip with Don in the back of that pickup truck and not have that accident happen; if I could just pick up my life at that point as opposed to living the life I've lived since, I wouldn't take it.

It hasn't been easy. But in terms of personal growth, the experiences I've had, I think I'm a much richer, stronger person for it. I think I've grown because I've been challenged to grow. That's what life is all about. And gliding down that highway toward Williams Lake, thinking of where we'd been, what we'd done and what we hoped to do, I knew I wouldn't trade that now just for the use of my legs.

Of course, I'd like to have both. I still have recurring dreams that I'm running, sometimes with my braces, sometimes just running free. Those dreams may never leave me. But no, I wouldn't trade.

To get to Williams Lake from Quesnel, you have to pass the turnoff to Blue Lake, where my granny had her cabin. Could I pass that up? No way. As a kid it had been my playground. After the accident it became my sanctuary. You'd have to see it to understand how beautiful it is there, how clear and crisp the air. I had to show Amanda. So we played hooky for a night—Amanda, Don, Rico, Mike and me.

And the next morning, we wheeled into Williams Lake.

It was overwhelming: a sea of yellow ribbons and balloons and what seemed like every man, woman and child in the area lining the streets or crowding into the Stampede ground for the official welcome, or coming into the school gym for the official banquet. Williams Lake wasn't welcoming one local boy, it was welcoming two. This was Don's day as much as mine. He'd hung in for two years on the road, his natural reserve pulling him into the background. I know there must have been times when he wanted to leave, just as I know that loyalty to me carried him through those black patches. But he was home now, meeting old friends, accepting well-deserved accolades. I was so happy for him, and so proud that he was my friend.

We took a rest day back in the house on Pigeon Street, which was crammed with relatives and old friends, then another day at Blue Lake with the family and Tim and Lee, who'd come up for the border crossing and the homecoming. The fences between Tim and me were mending. I knew now that I could keep my promise: we'd started this thing together, we'd finish it together. And knowing it made me feel good.

Everywhere we went, the crowds swarmed around us and the money rolled in. My only worries now were making sure that nothing went wrong the rest of the way. The temptation to floor it was still there, but so was the project. "Maintain the routine," I told the crew. "Let's not make the careless mistake now. Look after the little details. Assume nothing. We're so close. Let's not blow it now."

Every day we'd meet someone in a wheelchair who had overcome a disability or was working his or her butt off to do it. We met a man in a wheelchair who ran his own farm. Hairdressers, wrestlers, strippers, church groups, swimmers, rock groups, school groups— everyone was involved.

Professional singers wrote and recorded songs about us. Amateur songwriters crooned or croaked into hand-held tape recorders. Songs on records or tapes, lyrics scrawled on foolscap paper—they poured into the Man in Motion office. Kids walked dogs, mowed lawns, washed cars, skipped rope, collected paper, pop bottles and cans . . . one little girl in Vancouver held a slide-a-thon on her back yard slide, getting pledges for so much per slide and keeping at it until a queasy stomach did her in.

Some of the dollar figures were boggling: $230,000 from Prince

George and vicinity; $70,000 from Quesnel, B.C., population about 20,000. And in the Williams Lake area, where they'd optimistically thought that a town of 22,000 might possibly raise $100,000, they were at $175,000 and counting when we left. The message had gotten through.

There was only one flaw in the border reception and the tumultuous welcome in Williams Lake. Stan Stronge wasn't there for either of them. He'd wanted to, so badly, but he had other fights on his hands. He'd had a leg amputated, and undergone surgery so serious there was some doubt he'd make it. His friends said the desire to see me and be there for the finish were the threads that kept him going.

And finally, in Princeton, B.C., he made it. Stan Stronge, the man who'd brought me into the wheelchair sports he'd pioneered so long ago. Stan stood for everything I was fighting for. We get greedy sometimes, and want more. Stan was the link, the man who lived through it the way it used to be, fought to make it better, and still carries the dream of how much better it can be.

Stan had more or less passed the baton to me. I hope I'm worthy of it, and can carry it half as well.

On Thursday, April 7, 1987, at the entrance to Glacier National Park, I rolled the chair through the second-last banner, the one with 24,000 miles written on it. The next day, Good Friday, we climbed through Rogers Pass, the last real mountain challenge. There were two more mountain passes after it, but I knew that once we made that one, the momentum would pick me up and carry me the rest of the way.

It was a tough climb, from an elevation of 2,000 feet to 4,300 over the 23 miles, but not as tough as some. The real challenge was to get to the top in good physical condition, because I felt as good as I'd felt in months, and was determined to stay that way.

We'd planned it carefully, breaking it into segments of 9, 10 and 4 miles with two rest breaks. We had an advantage now: Amanda could check our records to see how the chair had been set up on previous climbs. It was all very scientific, but we couldn't take credit for what happened up there during the two rest breaks. On both occasions, it began to snow just as I stepped into the motor home, snowed all the time I was inside—and stopped each time I came back out to wheel. We had sunshine, a breathtaking view, and winds from the west at our back all the way. I passed three-inch dents in the road where rocks had come tumbling down the virtually perpendicular walls. For a minute there I felt like Wily Coyote in the "Roadrunner" cartoons. Whenever he appeared to have caught that pesky bird, he wound up under a boulder.

187

Not this time, though. Not with our bird just inches from our grasp. Every time I looked back at the motor home, I laughed. The sign on the front no longer read Miles to Date, it read Miles to Go, and it was down to three figures and sinking. By gosh, we really were going home.

It wasn't all work in B.C. We knew now that, as long as we didn't do anything silly, we basically had it whipped. There was time to savour the moment.

We were offered the use of two houseboats to spend the day fishing on Shuswap Lake. Well, I guess! We had a great day in the sunshine. Amanda caught a five-pound rainbow trout. The two of us cruised home and were settled in nicely when we got a radio call from Nancy. Getting back required staying to the right of the buoys, or you'd hit the sandbars. Simon had tried a shortcut. The engine was spewing smoke and they were aground on a bar. Yo ho ho. Fortunately, there was no serious damage.

But it wasn't all fun and good news. I also got word that my car— my beloved 1981 Honda Civic, which I'd left in the care of my sister, Christine—was dead. I think it was murder.

I got the word through a memo from the Vancouver office: my car had been picked up and hauled away for scrap. The mechanic said it wasn't worth fixing, that my best bet was to sell the parts and forget it.

"That car was in great shape!" I protested. "Maybe a dent or a rust spot here or there, but . . ."

The crew just collapsed with laughter.

"Rust bucket," Don said. "It was a rust bucket when you had it, and it was a rust bucket when we left."

It seems the crew had known for a year that my Honda was dying. Christine must have had it magnetized: it attracted every bump, rock or accident in sight. They knew, but they didn't tell me, because they knew how I felt about that car, and my frame of mind at that time.

Well, maybe it said something about how well things were going that I could laugh at the situation. But now I had two things to look forward to: crossing the finish line, and talking to Christine about my car.

There could never be an accurate count of the people who formed the pieces of the Man in Motion tour. The crew, of course. The people at the office. Chunky Woodward, the troubleshooter, the man who was always there when we needed him, with his friendship and support and endless generosity. The corporate sponsors. The organizing and support teams in the various countries. Service groups. Organizations for the disabled. Local businesses. Schools. The thousands who lined the streets and pushed us along on the strength of their enthusiasm and understanding. The radio hams who kept the communication lines open in the U.S., the Telephone Pioneers all over North America, out on the road with us and scurrying to do any little thing that might make it easier for us. The Kinsmen, who played such a vital role in the fund raising and merchandising. The police who provided the escorts, controlled the crowds and led us through the red lights. The media—particularly Fred Cawsey, Pat Bell and John Collins of the cbc, who were there before the public really knew about us, and used their own money to join us in several countries, filming a documentary and, more important, sending tapes back to the cbc to spread the word and keep the interest at home alive and growing.

So many people—most of whom I'd never met and never would—working in the background, sharing our dream . . . The number was beyond counting—but not beyond remembering. As I wheeled closer and closer to home, I tucked them away in a special corner of my heart. As long as I live, they'll stay there.

The phone rang one day in the Vancouver office. The lady on the line had a problem. It was her son, she said. He wanted a wheelchair.

"Well, what's his disability?"

"He doesn't have one," she said. "But he's seen Rick wheel, and now he wants his own wheelchair . . ."

As we crossed Canada, I'd see kids and adults on crutches, grinning and waving them at me and pointing down at their legs. They were telling me they were disabled, too, that they weren't ashamed to be seen, and that they weren't letting it beat them, either.

In Vancouver, a twenty-five-year-old able-bodied man named Kelly Gordon, a disk jockey out of Edmonton, won the wheelchair division of a marathon. He'd trained with a disabled friend, then tried the wheelchair himself. The athleticism of wheelchair sport fascinated him. Now he was a full-fledged wheelchair athlete, training just as hard as any in an able-bodied sport. "My ambition," he said, "is to have racing wheelchairs on display in sporting goods stores, right next to the racing bikes."

Everywhere we went, we could sense it: this wasn't a one-time thing. The awareness level was growing higher and growing roots. The war wasn't over, but we were winning the battle.

And then, on May 22, 1987, we crossed the Port Mann Bridge and came into Vancouver.

How can I describe to you the feelings that were rushing through me in waves?

The thrill of having an honour guard of my wheelchair buddies pushing with me up a final hill in Port Coquitlam, a hill as steep as any we'd encountered, and of hearing Ron Minor driving me on as I'd driven myself so many months ago on the slopes of the Siskiyous: *"Push! . . . Push! . . . Push!"*

The thousands and thousands who formed a human chain on both sides of the street from the suburbs to the Pacific National Exhibition grounds, our last stop before B.C. Place. The moment when I almost broke down as I heard for the first time the hauntingly beautiful new song dedicated to the Man in Motion tour, "The Dream Will Not Die."

Coming over the hill and looking down Hastings Street to the city itself, a view I'd ached for so many times. I'd received all kinds of offers to come back for a day or two and turned them all down on principle. That one moment made all that worthwhile . . . wheeling into the heart of the city through mobs of people from every walk of life. Business offices emptied, pubs cleared out, those who couldn't escape their offices leaning out the windows and cheering . . . horns and sirens blasting . . .

The final turn for the trip down Cambie Street to Oakridge, touching as many hands as I could, misting up as I passed a group of patients and staff from G. F. Strong, where I'd fought and worked and forced myself to push on—and thinking that I'd come full circle in more ways than one . . . Maybe some day I'll have it all sorted out. But not then. I was on sensory overload.

And the last right turn into Oakridge, wheeling up the podium and breaking through the ribbon that said I was home and it was done. Looking around at the team on the stage with me—at Don and Mike and Rico and Nancy and Simon and Derrick. And Amanda. Always and forever, Amanda.

We'd done it. Together, we'd done it. The people on the stage. The part-time crew members who'd come aboard for a time and contributed so much. And Tim, who'd driven the motor home on the last leg, with Lee in there with him or hopping out to take pictures as he'd done so many times before. We'd done it, and we'd kept a promise. We said we'd start and finish together, and we had.

And there was a moment, someone else's moment, that told the story of Man in Motion as simply and truly as it was possible to be told.

Eighteen-year-old Kerris Huston, badly injured in a car accident two years earlier, pushed away the hand of a would-be helper and walked slowly and haltingly to the microphone.

Her voice was slurred. She was obviously nervous. But she spoke to me, and she proved again that the effort was worth the prize:

"One year ago I was in a wheelchair. You showed me how to reach for the stars. You gave me that encouragement to be the best I can. I thank you for letting me share a part of your dream."

Then she walked back to her chair and sat down.

I spoke, and thanked everyone. I got Don to come over and pinch me, to make sure it was all really happening.

The next day at B.C. Place 50,000 people turned out for a welcome home party full of musicians and dancers, some of them disabled themselves. My honour guard was there, the elite of wheelchair athletes in Canada, and I was so proud to be sharing the moment with them because of our common bond. They, more than anyone, understood what the tour was all about. There was a parade of nations, hundreds of disabled persons front row centre as honoured guests. David Foster and John Parr were there, playing the song that had become our anthem. We made a circle of the stadium, waving to the people, trying to show them how much it all meant.

The premier confirmed the matching grant. He announced an additional grant of $1 million for upgrading the spinal cord unit at Shaughnessy Hospital and the formation of a premier's advisory council to give disabled persons direct access to government. Although I hadn't wanted the Legacy Fund mentioned on this day that was to be a welcome home and a gathering of friends, he couldn't resist giving the latest figure: $18 million, not counting the $2.45 million matching grant left in Alberta.

It was a warm and wonderful celebration, a meaningful recognition of and commitment to the disabled of our province and our country. For me, it capped two days as perfect as I'd dreamed they'd be when I first dared to think about the finish line. And when all the speeches were over, no one had said it better than Kerris Huston did by walking unaided across that stage at Oakridge:

"Thank you for letting me share a part of your dream."

And thank you, all of you, for sharing mine.

The work was not over, only the journey. Life had changed forever for the boy from Williams Lake. Like it or not, he was a celebrity now. The business of shutting down the Man in Motion tour, of setting up the advisory board to administer the Legacy Fund, of sorting through the hundreds of requests for appearances and assistance and support would take months. And, of course, there was a wedding to plan.

On the sunlit balcony of their ninth-floor apartment, Rick Hansen sits in a wheelchair that is locked into place on rollers. He is pumping away in the old, familiar stroke, putting in the miles as he does every day that time permits. The 1992 Olympic Games are not that far away. And he is still not afraid to dream.

Afterword

"Yesterday I was twenty-five. What happened?"
—legendary showman Billy Rose on his fiftieth birthday

Yesterday, Tim and Don and I sat around talking over this nutty idea about wheeling around the world. Yesterday, we figured if the support wasn't there, the three of us would just take off in the car and live in it when I wasn't wheeling. Yesterday, we were very young.

We're not young anymore.

Maybe we had to be, back then. If we hadn't been so naive, so youthfully cocky, we might have looked at the whole idea objectively, cracked another beer and gotten back to figuring how I could trim a few more ounces off my racing chair. The tour idea was a challenge, sure, but I'd never been short of challenges. If I'd been ten years older, with adult responsibilities, there'd have been every reason to decide it couldn't be done.

But that was yesterday, and yesterday's gone. So who put my life on fast-forward?

It's not 1985, when we left Oakridge, or even '87 when we came back. It's 1999.

Suddenly, I'm an old married man of forty-two with a gorgeous wife, three beautiful, healthy daughters and a home in the 'burbs, commuting to the office every day. The Man in Motion tour we thought so huge at the time has become a single facet of the Rick Hansen Institute, which establishes and oversees projects in the field of disability, nationally and internationally. The $24 million in the Legacy Fund has swollen over the decade to an impact of $107 million. There's a Neurotrauma Initiative, an ongoing campaign to give full medal status to wheelchair athletes in the Olympic Games, and a school Lifeskills program.

No one could have foreseen this, least of all me.

The big day! Wedding photo of Rick
and Amanda Hansen, October 10, 1987.

Rick and family: wife, Amanda, daughters Emma, Alana and Rebecca, during the
Man in Motion World Tour Tenth Anniversary Celebrations at the unveiling of the
sign commemorating Williams Lake as Rick's home town, B.C., 1997.

Rick Hansen with Dr. David Strangway, President of the University of British Columbia, at the announcement of the opening of the Disability Resource Centre at UBC, 1991.

International Congress and Exposition on Disability – Independence 1992 International Advisory Committee.

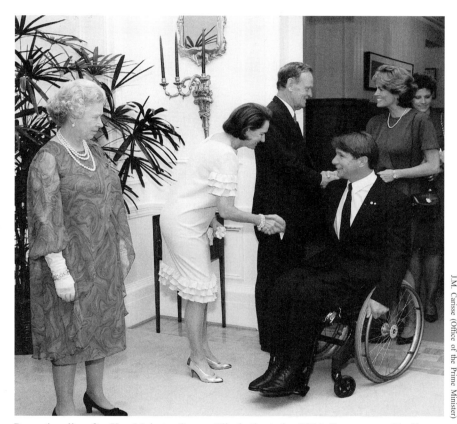

J.M. Carisse (Office of the Prime Minister)

Reception line for Her Majesty Queen Elizabeth at the 1994 Commonwealth Games in Victoria, B.C. (Rick was proud to serve as a member of the Board of Governors for the Commonwealth Games. He was also honoured by his appointment as Secretary to the Queen during her 1989 visit). Also shown are Canadian Prime Minister Jean Chrétien, Mrs. Chrétien and Mrs. Amanda Hansen.

Rick meeting with Deng Pufung (son of Deng Xiaoping, Chairman of China), during the Man in Motion World Tour Tenth Anniversary Tour, to continue ongoing relationships in China, October, 1997.

Rick with Ontario Premier Mike Harris, following the May 1998 news conference announcing the national distribution of the first $7.5 million of a $36.8 million Rick Hansen Neurotrauma Initiative commitment.

Rick pictured on his hand-cycle, 1996. Rick is involved in the development of hand-cycles as part of a line of assistive device products.

Big Catch! Sturgeon caught, tagged and released as part of a program initiated by the Fraser River Sturgeon Conservation Society (which Rick chairs). Photo taken during the taping of the *Shelley and Courtney Show*. Also pictured are Rena Vandenbos, local guide Fred Helmer and Michael Hildebrand, Fraser River, B.C., 1999.

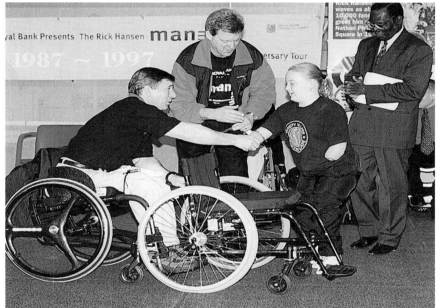

Rick with George Gaffney, Executive Vice President, Ontario, Royal Bank Financial Group (a long-standing corporate sponsor), presenting a wheelchair at the Man in Motion World Tour Tenth Anniversary Celebrations at the Variety Club in Toronto, 1997.

Dr. John Steeves, Director of CORD (Collaboration on Repair Discoveries), at UBC with Post-Doctoral Fellow Dr. Gordon Hiebert, 1999.

Dr. Judith Hall, Medical Research Council, the Hon. Allan Rock, Minister of Health, and Rick at the announcement of the first year of the Canadian Neurotrauma Research Program funding partnership of over $2.5 million. Vancouver, B.C., February 22, 1999.

Rick and Amanda Hansen accepting a cheque from the Toronto Blue Jays on behalf of the Ontario Neurotrauma Foundation.

The Rick Hansen Plaza at General Motors Place in Vancouver, B.C., 1997. Rick with the sculptor, Bill Koochin, landscape architect Illarion Gallant and tile artist Blake Williams.

Raising funds for research: Rick with participants of the inaugural Rick Hansen Fishing Challenge at Langara Fishing Lodge, Queen Charlotte Islands, B.C., 1998.

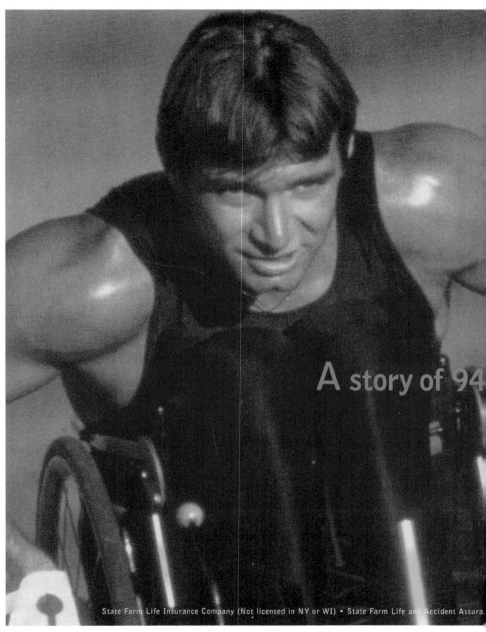

A story of 94

The 1997 State Farm advertising campaign portraying Rick was featured in print in *Life*, *Time*, *People* and *In Style* magazines; it also played on television and radio.

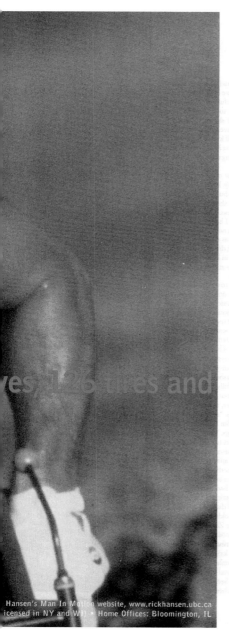

When told he would never walk, he swore he would never be still. And for 2 years, 2 months and 2 days, at an arm-numbing 9,000 wheel turns a day, he pushed himself around the world. Travelling over 40,000 kilometers through over 30 countries, he raised over 20 million dollars in donations for spinal cord research and rehabilitation. And today, Canadian Rick Hansen is still a man in motion and the constant proof that courage knows no handicap.

1 indomitable spirit.

To get where we're going in life, we all need a dream. And at State Farm, we can help you turn those dreams into plans, and those plans into futures. State Farm Understands Life.™

STATE FARM INSURANCE

SALUTES **LIFE** HEROES

lifeheroes.com ■ www.statefarm.com

Hansen's Man In Motion website, www.rickhansen.ubc.ca
Licensed in NY and WI • Home Offices: Bloomington, IL

Roger Gould: Nike International. Produced by DDB Needham – Chicago for State Farm Insurance

Rick meeting with schoolchildren as part of the Life Skills Program, an educational resource created in partnership with the B.C. Ministry of Education and supported by Royal Bank Financial Group, 1997.

Rick celebrating with B.C. gold medal winners at the Canadian Wheelchair Basketball Championships, General Motors Place, Vancouver, May 1997.

Rick gets a big hug from students at Rick Hansen Elementary School in London, Ontario.

Rick Hansen and Christopher Reeve at the kickoff of Toronto Hospital's "Spark of Life," a $21 million fund-raiser campaign to support research into finding the cure for brain and spinal cord injury and diseases, September 4, 1996.

I was determined to wheel around the world, sure. I wanted to see if I could DO it, and with luck maybe we could raise some money to focus public awareness on the disabled and the issues they faced every day. Maybe we could kick-start a cause.

But not even our wildest dreams prepared us for this. We were buds off on a great adventure—so young, so excited, so green.

Even the idea for this book wasn't finalized until the night before we left. Jim Taylor was sitting with me in my apartment, off in a corner of the chaos. I didn't know him, but I'd read his sports columns for years and knew he had a daughter in a wheelchair after a skiing accident left her quadriplegic and brain damaged at fourteen. That was important.

"People keep saying they know what I must be going through," I told him. "They don't, and you don't either. But you've pushed wheelchairs. You come closer than most. I want you to do this book."

Then I asked Jim how much it would cost.

He thought about it.

"I'll do it for nothing if you will," he said. "But nothing is my final offer."

Since we didn't know how much money the tour would generate (we didn't know if it would generate any), we agreed to throw the book royalties into the fund unless it hit something fantastic. Then we thought about what would constitute fantastic. Neither of us wanted the royalties anyway, so we put it at a ridiculous $8 million. Then we shook hands, and he handed me a tape recorder and a bunch of cassettes with orders to speak into it every night without fail and ship him the tapes as we travelled.

And that was our book deal.

"Shouldn't we sign something?" I asked.

"Why?" he replied. "Are you going somewhere?"

Yes, we were. But as it turned out, even 24,901.55 miles and thirty-four countries later, I still had no idea where . . .

On the Road Again

Let's see . . . where was I?

Oh, right. Sitting on the balcony in the old training chair on the rollers, pumping away and dreaming of competing in the 1992 Olympic Games. The tour was over. I could get back to racing, concentrate on re-setting the world record that had been broken while I was gone. Get the old bod out of world marathon mode and into racing shape. Twenty-nine years old—prime of life. Just give me a few months, boy, and . . .

A great idea, but it had a few flaws.

I was broke, with no job and no prospects.

And I didn't want it anymore.

That took a while to figure out. When I quit halfway through the first workout, I thought: bad day. Next morning, same thing. I finished, but there was no zest, no sense of progress or satisfaction. Every day it got harder to get up, harder to look at the chair, harder to force myself into the routine.

When I stared into the mirror in front of the chair, the guy looking back at me said: "Well, now. You're going to have a wife to support, you're broke, in debt and unemployed, and you're sitting here trying to get in shape to go back to chasing other people in wheelchairs and trying to get to where they'll be chasing you. Right."

There was nothing left in me. My confidence level had gone from top of the world, slay any dragon, to a tired and drained stranger. I was sitting there wondering "What now?" and suddenly realizing that it wasn't going to include getting back into athletics. I didn't want it anymore.

In fact, I didn't know what I wanted. In a sense I was a soldier coming back from the war, changed forever by his experiences. The world tour had done that to me. Now all I wanted was to be with Amanda and have some space and time with no one making any demands and no schedules to keep. I wanted time to take a deep breath, exhale and figure out the rest of my life.

There was an easy way. I could sell out, do all the endorsements and the commercials, live off my name while I was still the flavour of the month, the year or however long it lasted. But for two years we'd been avoiding that, protecting the integrity of the tour. Even if I wanted to, how would it look? How long before the critics were saying: "I told you so. The tour was about cashing in."

I had to find a job that was meaningful, something with goals I could get passionate about, because that was where I got my strength. I had no idea what it was going to be. Not a clue. And Amanda and I had a big problem. We couldn't get out of the fish-bowl.

People wanted to see us, to talk to us, to touch us. It was gratifying, but it was also maddening.

Early in the hunt for an apartment, we were spotted in the lobby of a high-rise by two elderly women. "Rick Hansen!" one gasped. "Are you going to live here?"

"Just looking," Amanda assured her as we stepped into the elevator. Thirty minutes later, the apartment checked out, we returned to the main floor. The lobby was full of people, all wanting autographs. As we'd been going up, the two ladies had been hitting the apartment intercoms, one by one: "Rick Hansen is here! Rick Hansen is here!"

When we found a place, the media wanted the address, and could they please get a picture of the furniture being moved in? We declined with thanks, but for days afterward, newspaper, radio and TV types were scrambling around checking rumour after rumour that we'd moved upstairs, next door, around the block.

We left the mailbox nameless. Our unlisted phone number was given out only on pain of death for revealing it. Partially because we needed the rest, partially because we'd be mobbed if we did anything radical like go out to a movie or a shopping mall, we went into tour mode: phone-ordered pizza, Chinese food and fried chicken, taco chips and salsa for snacks.

Finally, after a month, we took a chance. The Hansens and the Taylors would go out for dinner. We picked an accessible restaurant and agreed to meet there. And we made an amazing discovery.

I left my chair in the car and walked in on crutches and braces, Amanda by my side. People turned their heads, nudged one another and began to whisper as we headed toward the table.

"Hey, isn't that . . . ?"

"Nah, it can't be. Where's the chair?"

"That girl looks just like Amanda Reid, but who's the guy with her?"

"Is that Rick?"

"No way! He's standing up."

The mental picture, the one they'd seen on TV and in the newspapers a thousand times over the past two years, didn't mesh with what they were seeing in real life. Rick Hansen used a wheelchair. That man was standing up. Ergo: that couldn't be Rick Hansen.

We had a nice, quiet dinner. Only one man came up for a closer look. He shook my hand, bowed slightly to Amanda, said "Congratulations," and left.

We clicked glasses and drank to a quiet, normal life. Eventually. Because first we had to go back on the road. It was time to start selling books.

Something about the bearded guy made us nervous. Maybe it was the prospector's cap and the army jacket, both covered with newspaper headlines held in place with Scotch tape, or the hammer hanging like a six-gun from a carpenter's belt. Maybe it was the fact that everybody else in the lineup held a book to be autographed and he was shoving his way to the front empty-handed.

"Mike?" Jim Taylor whispered, rolling his eyes toward the line.

"Got him," Mike Reid said. Mike was with us on the book tour, still handling security. He is big and dark and mustached. When he quits smiling, people develop this incredible urge to do what they're told.

The closer the guy got to the table where Amanda, Jim and I sat signing our little fingers to the bone, the closer Mike got to him. But as the guy drew close enough for us to read the headlines on his coat and hat (everything from Ban the Bomb! to Life Begins at 40), he reached into his pocket and pulled out two toy sets of military stripes, the kind you might fish out of a box of Crackerjack.

"Rick," he said, "I want to make you a general."

"Uh, pardon?" I said, shaking his hand.

"I want to make you a general," the guy insisted. "Hold still."

He leaned over and pinned the stripes to my sweater. "There," he said. "Now you're a general."

He took two steps backward, came to attention, snapped off a crisp military salute, pivoted and marched away.

There was a moment's stunned silence.

"Well, look on the bright side, Rick," Mike said. "You just got pinned. If he was a French army officer, you'd have been kissed."

Such is life in the book business. Four months after the tour ended, we were on the road again—Jim, Amanda, Mike and me on a nine-city, twelve-day cross-Canada tour, Halifax to Victoria, promoting the first edition of this book. ("Quit bitching," Jim said. "At least this time you can fly.")

It was like a tour rerun: meet a guide in every city, zip from radio station to TV station to newspaper to bookstore to autograph session, go back to the hotel, grab a few hours' sleep and get up to catch a plane so we could go somewhere else and do it all over again. Sign. Sign. Sign. Sign.

"Hi, Rick. I'm your greatest fan!"

"Rick, I'm so proud."

"Can I have my picture taken with you? Fred, hurry up and take the picture. Hurry, now! Oh, thank you!"

"And this must be Amanda! Will you sign, too? Gosh, I've got a daughter as good-looking as you! Just think, she could have been Mrs. Rick Hansen!"

"I bet your fingers really get tired doing all this signing, eh?"

To be honest about it, I don't know how many were there for the book and how many just to get our autographs. At first, Amanda stayed in the background. "Who'd want my autograph?" she protested. Answer: everybody.

Nobody wanted Jim's. He told me from the start it would be that way and it didn't bother him. I'd sign and then point to him and say, "This is Jim Taylor, who wrote the book." The general response was nicely summed up by the little boy in Halifax who looked at him, solemnly shook his hand and then said, "You can sign, too, if you want. But not on Rick's page."

Invariably, we ran past the allocated time, which meant frantic, tire-screeching dashes to the next appointment. It was tiring, frustrating—and wonderful. Because everywhere we stopped, there were incidents that told us something of what the tour had accomplished.

A man wheels up to the desk. "No accident, Rick," he says, leaning forward to put down his book. "I was trying to commit suicide. Screwed that up, too. But I watched your tour, and I'm coming back." He grasps the arms of his chair, lifts his body clear of the seat, and swings his useless legs. "Thanks for that," he says. "Thanks a lot . . ."

A single tear splashes the open pages of her book as a lady in her late twenties puts it down for signing. She refuses to say what's wrong, but later, in a quiet corner, she explains to Amanda. "I'm dying," she says, "but I've watched Rick and read the book, and I know how bad it is for my family and my friends. So I'm doing the best I can . . ."

And always, there were the children. Disabled and able-bodied, little kids to teenagers, they were there by the hundreds with books and autograph collections and posters and scraps of paper, giggling or gushing or staring silently, just wanting to say hello and show they cared.

One afternoon in Victoria, when the crowd was particularly large, Jim leaned over and whispered in my ear: "I wonder where they are," he said, "all those people who said the tour wouldn't work and would be forgotten? Wherever they are, they're awfully quiet."

We came home and tried to relax. Fat chance. In two weeks, we were getting married.

Poor Amanda. I couldn't have blamed her if she'd gone looking for another bowl of salad to heave at me. I'd yanked her out of her career, parked her in a van for two years, worked her like a galley slave, stuck her with me for almost every hour of every day. And when we got home, all geared up for the tour to end so we could start putting together a normal life—nothing changed.

Now we were getting married. But even then, we couldn't do it like normal people. The Man in Motion's success turned what we'd always thought of as a simple ceremony with friends and relatives into The Wedding. Now it wasn't "Who do we invite?", it was "Who DON'T we invite? And how do we keep this from turning into a circus?"

Our wedding began at 3 P.M. with more than three hundred guests crowded into the flower-decked B.C. Club and ended at approximately 2 A.M. with Amanda's dad, Patrick, and photographer Pat Bell arm-in-arm at the elevator, singing Roy Rogers's "Happy Trails" to the final stragglers. In between, a great time was had by all.

I gather there'd been a lot of public speculation as to whether I'd come down the aisle in the chair or on crutches and braces, and more on how we'd handle the traditional first waltz. Anyone who knew me knew I wouldn't be sitting down at my own wedding. Of course I'd be on crutches. As it turned out, it didn't matter. Brad was my best man. We wore tuxedos. Who knew? Amanda was so gorgeous in creamy white silk that I could have been wearing a Ronald McDonald suit and no one would have noticed. Reverend David Spence read a passage from a love poem by Elizabeth Barrett Browning and reminded the assembly of the parallels between that historic love story and ours: that Elizabeth Barrett had broken her back as a child and began writing poems as she battled her disability, and that Robert Browning had first come to admire her through her poetry, then met and fell in love with her.

We exchanged vows. We kissed. Three and one-half years after I met this girl in the rehab ward, we were married.

We'd closed the wedding to the media. We knew people would

like to see the ceremony, and we appreciated that. But we'd been in the fishbowl for two years. We weren't about to turn our wedding into another tour event and photo-op. We made a quick trip outside to wave at the crowd and the cameras, then went back in to launch the reception.

The music for the first waltz was "It's What They Call Magic" by the Nylons. I wheeled out onto the dance floor. Amanda sat in my lap, put her arms around my neck, and we wheeled around the floor to the music, the only two people in our universe.

Then we partied and laughed and cut the cake and ate and laughed some more, trying to meet everyone. By 10 P.M., when it was time for the last waltz, many, many toasts had been proposed and answered, most notably by my racing buddies and friends down from Williams Lake.

So there we were, Amanda and I, whirling around the dance floor again, this time to "Amanda" by the group Boston. Things were going swimmingly, I thought.

Two lines into the song, somebody yelled, "Rick! Do a wheelie!"

Who, me? Tilt up the chair and roll around only on the back two wheels, with my bride in my lap, on the biggest night of our lives, when a single slip could put us both on our butts on the dance floor?

I leaned over, kissed Amanda on the cheek, and whispered tenderly into her ear.

"Freeze," I said.

Then I leaned back, threw the front wheels high, and we waltzed around the floor on the big ones until the song was over.

A lot of the guests had trouble believing it. Looking back, it probably wasn't the brightest thing I'd ever done. But, hey, the man challenged me.

Maybe this is a good time to turn things over to Amanda. From the day the tour started, she was my lodestone, my rock, the one I could turn to for a dose of perspective when it felt like I was being squeezed like a toothpaste tube and was one pinch away from squishing apart at the seams. Mrs. Hansen, how was it for you?

About a week after the tour, I went back to the Man in Motion office. It felt like a trip to the dentist. Everyone else was cutting their ties and trying to pick up their lives where they'd left off, but Rick couldn't. And I couldn't because I was marrying the guy. So I took a deep breath, walked in, and there was all this STUFF. Piles of letters and thank-you notes and posters and plaques and cards from all over the world, all from people who deserved a reply.

I looked at it, and just for a second I panicked.

199

I couldn't DO this. It was supposed to be OVER, dammit! I couldn't get sucked into it again. I wanted to move on. There was the wedding to plan, a career decision to make. Did I go back to being a physiotherapist? Could I?

I did a short stint in November, which was fine because it had a beginning and an end. But I couldn't see just picking up where I'd left off, seeing patients and working on disabilities. People were looking at me differently now, co-workers and patients. The tour had set me apart, and that wouldn't be a good working environment for anybody.

So, okay, I wouldn't go back to physio. But we couldn't just keep going on as though our life was an extension of the tour. I wouldn't.

We joke about it now. Rick would come to me looking for answers, and I'd say, "Sorry, shop's closed. I can't do this anymore." He'd tell people, "I got married, and that was my last massage." He was right. I'd done it day in, day out, for two years. Now I beef and complain when he asks me for a little back rub. "Are you CRAZY?"

But I wasn't going to have him running off to have some cute little physio give him a treatment, either. "Go see Clyde," I said.

This is going to sound crazy, but we weren't even married and we had a separation issue. For two years we'd literally been together almost every moment of every day. Even if I went off by myself to do something, it was related to the tour, to Rick. Now, even the thought of taking on a job that meant physically leaving him was, well, unnerving. So there I was. Trying to get my head around what I could do now, something that would keep me fulfilled and ordered, knowing it couldn't be my old career but not knowing what it could be.

We were both running on fumes. Planning the wedding, I was getting freaked out and being totally irrational. Looking back now, I know I wasn't playing with a full deck. I was fried, emotionally wasted, so I wasn't making good decisions. We honeymooned in Bali, and after travelling all that way we just sat and stared at each other like zombies. We didn't go out to see and do all the neat things we could have done. We had no plans, no prospects. It was like our life was in park.

Thank goodness for family. Especially, thank heaven for my grandmother, Lady Jean Lennard. When we were floundering, she bailed us out big time, gave us what amounted to a little pay cheque every month for a few months so we could make our rent and buy our groceries. But something had to give. There were a lot of people out there looking for innovative ways for Rick to work. If it didn't happen soon, if we didn't burst out of this cocoon pretty soon, we were both going to explode.

Something did. Rick got a job, and guess what? We were back on the road . . .

Fixing the Dumbwaiter

So I'm sitting there being idolized and wondering how I'm going to put food on the table.

The awards and honours kept rolling in and believe me, I appreciated them all. I received the Order of Canada. In New York, the Millennium Society named me one of the ten most inspiring people of 1987 along with Pope John Paul, Elizabeth Taylor, Nobel Peace Prize winner Oscar Arias, singer Paul Simon, basketball legend Julius Irving, oceanographer Jacques Cousteau, Harlem charity worker Mother Hale, baby Jessica McClure and, symbolically, the U.S. Constitution. Movie producers started calling. *Chatelaine* magazine called me one of Canada's ten sexiest men. (Must have been a slow year.)

But the tour was never meant to be about me. And now Amanda and I were married. We wanted to raise a family. We were broke. And then, just like that, I had a job: commissioner-general of the Canadian Pavilion at Expo 88 in Brisbane, Australia.

Again, the quotes were flattering. "Rick was the unanimous choice of the cabinet," said International Trade Minister Pat Carney. "We wanted a commissioner-general who had solid credentials in the field of sports and recreation and would, at the same time, be an exceptional ambassador for Canada." Gulp. How's that for a job description? For us, though, the appointment was special: Amanda's father, Patrick, had spent much of his career involved in running world expositions. He'd been commissioner-general for Canada in cities around the world, and for Expo 86. We were sort of carrying on the family tradition.

Start to finish, it was wonderful. Hectic, but wonderful. The string of official dinners and functions seemed endless, either as host and hostess for Canada or representing the country at dinners and functions hosted by other nations. In hindsight we might have been better to just move to Australia when the appointment was announced. Not us. We commuted, Vancouver to Brisbane, five trips in sixteen months, averaging about one month per visit. And, as a government employee, I couldn't even keep my frequent flyer points.

But things were slowly starting to come together. Every trip back from Australia, we were able to stop in Hawaii for a couple of days, the last time for a month, giving the old nerves time to restring. And when we got home, I was presented with an intriguing proposition that just might solve the groceries problem . . .

The call came from the office of Dr. David Strangway, the president of the University of British Columbia, offering me a job as a consultant on disabilities.

"Aha," I thought, "he wants to fix the dumbwaiter."

Remember? The day before we left on the tour? The speech at UBC's Faculty Club? No wheelchair access, so they jam me into the dumbwaiter to lift me up to the reception area, but they hoist me to the wrong floor, and there's nobody there to let me out so I have to pry the door loose to get out and scare the living daylights out of the cook?

I'd never been angry about it. Truth was, it had given me the ideal opening for my speech about the university's lack of facilities for the disabled. But you don't forget being mislaid in a dumbwaiter. So, when the call came, there was a bit of a flashback.

Dr. Strangway and I met several times. He was sincerely committed to change. I was just as determined not to be some sort of figurehead on a Band-Aid project, some little Dutch boy jamming his fingers into holes in the dike until he runs out of fingers and never gets to the cause of the flood. If I accepted, it would not be to do crisis management but to develop a plan for UBC to handle its own issues. No problem, he said.

So I jumped in. At first look it didn't seem too promising. My office was a windowless room about 6 x 7 feet, with lights that flickered. If I wanted to meet with my entire staff, I looked in a mirror. In the back of my mind was the realization that a consultant's salary wasn't enough to cancel out the fretting that I'd have to look for something else in addition. But I hired a secretary and brought in Nancy Thompson, our road manager on the tour, and began work on establishing the Disability Resource Centre, to create access for disabled students at UBC and other universities. We started with a staff of four or five. Over the years it grew to ten or fifteen, allowing us to deal with issues as they developed. We made progress, lots of it.

Meanwhile, I sort of stumbled unwillingly into something that could possibly generate a little extra income. The down side was that next to wheeling around the world again, it was probably the last thing I wanted to do.

Even before the tour I'd done a lot of public speaking—small stuff, schools and things. During the tour, of course, I had to do a lot more. Now I was back, and a lot of corporations were calling, asking me to speak to their employees or their annual meetings. I kept saying no. Then IBM called, inviting me to come to Montreal and speak to two different employee groups. I didn't want to do it, but I didn't want to be rude, either. So I said yes, but set a fee so outlandish they couldn't possibly agree.

They said yes. What kind of a dirty trick was that?

Montreal. The IBM employees were out there in the darkness—eighteen hundred of them, staring up at me in dead silence. They were waiting for me to open my mouth and say something. That made two of us. Unfortunately, my tongue was cemented to the roof of my mouth.

What was I doing here? This wasn't a bunch of school kids. This was a big, corporate gathering. I'd told Amanda I couldn't do it. Why hadn't she stopped me?

I had this speech written for me. Jokes and everything. Patrick told me I didn't need it, that I wasn't a belly-laugh guy. "Be yourself," he said. Easy for him. He wasn't sitting here looking out into pitch black wondering if those people were carrying heaveable fruit.

I've experienced terror before, but never anything like this. My heart was in my mouth. Any second now, it would explode and splatter all over the stage. Everything was magnified by a hundred, but in slow motion.

That morning I'd kind of figured out what I wanted to say. Finally, I croaked out a few words and started the speech. Immediately, I got lost.

Oops! Better look at the notes in my lap. But if I did that, they'd know I screwed up!

Okay, Rick, don't panic! Stall! Have a sip of water. Wait a minute! I don't think I can move my arm!

To me, the silence lasted an eternity. If I didn't do something pretty soon, people were going to get up and leave. Actually, it was just a few seconds, according to Amanda. Then I pushed my way through to a lesser degree of terror and got on with it.

The speech was supposed to go forty-five minutes. That night, I asked the head of the IBM group how it had gone, and if he had any suggestions for the repeat performance the next day.

"Oh, it was great," he said. "But maybe for the second one you could shorten it up. You ran twenty minutes over. People had planes to catch, but they didn't want to walk out while you were speaking. I think some of them missed their flights."

Well, giving the speech hadn't killed me. So, on the theory that it could never get any scarier than the first time, we formed Rick Hansen Enterprises, operating out of the apartment, then out of the house we scraped the down payment together for in '89. I began to accept some of the speaking requests I'd been turning down. One of the first things I learned was that tour issues didn't go away just because the tour was over.

People were still trying to figure ways to get a guy in a wheelchair out of the back room at an event and up onto the stage. I was lifted by football players and forklifts, wheeled up little ramps and big ramps. Once, at a fund-raising dinner for the David Foster Foundation, I fell off the ramp onto Wayne Gretzky's table and wound up with Lee Majors, the Six Million Dollar Man, lifting me back into the chair and pushing me up to the stage.

Amanda, pregnant with the first of our three daughters, was RHE's operating officer, soldiering on even though she knew she'd have to make a career move eventually or, as she put it "get swallowed up by this machine and never come out the other end." We tried to be sensible about it, keep the number of appearances down. After a lot of trial and error we now have my travel quota down from ninety to thirty nights a year, most of it in North America, off the continent only if the issue is high on the importance list. (I actually suggested cutting back to twenty, but Amanda grinned and said she didn't want me around that much.)

At first I chose the ones that sounded interesting and gave me a chance to meet new people, to keep the Man in Motion Fund in the public eye, to hear and put forward new ideas to further it and, of course, to generate some income. Now it's limited to opportunities to reinforce a current association, support a specific project, or court a potential client for future projects—relevant companies that are in a position to get involved, like the auto industry, alcohol-related businesses or insurance companies, because they're the ones on the front line in terms of so many disability injuries.

Overnight, it seemed, we were a Family in Motion.

Emma Kathleen Hansen was born on March 23, 1990. Alana Victoria followed on January 17, 1992, so impatient to get here that she arrived six weeks early. Amanda ruptured a disc delivering her and was incapacitated for six months. Rebecca Jean, thank God, emerged safe and healthy on July 6, 1995, because modern science allowed doctors to discover that through some freakish circumstance the umbilical cord was wrapped around her neck, and they were able to do an emergency Caesarean section.

Like the family, RHE was growing in a hurry. We hired Liz Mitchell, who'd been media and public relations consultant at the Australian Expo, to handle the day-to-day operations and let Amanda concentrate on the Mom business. At first Liz worked in the back bedroom, then out in the garage, which we converted to an office. From there, we moved briefly into what was technically a real office—a basic under-the-stairwell nook in a building where the rent was cheap and we were just far enough inside the city limits to claim a Vancouver headquarters.

Things were mushrooming. Work at UBC progressed from consultant to creating the Disability Resource Centre, then into the National Fellow Programme, an ongoing position established at UBC by the federal government to help remove barriers for people with disabilities in Canada and internationally. Dr. Strangway asked me to be the first incumbent. Perfect, or darn close. I could continue the barrier battle, take part in disability issues across the country, and still work on resource and accessibility issues at UBC. No more fingers in holes.

That became home for me, where my salary was going to be coming from. It allowed me to continue to work as a volunteer with Man in Motion, speak at schools and community projects, talk about the issues and develop new endeavours like the Life Skills program, the world-wide Independence '92 conference in Vancouver, and the ongoing campaign for inclusion of disabled athletes in the Commonwealth and Olympic Games with full medal status.

And, like Dick Whittington's cat, I got to go to London to see the Queen.

Queen Elizabeth II was coming to Canada in 1992 to commemorate our country's 125th anniversary, and I was named by the federal government as Secretary to Her Royal Highness during her stay. Royal tours don't just happen. It was about a year in the planning, which included my going to Buckingham Palace to meet her.

Right away, we had a protocol problem: once the visit was over, how did I make my exit? You don't turn and walk away from the Queen, you walk backwards. Did you ever try walking backwards on crutches? What if I fell on my butt trying to get out the door? How big a protocol blunder would it be to turn around and hop out with my back to Her Royal Highness?

I got through it somehow. (Look, Ma! I'm playing the Palace!) and exited with a sort of sideways hop-and-sidle. But fate wasn't through with me yet.

About a week before I was supposed to go to Ottawa to greet the

Queen, I was visiting the family at my brother's house when one of my nieces bumped into me. I fell over on the crutch, flailed for the wall and missed, hit the floor, and broke my hip. When the Queen arrived in Ottawa for what was going to be my big moment, I was sitting in a hospital back home recovering from an operation to put a pin in my leg.

You don't make one lump-sum payment on adversity and live happily ever after. The bumps are always there. I'd missed greeting the Queen. My life as a wheelchair athlete was over, and that stung, particularly when we went to Japan as part of the book promotion and watched hundreds of wheelchair athletes competing in Oita. Thirty-one years old, still potentially not at my athletic peak, and I was there as a dignitary. Too many things were going on in my life to give proper time even to recreational basketball, and I finally gave it up.

But all in all, things were pretty close to perfect. Until I noticed that I'd earmarked time for everyone but myself.

Remember that old TV commercial for the finance company? The one that had the guy juggling the house and the car and the mortgage and the ambulance and a bunch of other stuff, and one piece fell and the others came crashing to the ground? I knew how he felt. I had the Man in Motion Foundation, Rick Hansen Enterprises, the National Fellow Programme, the Disability Resource Centre and the Life Skills program, all completely different in the way they were structured, all led by me and none of them working together. I was reporting to two advisory committees and one board of directors and assorted superiors. Every minute I could spend with my family was a joy, but there weren't enough of them. Not for family, for business or for any kind of a life.

My workout schedules had gone from shambles to zero. I didn't just get out of shape, I put on forty pounds and developed high blood pressure. I was supposedly in the prime of my life, and I was in deep trouble. I may have to have my head banged against the wall a few times, but I don't have to get kayoed to get the message. It was time either to abandon some stuff, get really focussed on one issue, or build an organization that would allow me to be more than a manager putting out fires, to be a leader.

Easy enough to say, but before I could do it I had to figure out where my real strengths and interests lay. So we brought in Bob Johnston, a guy whose business was developing personal and organizational strategies. Right away, he threw me a curve.

I wanted him to get the organizational end of my life going, but we sat around for hours dealing with personal stuff. I'm tapping my fingers, looking at my watch and thinking, "Hey, the meter's running." Finally, I couldn't take it anymore. "Bob," I said, "let's get on with it!"

He just looked at me.

"Rick," he said patiently, "you've just spent the last four hours telling me how frustrated you are, that you're tired, that you don't have any time for your personal activities, that you're burned out, that you're involved out of necessity in things you don't want to do, that you don't have enough time with your family. So let's figure out those issues, develop your own life strategy, remind yourself what you need to do, and then build in your leadership of the organization knowing that."

"Oh," I said weakly. "Uh, that sounds pretty good."

So that's what we did. We built a life strategy. It wasn't rocket science and it didn't happen overnight. What it did was give me a chance to get my head out of the sand and look around. My salary was from two sources, the university and RHE. We wanted to wrap it into one income source where I could do things either for profit or not for profit, things that tied in with where my values were. And, with my head finally screwed on straight, we found it.

What we did, basically, was bring the four organizations—the Disability Resource Centre, the Man in Motion Foundation, the National Fellow Programme and the Life Skills program—under the umbrella of a new one, the Rick Hansen Institute. Getting to that point took the best part of seven long and hairy years. My shares in Rick Hansen Enterprises were donated to The UBC Foundation, with net proceeds coming back to the Institute to support research and development.

The potential is there to expand RHE and make it a revenue-generating centre for the Institute, to continue the speaking and the sharing of knowledge and experience from the tour, but also to get into things like consulting, speaker bureaus and selling disability assistance devices and technology, and have the profits come back inside the Institute instead of outside into private business.

Complicated? Not really, once you get your teeth wrapped around the assorted sets of initials. It wasn't an instant fix, more like the way they steer those big oil tankers. The captain gives the order, but it's a long time before the course change becomes fact. Ours took about eighteen months, but when it got done it was as though my life had done a 180.

I joined a fitness club, even got myself a personal trainer. That way the exercise and fitness times had to be booked just like office appointments, no excuses. The weight came off. The blood pressure dropped. Gaps of time opened, time to be with the family, go fishing, see my old buddies, get back into wheelchair basketball. Yet, with all those things happening I was doing a better job at home and at work.

Not that the work didn't follow me home. Fortunately, Amanda was there, and she got pretty ruthless. She'd been officially out of RHE since shortly after Alana was born. We had a family to raise, and home was home, thank you very much. Whatever office things come in by phone or faxes go into a pile. When I get home, I deal with it or shove it into the briefcase to handle the next day. But she has threatened me with surgery to remove the telephone growing out of my ear.

I wasn't the only one who turned a corner. Amanda had worked hard for years in physiotherapy, reached a certain level and dropped it because of me. Finding her post-tour place wasn't easy for her, either. It took her until after Alana was born to realize that for now her place was with the girls. And that opened so many other doors.

She's deeply involved with the school, charity work, some television host assignments for which she's a natural, and as a spokesperson for Kids Help Phone, a crisis line for troubled kids. She's also kept up her physio ticket. One day she'll come back to the Foundation's work in some way, but as Amanda Hansen, not as Mrs. Rick Hansen.

Funny thing. People, I gather, have always wondered (a) how much money I earn and (b) how much money I made out of the tour. The answers in order are (a) enough so that like a lot of people we've got a mortgage, a twenty-year-old three-bedroom home that's a forty-minute commute to work, and a sixteen-foot boat that's inefficient in two-foot seas, and (b) zero.

Some find that last one hard to believe. "How much did you get?" Brad asked me when the tour was over.

"Nothing," I said. I'd spent all my savings and gone into considerable debt preparing for the tour. When we came back, I was recompensed for some of that, but that was it.

"Well, you should have taken a percentage," he grinned, "because everybody I talk to thinks you did."

Sorry. I draw my salary in one cheque, from the National Fellow Programme, and that's the way I like it. I haven't assigned my name lock, stock and barrel. There's a firewall in there that will give my family some control when I'm gone. There was a choice, and I made it: pursue the big-time bucks—and they were there—and turn myself into a corporate machine, or draw a salary, do what my beliefs and conscience dictate, and have a life.

I made the decision before the tour began. For a while there, with RHE, I got pulled a little to one side, doing the right things for the wrong reasons, doing them for the money because it was part of how

I was making a living. Now, with everything under the Institute, I can pursue the same goals, develop new initiatives that will turn RHE into a more diversified force for the disabled, and know that the reasons are solid and right because everything that accrues from them goes directly into the Institute and its programs.

Yes, it could have been done in a way to generate more money for the Hansens. But I have four proofs that the choice was the right one. Their names are Amanda, Emma, Alana and Rebecca. We don't have millions, but don't tell me I'm not rich.

The End Is Just the WHAT???

Looking back, the end of the tour had to be one of the more emotional moments of my life. There I was, pushing through the crowd and the balloons and the cameras and the uproar on the last 50 yards of a 24,901.55-mile odyssey and into the Oakridge shopping mall where it had all begun two years earlier. And there was this huge banner stretched over the podium:

Welcome Home, Rick.

Then I noticed the line above it:

THE END IS JUST THE BEGINNING.

And I thought: "What idiot came up with that?"

Didn't they realize I'd just given up two years of my life, that the dream had been ten years in the making? We'd DONE it, dammit. There was $24 million in the Man in Motion fund. The public reaction had been fantastic, greater than we'd ever dared hope. Just the beginning, my butt.

To whoever designed the sign, my apologies. It didn't take long to realize that you were exactly right. Because the dream behind the tour hadn't become a reality at all.

Oh, we'd pushed the edge a little. We'd raised public awareness. We'd generated a lot more money than we'd ever dared dream. But it was like a garden of hope: without constant weeding and watering it would crumble into dust. The message came through loud and clear after we made the first annual fund disbursement—$1,558,120, representing one year's interest from a principal that would be there forever—in a Viewpoint item (unsigned) in the North Delta (B.C.) *Sentinel*. Commenting on the fact that some money went to a project

210

for a process that would help paraplegics recover use of their reproductive organs, the author wrote:

> *Common sense would seem to intimate that for a paraplegic to have a child would involve just more problems. A paraplegic needs constant care and having a child would infer that someone else would now be needed to look after the child as well as the paraplegic. Trying to make un-normal people normal is a laudable idea, but trying to give the impression that there is nothing wrong with a paraplegic is not logical.*

Ah, the almighty stereotype: disabled people meet, fall in love with and marry only other disabled people. Able-bodied people could never look past a chair or a disability and see the individual inside. Having fought every day of their lives to overcome their disabilities and gain acceptance in the "normal" world, disabled parents could never cope with the everyday problems of raising a child they love. And a happily married man turned paraplegic by an automobile accident or twist of fate, as hundreds are somewhere every day, should give up any hope of raising a family.

The problems were not all on the outside. Some advocacy groups still viewed the journey as a McTour sponsored by Ronald McDonald and other corporations who saw a high-profile bandwagon and jumped aboard. Others resented the fact that the federal government had handed us $1 million, just like that, after turning its back for years on organizations that had been trying to achieve the same goals through normal channels.

If we'd finished this thing and all that people were going to remember was me and my name, then we'd blown it. Clearly it was going to take a life's work—and generations after that. There was an obligation. This was going to be part of me forever, a road as uphill as the Siskiyous, as daunting as the Great Wall. But it was there to be travelled, and travel it we would.

Great revelation. Now all we had to do was make it work.

The first hard lesson in refocussing and thinking long-range was a crash course in what you might call Reality Mathematics 101. Bottom line: long-term, the money the Man in Motion tour had generated and the annual grants it engendered were jack squat.

Don't misunderstand. We were proud of the initial $24 million and the generosity of the people across Canada who'd reached into their pockets and hearts and handed over what they could afford and often what they really couldn't. But what you're generating from it is six per cent per year because you recapitalize the rest to stay abreast of inflation. Statistics tell us that there are 41,000 new spinal cord and brain injuries in Canada every year, and that the direct and indirect cost of those injuries annually runs into billions—not millions, but billions of dollars. So whatever amount of money we put out there, it had better be bringing something back in.

And with the best intentions in the world, we'd been doing it wrong. We were looking at the whole broad field of disability and trying to fix it with money.

It wasn't done casually. Every grant proposal was studied, and there were always far more proposals than grants. It was just that handing out what money there was available was like the end of the process for us. Progress was being made, but we just weren't taking it far enough. What we needed to do was say: "All right, this looks like a worthwhile project. Let's put it in the context of a plan, get the people with the expertise together with the money, and go from there."

Strange as it seems, we'd been thinking too small. Because most of the money on the tour had been donated in the home stretch from Cape Speare to Victoria, the old Man in Motion philosophy had been that it's a Canadian issue and we're just going to disburse the funds each year and see what happens. Now, on the research side, for example, we're thinking worldwide big, but with a major philosophical difference that starts off with the understanding that money alone won't get it done.

Take spinal cord research. No random flailing and tossing of money. Now we're looking for a plan that will give us the best chance for success. That means gathering the best researchers, the best people to push forward the cause, people like Christopher Reeve, who since his accident has become perhaps the world's highest-profile advocate on spinal cord regeneration and cure issues.

We're saying, "All right, if we're going to be successful over the next ten, twenty or forty years, then here's what we have to do, here's how much it's going to cost. So we've got to somehow get that money in, then we've got to make sure these people are doing what they said they were going to do, and if we're not being successful then we have to change."

It's the same on the rehabilitation side. It's not that we didn't have success. We've made great progress. But we want to stay close to what was behind the Man in Motion tour in the first place: set goals, zero in on them and get them done. And if you don't, you go down swinging.

Having everything under the Rick Hansen Institute umbrella gave us the base to put the concept into play, every arm of the organization pursuing its goals within an overall framework, so everyone

212

knew where everyone was going. And slowly, turning that tanker again, we began to inch forward, then to gain momentum until, as we celebrated the tenth anniversary of the tour, we were able to look with pride on the things that had been accomplished and with hope for the challenges that lay ahead.

So how do you celebrate the tenth anniversary of the Man in Motion tour? You go on another tour, from Newfoundland to Vancouver. By plane.

There was also a television special, and background work on a movie that had been on and off the back burner since Sherry Lansing stopped work on a movie she was making in Vancouver to watch us wheel into Vancouver the day the tour ended.

Basically, the anniversary tour was a chance to reinforce the awareness message of the first one, to say thank you to everyone across the country who'd been involved and given their support, to check on and showcase the legacies created across the country either by local governments or through Man in Motion grants, and to remind everyone that there was still a long way to go.

But there was something else, the major step in our new go-big-or-go-home game plan: I was after financial and moral support from every provincial government in the country for the Rick Hansen Neurotrauma Initiative.

About half of the 41,000 new brain and spinal cord injuries every year are the result of motor vehicle crashes. So why not take a portion of funds raised in each province from relevant traffic fines, and pool them for research, rehab and injury prevention?

British Columbia premier Glen Clark saw it that way and was first in with a pledge of an annual $2 million from traffic fines revenue. Others found the revenue in other areas. What counted was that they were there. Premier Mike Harris of Ontario pledged $25 million over five years. Newfoundland and Labrador premier Brian Tobin committed $500,000, and Saskatchewan premier Roy Romanow $1 million. One by one, other provinces came into the fold, to the point where we now have $36.5 million over five years. We're able to use our experience to set the agendas, establish the advisory committees, assemble the experts, vet the applications and get the money out.

In the past we were giving away $1.2 million each year from the Man in Motion fund. The year after the tenth anniversary we upped that to $7.5 million. In 1999 it went up to more than $8 million. That's the difference. What we did was put our endowment engine into the leadership aspect. We're also starting to attract other funders who typically have not worked together. And it all started with placing leadership first and working from there.

We can now turn money over to specific projects with a mandate and a responsibility. If the goal is finding a cure and you come to us with a promising research project and say it will require three years, we can provide the funding with the understanding that in three years there'll be a re-evaluation. If you haven't completed it, you tell us why, and we decide whether the progress rates continuation.

It's like looking at one of those paint-by-number or follow-the-dots pictures: the canvas is huge and mostly untouched, but at least we're connecting some of the dots, painting in some of the blank areas. And slowly, we can see that portions of the picture are starting to emerge.

So where are we now, twelve years past Oakridge, twelve years after the cheers?

First, understand that the pronoun isn't personal. We isn't just me. We is the Institute and all the people therein. We is the collective effort as it sits now after all the planning and the struggles and the streamlining and the emergence of what we are.

In short, we're smarter.

Not in the know-it-all sense. The field is expanding so quickly that even if you did know it all today, by tomorrow you wouldn't. We're smarter in that after a lot of trial and error effort, we're focussed. We've identified what we're good at, and that's important, because no matter how much we'd like to, we're never going to be able to do it all.

We're always going to concentrate on quality of life. One of the ways we're going to do that is to put money into research and develop programs that will make a difference by helping to get people with disabilities back in motion.

But we're also going to continue to focus on cure, and before we go any further I'd best explain something about that.

One of the things I did from the moment the tour was conceived was to work to protect the quality of life side, to make sure it didn't get washed out with all the tour hype. It was never that I wasn't interested in finding a cure. But if a cure is ever found, it is more likely to be for the disabled to come than for the ones already facing the challenges.

I couldn't let the present get lost in the hype over the cure possibilities of the future. And remember, in 1987 we were nowhere near the technology that is opening so many new paths today. And maybe I was so determined that the tour be about more than cure that I overcompensated.

Today, I look at the cure issue as part of the overall picture because I'm in the business of helping people improve their quality of life, and there are lots of people out there who really believe that cure is critical to that. To them, it's got to happen or life is a disaster.

So, concentrating more effort on finding a cure isn't a philosophical change. The timing and the technological advances coincide to say, "Okay, now!" It's kind of a three-pronged thing: the sheer challenge of it; the enormous benefits to so many people when we win— as we ultimately will, and (distant third) if it happens that the solution includes something that would get Rick Hansen out of the chair and off the braces, perfect.

The disabled community is full of people who've moved on and are having a great life. But if I was to say to them, "I can help you walk again," there aren't many who would say "No." They would see it as a dazzling value added to an already happy and challenging existence.

That's my philosophy. If at the end of the day I get a chance to walk again, I'll take it in an instant. But if I look back on it, it's not going to be the defining element of whether or not my life was meaningful and successful.

Which brings us full circle, back to the issues still hanging out there, where it is for the able-bodied as well as the disabled, the striving to improve the quality of life. The objectives vary according to the individual. For a bunch of athletes I knew, some I know now, and the ones who'll follow, one objective would seem to be simplicity itself: to be looked upon as athletes without the disabled in front.

But simplicity is a word that seems to have been erased from the dictionary of international athletics. Fifteen years after the '84 Olympics in Los Angeles, the wall of ignorance and indifference is still in place, and we're still batting our heads against it.

Some in the disabled community still don't understand the passion we've put into the Olympic inclusion initiative, the bid to attain full medal status at the Olympic Games for two events, starting with the 1500- and 800-metre wheechair races. Haven't we got our own Paralympics? What difference does it make, they ask, where the race is held as long as you're competing?

If they could have been with me in Los Angeles Coliseum, rolling down the dark tunnel and into the sunlight, the stadium jammed, the people roaring. There are no words to express the surge of emotion that came with the realization that, perhaps just for that day, but at least for that day and that moment, we were not world-class disabled athletes, we were world-class athletes on a par with all the other athletes in all the other disciplines from all the other countries in the world's greatest sports event.

"How nice for you," they reply. "But what's it got to do with the rest of us?"

Simply this: the power of the Olympics is that they reach millions upon millions of people. Television takes their message into every corner of the earth. One of those messages is that disabled people are either special and don't fit, or they're equal partners in every facet of the game of life.

You would think, with the scandal-torn mess the International Olympic Committee finds itself in heading into the new millennium, that the timing would be perfect for inclusion as a spot-lit move to return to some of the original Olympic ideals. But after better than twenty years of trying, you also have to wonder.

I really thought we had a chance for the 2000 Olympics in Sydney. We'd formed the International Paralympic Committee way back in 1989 to give our bid a world focus. We'd done our homework, submitted our proposals, met every objection with some form of concession. We respectfully submitted that staging disabled events as "exhibitions" in the Winter and Summer Games, as the IOC allowed since 1984, was no longer enough, that it was time disabled athletes were granted the same status as able-bodied ones.

And, in June of 1998, the IOC Executive Board had agreed to consider the proposal. Our arguments would be heard and assessed by the world's most powerful sports organization. Surely now, someone would listen.

We got our answer by fax. All three paragraphs:

Thank you for your fax dated June 14, 1998.

We would like to inform you that during its meeting held in Seville from 2nd to 5th June, the IOC Executive Board did not support the IPC request for full medal status for two events for your athletes at the Olympic Games.

We remain at your disposal should you need any further information.

Yours sincerely,
Gilbert Felli,
Sports Director.

Translation: "You've got your Paralympic Games. Go play in them."

A kind and caring group, the IOC.

Hadn't they let the disabled stage two wheelchair events—the women's 800-metre and the men's 1500-metre—as exhibitions, right in the middle of the Summer Games, so that people could see how fast those wheelchairs could go? And now they want MEDALS, just like they were real athletes with all their body parts intact? How ungrateful can these people get?

And so ended the latest chapter in a twenty-year dream.

For twenty years, the disabled athletic community had lobbied the IOC with a simple premise: we are people, and we are athletes. Let us compete as equals. Let us go for gold.

One by one we'd met IOC objections.

Too many athletes? We cut the number.

Too disorganized? We formed the IPC to marshal and channel the campaign.

Too many events? We trimmed our request to two.

Too political, because only wheelchair athletes were involved and what about the rest of the disabled community? We said fine, two events every Olympiad and revolve them so that athletes in other sports will have their chance.

Every objection, we met with compromise. And the answer remained a condescending tokenism: two events, exhibitions, no medals.

Never mind that the European Games have given disabled athletes full medal status. Never mind that the Commonwealth Games put disabled events on the 1994 program as exhibitions and have now voted to give them full medal status in the 2006 Games, and perhaps sooner.

The Olympics are the Olympics. They are special. They are for the elite, the high-profile, the physically whole.

When the two exhibition events were staged at the '84 Olympiad, the disabled had dared hope for a quick step up to demonstration status, then full medal. Instead, the IOC voted to maintain exhibition status for four Olympic cycles, through 1998.

The disabled waited. You get used to waiting when you're disabled.

And now they had their answer. Nothing changes for Sydney 2000.

There was room on the Olympic program for ballroom dancing, for cross-channel swimming, for snowboarding, for ski ballet, for curling. Those changes can be made without any problem. But give equal status to disabled athletes who are already there and competing? Sorry. Can't be done.

It made no sense.

The disabled athletes would be in Sydney anyway, competing in those same two events. Granting gold medal status would involve no extra people, no additional expense. All it would take is an Olympic official handing out gold, silver and bronze for two more events to athletes who have worked and trained and dreamed every bit as hard as the rest, and overcome obstacles the other athletes could barely imagine.

For the IOC executive committee, that was too much to ask. So now what?

We keep trying. Prejudices have fallen before: "I tell ya, we let one nigra in the front of the bus and pretty soon decent white folks won't be able to get a seat . . ." "Can't have women coming into pubs without an escort. It doesn't LOOK right . . ." "Equal pay for equal work? Women should stay home where they belong. They're lucky they're ALLOWED to work . . ."

This one will fall, too, eventually. Because we are never going to stop pushing, and as recent events within the IOC itself have proven—the bidding scandals, the tales of bribery and corruption, the subsequent investigation and the demand for massive reorganization—even the thickest skulls can be fractured.

They'd better get used to dealing with us. We're not going to go away.

The business of searching for an eventual cure was never about me, never "I need to do this tour because I need to walk again." Realistically, if they queued the line in order of the people who'd benefit from the research over time, I'd be at the end of it. But the cure issue has matured for me, become a dream and a challenge unto itself. It's another adventure, a chance to play a part as one of the pioneers in something enormously important and ground-breaking.

I'm not a scientist. But maybe through the Institute I can help figure ways to refine the vision of what has to be done. How to get the money, where to put it, how to pull people together into collaborations to go where the promising research takes them.

Amazing things are happening. New technologies have given researchers weapons they've never had before. Scientists are probing gene structure, pushing down paths unknown or closed a decade ago. We're encouraging NASA into looking toward taking a disabled person into space to study the effects of zero-gravity on spinal cord injury.

Every day, a new door opens. Some lead nowhere, and that will always be the case. But the sunlight pours through some of them, showing new trails to travel, new possible routes to the ultimate goal.

It's going to happen. The day is going to come when society accepts the responsibilities for preventing the injuries in the first place, and scientists solve the puzzle and can repair shattered nerves and lives. Ten years, twenty years, thirty—who knows? But if we keep working, keep planning, keep pushing, the time is going to come.

Sure, it's a big dream. And while we're working toward it, we're not going to forget the other half, the removal of the major barriers that stand between the disabled and their determination to have normal, productive and fulfilling lives. From the first push on the wheels getting over that door jamb at Oakridge all those years ago, that's been the objective—and will be as long as there's a barrier left.

We look back now, Amanda and I, and we shake our heads at the way we started out, full of excitement and a sense of adventure and expectation. We could never have imagined where the road would lead us, the paths along which the tour would take us, the way it would move from a two-year journey to a lifetime commitment.

It's been a wild and wondrous ride, and while the new directions and challenges mean it's not over yet, I go to work every day buoyed by a newfound realization:

On that last day of the tour, pulling into Oakridge, I couldn't accept the fact that "the end is just the beginning." But today I can see the beginning of the end.

Rick Hansen
I N S T I T U T E

Rick Hansen Institute

The Power of the Dream

The Man in Motion World Tour ended in triumph in 1987. Now, twelve years down the road, Rick's energies are focused on the Rick Hansen Institute at the University of British Columbia. Working in partnership with internationally renowned medical researchers, educators and government groups, the Rick Hansen Institute provides leadership, support and funding of advanced biomedical, rehabilitation and injury prevention research into spinal cord injury and disability issues.

Our vision is for a world in which people with disabilities can reach their full potential. Our dreams are a cure for paralysis and an improved quality of life for people with disabilities; and we will never give up on those dreams. The Rick Hansen Institute is committed to mobilizing the critical resources needed to find a cure for paralysis, primarily through research into spinal cord regeneration. We're also working to develop and pioneer innovative new projects that will improve the health and quality of life of persons with spinal cord injuries and other disabilities. We're focusing on research related to spinal cord injury and regeneration technology to enhance mobility, and innovative programs to help people to maximize their potential to participate in society.

We have always believed there is nothing that can't be achieved once you set your mind to it.

Achieving the "Impossible"

When Rick Hansen wheeled around the world, most people said that it couldn't be done—that it was impossible. In 1987, when Rick wheeled across the finish line after two years on the road, researchers said the same thing about regenerating the spinal cord. It simply couldn't be done. But Rick and the Man in Motion Foundation believed that it could and made a commitment to fund the best research in Canada. The original tour raised $24 million in support of spinal cord research, rehabilitation and awareness. To date, Rick Hansen's efforts have impacted the field of disability by more than $100 million, and the progress of spinal cord injury research findings in particular has been significant: 90 per cent of what is known in this field has been learned in the last 10 years.

Today, in 1999, we are confident that a cure is within reach. And like the Man in Motion World Tour, one of the most important success factors will be people working together in support of a common dream.

The Rick Hansen Institute has brought together expert researchers from across Canada to start to identify a clear strategy for finding a cure, and we will continue to raise funds and apply them to the very best research being conducted. In addition, RHI will play a leadership role in bringing international spinal cord researchers and funders together to support an international cure-focused research strategy. Through collaboration and by working toward common goals, we believe anything is possible!

For more information on Rick Hansen, the Rick Hansen Institute or the Rick Hansen Man in Motion Foundation, please visit our website at www.rickhansen.org

The Dream Lives On:
An Acknowledgement

I really thought that the end of the Man in Motion World Tour would be just that—the end. Instead, it was only the beginning of what has been more than a decade of new goals and dreams, complete with both challenges and successes.

I am continually rewarded by the progress I see in making our world one in which there are no barriers preventing people with disabilities from reaching their potential, and I am humbled by the courage shown by so many Canadians who are fighting for their quality of life. I am very touched that people around the world still want to hear my story and share my dreams for the future. We've come a long way and I truly believe our best work is still to come.

Above all, I am eternally grateful and thankful to the thousands of people who have given me their support and encouragement over the years, and shown such faith in what we are trying to accomplish. You've helped make my dreams come true. Thank you.

Our Team: 1985–1999

Individual and Corporate Donors
Man in Motion World Tour Board of Directors
Man in Motion World Tour Patrons
Man in Motion World Tour BC Provincial Homecoming Committee
Man in Motion World Tour BC Steering Committee
Man in Motion World Tour Provincial Coordinators
Man in Motion World Tour Honorary Chairs
Man in Motion World Tour Vancouver Volunteers

222

Man in Motion World Tour Crew Members
Man in Motion World Tour Headquarters Staff
BC Place Stadium Tribute Team
Rick Hansen Man in Motion Legacy Fund Advisory Panels
Canadian Paraplegic Association
National Access Awareness Week coordinators, government sponsors
and volunteers
Independence '92 coordinators, volunteers and delegates
University of British Columbia
UBC Foundation
Vancouver Foundation
Rick Hansen National Fellow Program Advisory Committee and
employees
Disability Resource Centre employees
1994 Commonwealth Games Board of Directors
Rick Hansen Institute Board Members and employees
Rick Hansen Enterprises Advisory Committee and employees
Rick Hansen Man in Motion Foundation Board Members and
employees
Tenth Anniversary Provincial Committees
Tenth Anniversary volunteers
Rick Hansen Neurotrauma Initiative Provincial Committees
Rick Hansen Neurotrauma Initiative Adjudication Panels
Canadian Brain Injury Coalition
Spinal Cord Injury Network Transition Team and Committee
Provincial governments
Federal government
British Columbia Ministry of Education
Rick Hansen Life Skills Program development team
Rick Hansen Role Model Resource—role models and development
team
Telephone Pioneers of America
Canadian Wheelchair Sports Association
Canadian Wheelchair Basketball Association
BC Sports Hall of Fame
Canadian universities
Corporate supporters
Individual supporters
Reporters and cameramen
Spinal Cord and Brain Injury researchers
Rehabilitation organizations, institutes and practitioners
Injury prevention groups